Walking On Custard
& the Meaning of Life

WALKING ON CUSTARD & THE MEANING OF LIFE

A GUIDE FOR ANXIOUS HUMANS

by Neil Hughes

Published by Enthusiastic Whim
www.enthusiasticwhim.com

Print edition ISBN: 978-0-9931668-0-8

Featuring cover art by Tom Humberstone
www.tomhumberstone.com
Chapter opening art by Tom Humberstone & Neil Hughes
Unprofessional doodles by Neil Hughes

"You're Beautiful" © Kelly, Johnston, Emmausongs/IMRO 1999, recorded by Emmaus from the album "Closer Nearer", excerpt quoted with kind permission.

"I'm Intense" © Smith, Luke. Originally published with Beautiful Jo Records 2000, recorded by Luke Smith from the album "It's Not Wrong It's Just Different", excerpt quoted with kind permission.

"Time Trades" © Lewis, Jeffrey. Rough Trade Records 2011, recorded by Jeffrey Lewis from the album "A Turn in the Dream-Songs", excerpt quoted with kind permission.

The author gratefully acknowledges the creators of the following typefaces, which were used for the text of the book and in the production of some artwork: 'Neuton', 'Gentium Basic', 'Euphoria Script', 'Condiment' and 'Cabin', all available under the SIL Open Font Licence, and 'Florante at Laura' ("Nyek!"), 'Quikhand' (no named licence), 'Belligerent Madness' (Font Monkey) and 'Drafting Table' (paid licence).

For Dad, who would have been very proud.

And for Mum, who has selfishly given me more patience and love than I could ever repay, thus leaving me forever in her debt.

ACKNOWLEDGEMENTS

I am lucky to have had the support of many wonderful people in taking this book from initial idea to completion. In no particular order, I'd like to publicly thank:

Alasdair Dawson, Ellen Spaeth, Jon Matthias, Caitlin Watson, Tina Hannemann, Oscar Robson, Paul Dormand, Joshua Keel, Steph Pickerill, Pauline Potter, Lily Rattray and all the various Wrights and Hugheses.

Many thanks to each of you for your encouragement, ideas, comments, corrections and general excellence.

The fantastic cover and outlines for the chapter art are courtesy of the magnificently talented Tom Humberstone. Please don't blame him for any of the dodgy illustrations I attempted myself.

Thanks also to Glenn Thomas Davis, Ray Lardie (and all at the Puttytribe), Albert Johnson and John Rogers, who are always there to provide morale when hope fades.

Special acknowledgements must go to Bob Ginger and Gemma Scott for their expert assistance in eliminating errors and ensuring that no sentence ever trailed off without

... but seriously, despite all this hard work it is impossible to entirely avoid mistakes, and so I can only apologise in advance for any errors that have accidentally crept in, be they typographical, factual, or simply terrible jokes.[1]

---

[1] To everyone who knows me: enjoy this public admission that I make mistakes while it lasts... it won't happen again!

Walking On Custard
& the Meaning of Life

CONTENTS

Before We Start	1
An Apprehensive Visit	3
The Ominous Bit	8

CUSTARD — 13

Me, Myself & Anxiety	14
Non-Newtonian Fluids for Novices	21
And Making It Visible	31
Both Growth Oaths, and Sloths	37
A Sweet Summary	42

SELF — 43

Hero-At-Large	44
Mea Culpa?	47
Brains. Braaaaiiiiiiiiiiiiins!	56
"Only"	66
The Unbearable Lightness of Bananas	68
Are Thoughts Good, Or Are They Bad?	77
A Critical Interlude	88
Crisis	90
The Inner Cuddle Dilemma	101
But What if I Actually... Kinda... Hate Myself?	111
And Her Brother Stuck In The Past	113
The Gift of Presents	115
The Full Revelation	126
Voices In My Head	127
An Adventurer Seeks Fulfilment	135
Cleave La Resistance	138
Limited By Belief	143
Being Ourselves	153
Questions That Occur To Me At This Point	155

OTHERS — 157

A Small Thing That Happened To Me Once	158
An Introduction to Other People	161
Approval For Everything	173
Growing Solo	174

Another Critical Interlude 184

That Grew In The Mud 186

Apples & Pomegranates 187

Hero-Still-At-Large 198

The Unbridgeable Divide 200

But Life is Complicated 212

In Fantasy Form 214

THINGS **217**

A Superficial Baptism 218

Where NOT to Find Happiness: Part One 220

Advanced Material Science 221

Where NOT to Find Happiness: Part Two 234

Being Without Flaw 235

To My Fellow Perfectionists 237

No Subtitle Required 240

Where NOT to Find Happiness: Part Three 243

The Boy & the Teacher 247

Dying of Laughter 248

A Breakthrough 258

Valuing Time 259

Hero-At-Last 272

FINALITY **275**

Gotta Keep Going 276

The Meaning of Everything 277

The Meaning of Life 287

A Guide for Peaceful Humans 289

Hero-At-Rest 290

A Note to the Reader 291

For Anyone Interested 292

AN OMINOUS NOTE
Before We Start

Er, hello.

I'm a bit nervous. I've not done this "book" thing before.

I hope I don't mess it up.

That is, if I haven't messed it up already. Are you supposed to start a book by saying hello?

I'm not sure... reading it back, it doesn't feel very professional.

On the other hand, it feels polite to be welcoming. And even though I planned this bit to be dark, ominous and foreboding, politeness is important, right?

Just because I've heard 'proper' authors saying over and over again "You don't have to start books with 'hello', you know, and how did you get my private email?" doesn't mean I ought to let my standards slip.

So, hello it is, I guess.

But then again, maybe those authors I just made up had a good point.

I think I've accidentally killed the ominous atmosphere before I even got it going.

Especially as I keep saying 'ominous'. That's three times already. All this repetition might dislodge the meaning from the word. Ominous. Ominous. Ominous. Yeah... it's gone. It's just a collection of sounds now. Ominous. Ominous.

Damn it. I was *planning* to warn you about a difficult bit coming up where we discuss a potentially upsetting topic. I thought it'd be fun to be all dark and mysterious. But I've completely screwed up the mood.

Okay... don't worry.[2] I have an idea...

Maybe there's a way I can rescue this.

---

[2] Well, worry just a bit, if you want. That's kind of the whole point of ominous foreshadowing, even if I am bungling it so far.

What if I draw a graph of the emotions associated with the first few bits of the book?

That way you'll know about the ominous bit coming up, and you can prepare yourself accordingly.

(This is a *great* idea. I don't want to speak too soon, but I am *one hundred percent sure* I have saved this opening bit from disaster.)

Here we go:

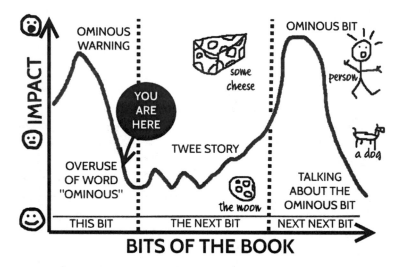

Hm. Oh dear.

Looks like I screwed up again. Even more than last time.

That graph is *terrible*. It doesn't clarify anything at all, except, possibly, something to do with cheese.

And the only thing it successfully warns you is that I'm incapable of drawing graphs under pressure.

Here's a better idea: let's forget that this whole opening ever happened. It's been an utter catastrophe.

Instead, let me tell a story...

THE SHOP BEFORE LIFE
An Apprehensive Visit

The shopkeeper twisted the lid tightly shut as she placed the jar in the final gap on the immense shelf. She paused, swiping away a little accumulated dust with her finger, before carefully settling the jar in its new home with the label proudly facing outward: EXCITABILITY.

She peered at the vessel, enjoying the sparkle and fizz of the contents, before shuffling back down the ladder. It had been a demanding day, but somehow amid the endless stream of customers she had managed to restock her supply of everything from ENTHUSIASM to IRRITABILITY.

She was a little low on PRUDENCE - and FICKLENESS, for some curious reason - but there was already more on the way from The Supplier, so there was no sense in worrying. Time to close the till for the night.

There was a boy standing at the counter. Surprised, she stared for a moment before breaking the nearly-awkward silence.

"Hello...! Have you been here long?"

The boy shuffled nervously.

"I've, I've been here all day. I, I, couldn't decide, you see."

Ah. One of *those*. It was getting late, but it was more important for him to get this right than for her to finish up on time.

"No need to worry, it's okay."

She smiled, in the kindly manner of a wise old shopkeeper from a story. After many long evenings perfecting her traditional facial expressions she took every chance she could to use them.

"So. What can I help you with?"

The boy hesitated before spilling all of his words out at once.

"It's just, I saw everyone else arriving and choosing and leaving and they seemed to know what they were doing and they chose all those jars and I'm afraid I won't pick the right ones and there's so *many* to choose from and I'm scared it'll all be a disaster and..."

He was gathering pace alarmingly, like a plummeting chicken that'd never been told chickens can't fly.

She somehow interrupted him mid-flow. "Whoa whoa whoa! Hold on, hold on! It's alright! It's alright," she said, "Everyone comes through my shop. *Everyone.* If over one hundred billion people before you managed it, I promise you can too, okay?"

The boy nodded, tentatively.

"Tell me. What have you seen so far that you like?"

He pointed at the solitary jar he'd placed on the counter next to the till. Inside, a gentle reddish-green mist swirled, like a super-heated plasma of gooseberry jam.

ROMANTIC

The shopkeeper grinned. *Great first choice.*

"Getting the most important things sorted first, then?"

She couldn't resist winking at him. He bristled at the gentle jab.

"I like the way it looks!"

"And that's as good a reason as any, believe me." She placed a hand on his shoulder and turned him to face the colossal array of shelves. "I know it seems overwhelming. But you've already picked one thing you like. You don't have to spend hours deciding over every last possibility. If you'd like to be born with SPORTING POTENTIAL or a SECRET LOVE OF BISCUITS then just go for it. Whatever you pick will work out down there."

She gestured toward the window at the far end of the shop, where an immense blue-green globe spun slowly against a distant starry backdrop.

"Biscuits sound nice."

He sounded a shade more confident. Time to push him into action.

"Well, off you go then... get choosing!"

He sprang towards the shelves. Before long, he'd amassed a creditable collection of jars. PERSUASIVENESS sat atop VIVID IMAGINATION, alongside IRREGULAR SHYNESS.

After a lengthy consideration, he added HESITANT. Shortly afterwards, he collected RESIGNED ACCEPTANCE too.

The shopkeeper examined the growing pile of jars, picking up OCCASIONAL OVER-INDULGENCE and swirling it around. She enjoyed the satisfying way the goopy yellow liquid stuck to the glass before peeling off, bit-by-bit.

"Excuse me," the boy said in a small voice. "I- I want 'PAIN-FREE' or 'WORRY-FREE' or something like that. Where are those?"

She leaned back against the counter before responding. She liked to make the most of any opportunity for a dramatic pause. Finally, she spoke.

"Ah, well, we don't have any jars exactly like that. But maybe if you take these two you'll experience much less pain and worry?"

With this, she pulled a pair of jars from an alcove beneath the counter. She didn't bother flourishing them, figuring that the earlier pause had provided enough of an effect. No need to go overboard.

The youngster examined the jars with a thoughtful expression. One churned with deep grey fog, declaring itself to be COMPLETELY EMOTIONALLY NUMB, while the other appeared to be empty, with only the label providing a clue to its purpose: INCAPABLE OF ANY THOUGHT OR REACTION WHATSOEVER.

The boy's face fell as he read the descriptions. Not literally, of course. The laws of physics must be obeyed, even in fictional magical shops selling human attributes to children who are yet to be born. He just looked a little sad as he spoke.

"I, I don't think I want those…"

The shopkeeper's eyes sparkled as she slid the unwanted jars back into their place.

"Good for you. You can't completely avoid pain without cutting out all kinds of good too. All you can do is learn to live with and handle it as best you can."

Anxiety flashed across his face as he considered this.

"What if I *can't* handle it?"

She picked up INFREQUENT BOLDNESS from his pile and twizzled it around. Out of the corner of her eye she saw him slide a jar she'd exposed to the back of the pile, out of sight. She smiled privately as she recognised the red material within: INAPPROPRIATE SENSE OF HUMOUR. One of her favourites, that.

He was still waiting for her answer.

"Well, everyone has some natural RESILIENCE. Not to mention you can develop any attribute you want even if you didn't pick it to begin with! And there are people down there -" she gestured towards the Viewing Area, where the giant planet hung, humming with activity, "- who will help you. Most of them, in fact."

"I'm not stuck with just these, then?" he said, waving at the heap of jars on the counter. "I can change later?"

"Of course you can change! In fact, I'd be very surprised if you don't. Changing and growing is pretty normal down there. Some people say it's the best part of the experience, learning to master traits they never even realised they had."

She watched as he stared at the world that would soon be his home. Finally he nodded to himself, as if making a decision.

This was because he had, in fact, just made a decision.

"Okay then," he said, his eyes darting around in a final search, "do I pick up my political opinions and sports team allegiances from another section? I haven't seen them yet. And is there a bit that teaches me how credit cards and mortgages work?! I'm scared of those. And..."

The shopkeeper couldn't help laughing.

"Opinions?! You don't start with those, kid. You've got to make them up as you go. And I'm afraid you don't get born knowing *anything*, least of all about finance! Plenty of people don't even know how that works by the time they come *back* through the gift shop."

And half of THEM even worked in finance, she thought to herself, in a moment of mild cynicism. She had been around for thousands of years so she felt she'd earned the right to occasional cynical moments.

The child somehow managed to flush with embarrassment and pale with fear at the same time. An impressive trick.

"Sorry," he said. "I guess I don't really know what I'm doing."

"You'll get used to it. Eventually."

The shopkeeper smiled, in a way she hoped was reassuring enough to puncture the poor kid's nervousness. *It's funny*, she reflected, *how varied people are*. Some confidently strode through her imaginary shop-before-being-born, picking jars as if they'd been born a thousand times before. Perhaps they had. After all this time she still didn't know where they came from, or where they went after their time in the Viewing Area.

Other customers appeared uninterested in making any choices at all, reluctantly grabbing at a scattering of jars before shuffling past. Then there were those - like this kid - who wanted to get everything right so desperately that they struggled to settle on any decisions at all.

Occasionally the shopkeeper liked to spend time in the Viewing Area watching how her past customers were faring. She liked that ultimately it didn't seem to *really* matter what people chose in their brief moments with her. Plenty of people had left seemingly well-prepared, with every possible eventuality covered, and yet they didn't seem any happier - on average - than those who had grabbed a few jars at random, or been hurried by enormous crowds.

"No, it's what they make of it when they're down there," she muttered.

(She liked to occasionally narrate things to herself, as if her life were being written down in some story, somewhere. She thought it'd be rude if all the most interesting things she thought remained purely in her head. "Dialogue is important," she muttered again, for no obvious reason.)

There was a nervous cough. The boy was standing determinedly by the counter, having added one final jar to his pile. The contents shined iridescently.

HOPE

"I think I'm ready now," he said, attempting his bravest face.

She grinned brightly and began ringing the jars through the checkout. (It had never been clear why this was necessary since, after all, the customers had no money. But it seemed like something a shopkeeper ought to do, and she didn't want to mess with Tradition. Besides, if the auditors ever showed up she would have a paper trail a billion pages high to keep them busy.)

"You're going to be alright, kid…"

CHAPTER ZERO
The Ominous Bit

Back in the real world, I've been having suicidal thoughts.

I appreciate that this is a harsh change of pace. Even after warning you - or trying to, anyway - that I was planning to say something dark, I feel guilty for bringing it up.

But I want you to know immediately that I'm not going to hold back on my deepest, most secret and most shameful fears.

I wondered about finding a way to mention it a little more casually, but it's not easy. It turns out there's a fine reason that classic opening lines over the centuries have steered clear of the subject of suicide. It just doesn't work:

> *In the beginning was the Word, and the Word was "AAAARGGGH".*
> *It was the worst of times, it was the worst of times.*
> *Call me, Ishmael... if you need to talk.*
> *It is a truth universally acknowledged, that a single man in possession of a good fortune, must be in want of a reason to go on.*

But that won't stop me from talking about it. We don't talk about this stuff enough.

I'm lucky. These extreme feelings only surface rarely. Though I've had some lows, I've never felt like actually acting on them.

It's just that, at times, a mood strikes, a cloud descends, and I feel helpless. As if life were pointless, as if it were too much hassle to go on existing, and like it would be easier - and almost preferable - to end it right now and get it over with.

Sometimes this mood would come with an apparent cause; at other times it would appear out of nowhere, like an unwelcome guest at a party I never wanted to throw in the first place.

This anxiety could pop up even in the midst of happiness, so I could never relax. A nagging sense of doom followed me like a surgically-attached fart, spoiling pleasant moments with terror of sudden disaster. I lived in a persistently agitated state I could neither explain nor shake off.

Mentioning suicidal or anxious moods would likely surprise anyone who knows me. From what I can tell, I come across as capable and 'together'.

And it's true: on the whole, I have a good life.

But this only made things worse. I felt pressured to maintain an illusion of strength whenever the anxiety built up beyond my normal background level of worry.

I was convinced I had to hide what was really happening from everybody. That I was the only one trying to hold it all together, while everyone around me had it all sorted.

Inner critic: Alright, Mr Dramatic, we get the point. Boohoohoo, poor you, life is hard. Get on with it!

Ah. There's something else I ought to mention. My numerous inner critics insisted on being included in the book.

Inner critic: "Insisted!" It was YOUR stupid idea.

We all have a continuous flow of thoughts in our heads: our inner voice. (Or, more accurately, our inner voices. As we shall see, there are a few.)

I'm sharing thoughts from these voices that I'd normally keep to myself. Some are awkward to publicise - such as judgemental thoughts about others, or about myself - and some are dark. Some are just plain embarrassing.

Inner critic: Some are probably true, fool.

Often, as you can see, they're merely irritating. It's my hope that putting my critics on public display will be encouraging. It's good to know we're not alone in clashing against our own thoughts.

Then again, I hope that *I'm* not alone in clashing against my own thoughts. That would be awkward.

Inner critic: This stupid plan is going to backfire. You're going to share all your secret fears and thoughts and it's going to turn out that it IS just you. Everyone will laugh, they'll all hate you, and you'll probably die.

Thanks, inner critic, for stepping up with some handy examples, just as they were needed!

So, there's an obvious question here. If my life is alright, then why do I have this stifling anxiety in the first place? What's with the repetitive worries, sudden terrors, the persistent feeling that I'm somehow screwing everything up, fear of the future, and inexplicable sadness when thinking of the past? What is that dark pit inside that occasionally makes me feel like everything is too much effort and suicide might actually be the easiest answer?

Is there something wrong with me? How can I be happy? What is the Meaning of Life?

This is the story of how I answered these questions; for me, and for anyone else fighting to stay afloat in their own lives. If nothing else, I want to reassure anybody else masking their anxiety that they are not alone. Nobody is immune from pain, not even those who seem to have it all together.

I find it perversely comforting to hear of the struggles of others, particularly when they appear 'sorted' to me. This possibly makes me a bad person, but it's not because I enjoy their suffering. Honest.

It's that we're all on the same level. No-one is exempt, no matter how rich, powerful or confident we appear on the outside; inside we are all hiding that we are broken to some degree. What a relief.

Coming Up Later On 'Walking on Custard'

As well as writing for anybody who's finding things difficult right now, in a way I'm writing for my past self of several years ago, who *really* needed to hear that he wasn't alone.

He was stuck in anxiety; in fact, long resigned to anxiety being inescapable. He was sceptical of self-help, of 'fluffy' advice, and of anybody claiming to have the answers. He wasn't sure what the problem was, and couldn't admit to anybody that there even was one. He was confused, overwhelmed and had no idea what to do.

All this meant he needed careful leading and encouragement to even begin tackling the problem.

As a result, it may seem that we begin a little slowly, as I'm helping my past self - and others like me - over the barrier of scepticism to where real progress can be made.

Don't worry: afterwards we'll get moving swiftly through an absurdly broad span of concepts, from thoughts to beliefs to relationships to contentment and even to death itself, before finally finishing by discovering the Meaning of Life itself. Sort of.

With such grand plans, you should be aware that I'm no professional. I'm not a psychologist, counsellor, therapist or philosopher. Sometimes I don't even feel like a 'professional sufferer of anxiety', as if there's some certificate I failed to get.

Yes, somehow I am anxious about not being anxious *enough* to write about anxiety. Sigh.

As I say, I'm not an expert; I just have some stories to tell, and some ideas to share which have helped me to live a happier life.

We are going to discuss the complete contents of the universe (more or less), which I've grouped into five clear and self-explanatory sections: *Custard, Self, Others, Things* and *Finality*.

In case that's too general, and you'd prefer something specific to look forward to, here are some spoiler-free previews of sentences you'll be experiencing later in the book:

"I soon found the right frequency and was happily whirling my fruity propeller."

"I arrived at Room 317, having evaded the mild disapproval of any monks, and knocked on the door."

"On balance, I prefer having clean, edible nuts that remain unburied all year."

Since our brains love the feeling of recognition, they ought to release a small happy chemical reward when you come across these sentences later on. The best bit is that telling you about this trick doesn't diminish it; in fact, it makes it more likely you'll remember this bit and go "oh yeah!" and get the pleasurable hit of completing the pattern.

At least, that's the idea.

*Inner critic: *rolling eyes* You are SUCH an idiot. Honestly...*

Now that we're all properly stoked with anticipation, we can get going...

WAAAAAAAIT!
Custard?!

Ah, sorry. I'm getting ahead of myself.

In case you're from a culture that isn't familiar with custard, all you need to know is that it's a tasty yellow sauce that is often poured onto puddings and desserts.

Admittedly, if you grew up some decades ago eating British school dinners, you might not recognise that description, instead remembering it as a yellow, lumpy and disappointing semi-punishment.

But it doesn't matter, so I prefer to visualise a gourmet sauce being served with a triumphant caramel pudding after a delicious meal. Just because it's tastier.

Anyway, relax. You don't need to be familiar with custard of any variety.

All will become clear very soon, I promise.

PART ONE
CUSTARD

"Poetry is a more philosophical and higher thing than history."
Aristotle

"Poets have been mysteriously silent on the subject of cheese."
G.K. Chesterton

CHAPTER ONE
Me, Myself & Anxiety

"Do not anticipate trouble, or worry about what may never happen,"
Benjamin Franklin

*"My arm feels a bit numb! That's weird...
Am I having a heart attack? I think that's a heart attack. Oh dear."*
Me

As long as I can remember, I've been worried.

Occasionally, this seemed like a strength. My obsession with avoiding risk helped me to dodge perils of all kinds. I rarely forgot my homework. My holidays were compulsively well-planned.

Worrying was simply my way of dealing with the world; through a haze of apprehension and imaginary worst-case-scenarios. And thanks to years of honing my worrying skills, if I'm ever in a building collapsing under the weight of a vicious zombie army I'll have a contingency plan ready to go.[3]

Sometimes I'd get stuck in loops of anxious fantasy, trapped in a maze of my own creation. The heightened stress would stay with me for days, taking away my ability to focus on anything but the imagined impending doom.

In between, I tried to forget about these anxious times.

But anxiety would sneak back up on me, even when everything seemed to be going well. One day I would wake with an uneasy awareness. That disquiet would expand and multiply until it was out of control for months at a time until finally - without obvious reason - everything would settle back to normal.

I never understood these anxious periods. I couldn't possibly talk about them, as I believed I was just being weak. I couldn't see any

---

[3] This is only a slight exaggeration; I have anxiously sat in cinemas imagining the floor giving way and sending me plummeting to inevitable messy death. This rarely improves the film.

excuse to feel bad, so telling anyone about it would only reveal how pathetic I was being. I just endured until everything rebounded close to normality, when I could resume not thinking about it at all.

I might go years between such episodes, and each time I'd believe - if I thought about it at all - that my anxious days were behind me.

This changed after one of the worst anxious episodes in my life, which lasted for nearly a year without explanation.

It was late 2010 and I was sitting at my desk at work. My life was broadly satisfying. I was cheerfully settled into a new job (after surviving an alarming year of fearing everybody would realise how little I knew when I was hired), and my social life in a new city was budding and full of fun. I was experimenting with writing a book (I wrote one, it was rubbish), and had just done my first proper stand-up comedy gig, to more or less universal acclaim (of the people who'd been there, obviously, which was more than enough for me). And I was dating a girl I'd secretly liked for months before we finally got together. All was well.

Yet, on this day, suddenly, I felt awful. I had noticed a slight unease earlier, but now my head was spinning and my heart was pounding. I was terrified. I wondered if I was going to fall over, or even collapse. I imagined the embarrassment of falling apart in front of my colleagues, and forced myself to sit still and stare at my monitor, hoping that no-one had noticed what was going on. Whatever it was.

I went to the little office kitchen and looked outside at some trees. Possibly somewhere in the back of my mind I thought this would help me connect with nature and make me feel better.

It didn't.

In fact, the normality of everything outside contrasted with my spinning sense of falling apart, and I felt worse still.

I returned to my desk. At lunchtime I liked to watch a comedy show, a treat I usually looked forward to all morning. As the familiar sound of the theme tune started up in my headphones I put my fingers to my neck to feel my heartbeat thumping. *What is that... like... 120 beats per minute? Am I dying?*

I couldn't concentrate. I closed the browser tab. I wasn't even in the mood for laughter. Something was seriously, seriously wrong.

I left work early and went to the doctor convinced I must be ill. Something was wrong with my stomach, perhaps. Certainly there was pain there. And I felt dizzy and tired and extremely scared. In the back of my mind was an insistent thought that I was severely sick. I could not shake the thought.

This non-event was the beginning of a lengthy anxious period. Every day was a conflict with myself. I woke up feeling a heavy dread, with my chest tight and my heart pounding. I couldn't concentrate on conversations with friends, only pretending to listen while my inner monologue was desperately screaming about how awful everything was. I said no to social engagements I wanted to go to because I felt terrified I'd fall apart there and embarrass myself and everyone would know what a fraud I was.

I dreaded everything. Mostly, I dreaded continuing to feel like this. But I couldn't see how it would stop, so I sought to explain how it started.

I was certain there must be a physical cause. There were physical symptoms: stomach aches, headaches, bowel problems, racing heart, dizziness and shortness of breath. There was a regular collection of unpleasantries on constant rotation.

Surely these must point to the underlying cause. I simply had to find what was wrong and then take some medicine, and all would be fixed. Or so I hoped.

I searched online. I diagnosed myself with every disease humans can catch, and probably some that they can't. I saw multiple doctors, and signed up for blood tests, urine tests, fecal tests, miscellaneous scans, allergy tests, reaction tests and the bar exam.

(Well, maybe not the bar exam. But I would have, if I thought it might help.)

One day I even had a surprise endoscopy.

I should probably explain the endoscopy. It wasn't *exactly* a surprise. Obviously I knew I was having an endoscopy. A certain amount of co-operation is required, after all.

The surprise was that, somehow, I hadn't really considered what an endoscopy meant.

If you don't know, it involves a scope going, er... in your end. Pleasingly, the word describes itself: *End-o-scope-y.*

I optimistically believed it would be a quick in-and-out procedure, so to speak. I'd nip to the hospital, there'd be a momentary discomfort, and I'd soon be on my way, finally armed with the answer to what's wrong with me.

Five minutes, at most.

Two hours later, as I lay in a hospital bed, naked but for a backless gown (having reluctantly been forced to hand in my clothes, my mobile phone and my wallet), I wondered if perhaps I should have told my colleagues - or in fact, *anyone at all* - that I was going to the hospital for a procedure and that I *might* be late to work.

I was the youngest person there, by far. In the beds surrounding me were men, maybe thirty to fifty years older than me, many of whom were quite clearly sick. Occasionally, I would receive a sympathetic glance from one of them, which I guiltily interpreted as pity that I was ill enough to need this procedure at my tender age. This just made me feel worse.

Several hours (and an astonishing amount of extra anxiety) later, I uncomfortably boarded the bus home. I never made it to work that day. But I did have a story that greatly amused my housemates that evening.

Some days in this drawn-out anxious period I'd feel better, some worse. But every day I awoke with a creeping alarm, fearing that today would be the day I'd "lose control" or "lose my ability to cope". I wasn't sure what I was failing to cope with, exactly, but it was clearly *something*. It felt as if every day I developed a new phobia. I became terrified of driving, of getting trapped in traffic, or being on a train, or in a crowded place like a theatre. I was afraid I was going mad, that there was something deeply and irretrievably wrong with me.

And every day I searched for more possible causes, figuring that if I could just understand *why* then I'd finally be able to fix everything.

Maybe it's some subconscious trauma. Maybe it's delayed grief for the death of my father. Maybe it's carbon monoxide poisoning. Maybe it's the onset of mental illness. Or brain cancer. Or an allergy. Am I getting enough exercise? Or doing too much? It could be my environment. My life choices. The place I live. Did I say brain cancer already?

Even - finally - accepting that there was nothing physically wrong with me didn't help. Now I couldn't understand how to fix myself *mentally*. Was I broken? There were a thousand different ways the anxiety manifested and I couldn't see any connection. My frightening online research indicated I had several anxiety disorders. At least.

I was afraid of the feelings. I was afraid they'd never stop. Or that they'd get worse. I was afraid of *everything*.

Nobody around me knew that this was going on. I certainly didn't let on. Not due to lack of trust in my family and friends, but out of shame.

It was essential that I maintained my image, and that everyone continued to see me as being "sorted". Capable. Able to handle whatever life throws at me. I couldn't face the idea of admitting I was falling apart for no explainable reason.

Finally, one night I lay awake, once more terrified for no evident reason.

The doctors had found nothing. I had found nothing. The anxiety wasn't pinned on any specific worry; it mutated to a new form every day. It didn't appear to be a medical problem. Not a stroke, stomach cancer, brain cancer, blood clots, environmental poisoning, gluten intolerance, AIDS or a mutated parasite attacking my brain. Probably.

It showed up without pattern, at unpredictable times, in irregular circumstances. For all my desperate hunting I was no closer to understanding why I was so scared of everything.

I lay in bed, afraid and furious in equal measure.

"I *shouldn't* be feeling like this! This makes *no sense!*"

Eventually, exhausted, I gave up.

I remember thinking "Okay. This is how I feel now. I am anxious. I guess I'd better just get used to it."

And - in that moment - it disappeared.

Not entirely - and certainly not forever! - but it lessened. For the first time in months, I suddenly felt peaceful.

This baffled me. I hadn't solved anything! I was no closer to the root of the anxiety, to that elusive answer I craved. But I was able to sleep that night, and this experience marked a turning point.

At the time, I had no idea what I had done, or why it had helped, but now I understand: I hadn't solved my anxiety, but in ceasing to fight I switched off my anxiety-about-the-anxiety.

It's achingly obvious with hindsight, but my constant worrying about anxiety was making me more anxious... which made me more worried... which made me more anxious. I was too mired in fear to recognise that this was happening. And so I didn't understand why I suddenly felt better.

I had inadvertently stumbled across the importance of acceptance on that particular evening. I'd love to say that it was a simple miracle cure, and from that moment on I never experienced anxiety again.

But that would make for a short book. And be a total lie. Not only was that not the only lesson I'd have to learn, I needed to re-learn that same lesson over and over. Possibly I'm particularly dense and anybody else would have understood immediately. But I hope I'm not alone in needing to learn important lessons repeatedly before grasping them.

For a while after everything calmed down, I stashed the drawn-out anxious experience in the far reaches of my mind, secretly hoping I could live in comfort now, forever. Predictably, it wasn't long before another anxious day came and the repressed fear of the inner black chasm returned. I still had not addressed any underlying issues whatsoever.

Deep down, I knew this. I occasionally feared that it would come back, which suggested I hadn't dealt with it properly.

There was no particular day when I chose to enter that black chasm to meet the possible monsters inside. I just got sick of living under the threat of anxiety returning, and I decided to do whatever it took to become free of the fear.

As I began, I found the sheer number of possible paths to follow overwhelming. I read widely. I took advice from the world of self-help, psychology, friends, family and therapists. It felt like unravelling a tremendous knotted string, where picking at any one part opened up several more that needed unpicking first. I'd follow a new strand and find yet more. And then I'd hit a strand that seemed to need one of the earlier ones to be untangled first. It was a crushing mess.

But, with time and effort, I slowly straightened out the knot. I understand the anxiety now. Mostly.

Your story will be different from mine, I'm sure. More anxiety, less anxiety, harder circumstances, easier circumstances.

Though each of us has our own individual struggle, many features are shared, such as a desire to appear strong. We pretend we can handle everything, even when we can't. This is a totally understandable, but harmful, drive. Not only do we shut ourselves off from asking for help and support, it can make us feel worse as we over-estimate how well everyone else is dealing with their problems:

"They look so in control. I can't handle things as well as them."

For all we know, they might feel just as broken as we do, and be doing a similarly great job of hiding it.

I was.

I hope that if you're in a similar situation that you can reach out and share your difficulties with a trustworthy somebody. The fear of being seen to 'not handle it' is almost always worse than the reality of being honest with someone we trust.

We don't have to undertake this journey alone. Many others have been down this path, and many more are travelling on it right now.

At the risk of getting uncomfortably poetical, this is a pilgrimage I've travelled myself, and I understand how arduous it is to pass.

But before we talk about exactly how, I'm afraid that there are things we must discuss regarding custard and physics.

CHAPTER TWO
Non-Newtonian Fluids for Novices

"Let's pretend there are only shear-thickening time-independent non-Newtonian fluids. For simplicity." - Me

This is stating the obvious... but in a non-Newtonian fluid the viscosity is dependent on the shear rate of the fluid.

We all know that, right? You can barely go down the pub without hearing someone talk about the relationship between viscosity and shear rate for all manner of fluids, if I remember rightly, which I *definitely* do. Viscosity is the talk of the town.[4]

But, on the miserably small chance you have no idea what I'm talking about, here's a quick reminder.

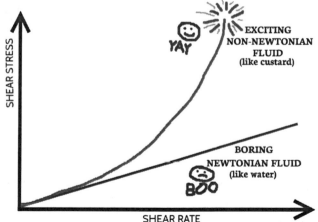

Figure 1. This doesn't really require a numbered caption, but I think they add nicely to the scientific atmosphere.

The viscosity of a liquid describes how well it *pours*.

---

[4] Please don't be afraid if you don't like science. There is no test, and barely any science.

Water isn't very viscous, so when after tipping a container of water it flows out, usually all over my crotch as I fail to impress a girl by drinking a glass of water without spilling it.

Some liquids are more viscous, like paint, shampoo or yoghurt. Ketchup is a common example. We've all turned a ketchup bottle upside down, shaking and bashing it with increasing annoyance until it suddenly comes free and spills, usually all over my crotch as I fail to impress a girl by squirting ketchup without causing an embarrassing incident.

In some liquids, known as non-Newtonian fluids, this viscosity changes depending on outside forces.

Put simply: *you can cause some liquids to harden merely by hitting them.*

This means you can perform impressive feats with non-Newtonian fluids. For example, you could fill a swimming pool with custard and walk across it, like a dessert-oriented Jesus.

Yes, it's entirely possible to walk on custard. If I stood on a vast pool of custard I could remain above the waterline[5] as long as I liked.

Hit it with my left foot. Hit it with my right foot. Each time, the liquid hardens beneath me, and I repeat. Left foot, right foot, left foot, right foot.

Custard is my servant, and I its master.

However... while it's *possible* to walk on custard, I strongly recommend against it.

Not for the obvious reasons, like getting your feet sticky with custard.

Or the understandable mockery from your friends and neighbours at how you choose to spend your time.

But because it's *exhausting*. Once you start, you CANNOT stop.

You slap your left foot down, and the custard temporarily hardens to take your weight.

Quickly - before it softens again - you slap your right foot down, hardening the custard beneath you once more.

---

[5] Okay, custard line.

By then, the custard underneath your left foot has absorbed the force and is returning to its less viscous mode. So you raise your left foot and slap it down once more.

But already your right foot needs to move. And so it goes:

Raise right foot. Slap.

Raise left foot. Slap.

Left. Slap. Right. Slap.

Left. Slap. Right. Slap.

You CANNOT stop. Walking on custard is an exhausting process. Sure, it's possible. It's even fun for brief periods. And it arguably may have some use.[6] But it *cannot* be a way to live your life.

You can't rest, you can't relax, you can't pause. You certainly can't build a shelter and live there. Once you are on a pool of custard, you have to either keep running to stay afloat, or escape to solid ground.

The longer you stay there, the more tiring it becomes.

Anxiety is like this. We exhaust ourselves, running, running, and running, just to remain where we are.

We get trapped in nervous patterns of thought that drain our energy and hurt us emotionally.

I liken these cycles to *custard traps,* which can manifest themselves in a myriad of ways:

We worry. We anxiously fantasise about possible disasters. We ruminate on the past, chewing over our hurts, heartbreaks and missed opportunities. We compare ourselves to others. We listen to the running commentary in our heads that criticises us for all our flaws and mistakes. And many, many more.

Inner critic: Aren't these just... bad things? Except for the helpful inner commentary, of course. What makes them traps?

The main feature of a custard trap is that it is a self-perpetuating cycle. The same pattern of thought that hurts us also prevents us from easily escaping. These cycles disrupt our inner peace and prevent us from living contentedly.

Let's observe an example of a custard trap in action:

- A passing bad feeling occurs, perhaps just a natural low mood.

---

[6] Perhaps after a freak boat accident with a pudding tanker, if those exist?

- Rather than let it go, my response is to search for an explanation.
- Because it's just a natural low mood - part of being human - I can't explain it to my satisfaction.
- I think "Why do I feel bad for no reason? Is something wrong?"
- This makes me feel worse as I imagine all the horrible things it could be.
- My coping mechanism again attempts to explain the new, worse feeling.
- In reality, nothing has changed, so I still can't find any reason for it.
- But I feel even worse, so I'm even more upset by the lack of explanation.
- I think, even more critically: "I'm *terrible*, there's *no reason* to get so anxious."
- This makes me feel worse still.
- And so on...

Left foot, right foot, left foot, right foot. No time to stop, think, or escape.

All my energy is spent on the repeated response of fruitlessly asking "why?"

Of course, there's nothing inherently wrong with wanting to understand myself - this is the seductive positive effect of this custard trap - but, in this case, it feeds the negative feeling and creates a cycle.

It's common for these traps to pretend to be helpful.

For example, we might justify ruminating on our mistakes by believing it helps us to improve. It hasn't worked any of the million times we tried it before. But maybe this time it will! And each time we are drained a little more, as we beat ourselves up for everything we've done wrong.

All custard traps have this seductive possibility of a positive effect. This isn't an illusion: perhaps the first time we ruminated on our flaws we *did* learn something useful. But we become trapped when we no longer experience these positives, but only the anxious, despondent, draining feeling of endlessly fighting to stay afloat.

Things get worse still when the negative feeling produced by the trap encourages us *back onto the trap*. If our habitual response to feeling bad makes us feel worse, then the cycle is complete. Our attempts to cope only generate more negative feeling to cope with. Unless we change something, we are fully stuck.

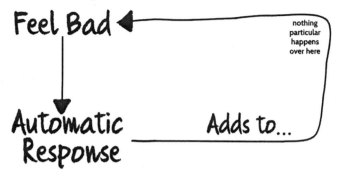

Figure 2. A simple custard trap, with another scientifically atmospheric numbered caption.

Looking at this diagram, the very idea that we might be caught by something so simple (and badly drawn) seems ludicrous, or even insulting. But, as we shall see, these traps are insidious and sneaky.

I appreciate that the word "sneaky" makes it sound a little like the custard is alive and plotting against us, for some unguessable reason. I've had some abysmal desserts, but none of them have gone so far as actively conspiring to imprison me. Or take me into custard-y.

Yes, take me into custard-y. Custody. Get it?!

Inner critic: Oh no. I warned you that if you tried to write a book you'd only humiliate yourself publicly. Though even I didn't think you'd be reduced to such dismal puns already.

You've caught me there. That was arrestingly bad. I've made a right pudding of myself.

Inner critic: Stop it.

Sorry.

Okay, so sneaky is the wrong word. But it's true that our automated responses are often invisible to us, along with the emotional effects they bring. We will see that we must develop the skill of detecting these internal patterns before we can learn to escape them.

Not everything that tires us is a custard trap. Everything requires energy. Externals such as family, career, chores, hobbies - or whatever we spend our time on - aren't custard traps. But our attitude towards them might be. We can never definitively list what is - or isn't - a trap: it is our thoughts, beliefs and habits that spawn them internally.

The custard, therefore, only exists in our minds. But that doesn't mean it's not real.

I mentioned earlier that after my prolonged anxious episode I hadn't solved, or even identified, any of my underlying problems. I was still unwittingly walking on custard. All my negative mental habits were exhausting me.

My anxiety was my body's reaction. It sought to jolt me into finding and fixing these hidden traps in my thinking.

I wouldn't claim that all anxiety hides such a helpful message (that kind of claim can be irritating, especially when in the midst of tough times) but it is true that if I had listened to it sooner I would have saved myself some pain.

My automatic response had been to explain the anxiety externally: it's my job, it's my home, it's my health, it's my relationships, it's the government, it's my diet, it's idiots on public transport, it's the terrible musical choices of the youth of today...

I got increasingly stressed as I ruled out each possible cause, each time redoubling my efforts to explain everything. My response encouraged me to look in the wrong places, and the resulting frustration added to my growing collection of negative emotion.

Yes... my search for the cause of my anxiety was itself a custard trap. This would be pleasingly neat if it hadn't been so bloody awful at the time.

Drowning In Custard

Because walking on custard requires constant effort, if we remain there long enough then eventually we are so drained of energy that we lose our steady walking rhythm and flounder. The ground melts beneath our feet and we stumble, slipping momentarily under. Our instincts kick in: we fear drowning. We kick, splash and lurch in an adrenaline-fuelled alarm.

These acute anxious episodes - such as panic attacks - mostly only last for minutes, though the associated trauma can haunt us for a long time afterwards. Some say they experience such panic for days, months or even years at a time.

We will explore techniques to manage these especially awful moments. But, while living without fear of panic attacks is an admirable goal, we can aim even higher than that.

Merely avoiding drowning is not enough: if we never take action we can waste significant portions of our lives on these energy-draining cycles. We can spend years anxiously existing, rather than truly living.

We avoid stepping back to solid ground for many reasons. For me, I was afraid of the journey.

Between my anxious episodes I pretended to myself that everything was fine. I feared waking the beast by poking at it; but instead of learning to tame it, I ineffectively imagined it wasn't there.

Maybe I could have continued with this series of anxiety-recovery-anxiety-recovery. I don't know. But I'm glad that I finally diverted some energy into seeking out solid ground.

Sadly, peace doesn't come easily. If there were a magic spell we could say to have someone rescue us in a boat (presumably with special custard-friendly engines) I'm sure we'd all say it. And I'd certainly love to pass it onto you. After saying it for myself, of course. I'm not an idiot.

*Inner critic: *cough**

But - unfortunately - this kind of self-work is exactly that: work.

Our minds resist escaping the custard traps. They tend to fly into a frenzy when faced with change, coming up with lies - and lies mixed with truth - about why we should stay where we are:

We can't afford to do this right now. We'll sink if we don't use ALL our energy staying afloat. This will open us up to more pain. Other people don't need to do this. Other people have it worse. Is this really such a big problem?

There may be just such a voice whispering to you "We don't have time to read this book now, there's too much to do," or "This sounds like too much effort".

We humans hardly need much encouragement to remain where we are, even if it's uncomfortable. But if we believe an alternative exists, we can move towards it.

It's likely that we will need help. While it is possible to reach solid ground ourselves, it's many times easier with help. If there are people in your life who can assist you then allow yourself to accept their help.

It is exhausting for every one of us to constantly run atop our own custard. We each have patterns of thought that drain us, so there is no shame in needing to share the load for a moment.

Many times in my most anxious moments I was too prideful to ask for any help, or even admit that I needed any. I struggled alone for far longer than necessary. I worried that asking for help made me weak, or deficient, or broken, or open to judgement, or that people would like me less. These feelings are common, and extremely unhelpful. Asking for help is a signal of strength, not weakness. It shows that you value yourself enough to do the difficult task of leaning on another and being vulnerable to them.

The amount of support that we need constantly changes. Each of us will go through rough times and smoother times. Often in the rough times we forget that life was ever smoother, or fail to believe that it can ever be smooth again.

In my bleakest hours I've labelled myself as permanently hopeless, forgetting that there were times when the worst I had to deal with were my own comical mishaps,[7] and that those times will likely come again.

For most of us even these dark times pass - or we find that we can cope with the new, harder reality - and we go back to needing less help once more.

Life, as usual, is unfair, and some of us will have a harder time escaping the custard. But nobody is so far from shore, or so without help, that they cannot make it if they are determined to do so.

EXERCISE: A Solid Dream

If, like me, you react nervously to the word "exercise", then relax. Hardly any exertion is required, I promise.

Having said that, I expect you'll get more out of this book if you play along with the exercises by considering the questions and trying the activities. But it's up to you.

Luckily, this exercise is a *very* easy start. You basically just have to read it.

---

[7] Much more on these later, unfortunately.

Inner critic: Given the quality of your writing so far, that's actually a pretty big ask.

Sigh. I'm going to ignore that. Let's begin this exercise with a question for the readers:

How are things for you, right now?

Maybe you feel broadly content, and are just reading idly out of interest. Or for entertainment.

Inner critic: Ha! Surely anyone looking for entertainment will have given up already? They'd probably prefer a real pool full of custard to this tedious rubbish.

Well, I can't really deny that a pool full of custard sounds like a hilarious way to spend an afternoon. However, while I can't realistically create a pool of custard for anybody, I am in a position to offer a few optimistic paragraphs.

Inner critic: "A few optimistic paragraphs"... Not the most poetic way to begin, but go on. This ought to be good.

Perhaps, right now, you are floundering under the custard with no hope of getting out. Or perhaps daily anxiety and fear - the endless, tiring work of staying afloat - is all you've ever known. Maybe you can't help but scoff at me, as you would to a passing sailor telling a tall tale of 'dry land', where it's possible to exist without habitual ceaseless running.

It's important to believe in the existence of solid ground. If you believed the sea of custard were infinitely big, why would you bother heading for the edge? Trust that solid ground exists, along with the promise of a more contented life there.

No matter how you feel, I'd like you to imagine a more ideal version of yourself.

A more resilient self, who isn't affected by the setbacks that currently send you reeling when they come along. A more fulfilled self, who enjoys all the good things in your life and sets the direction your life is heading in. A less fearful self, who is more able to do anything that feels insurmountable at the moment.

Imagine being that idealised version of yourself as you get up and out of bed. How do you feel at the start of the day? What are you looking forward to? Imagine this person - this ideal you - peacefully getting on with things, even in the face of your problems. Put yourself inside their mind and glimpse the feeling of security.

Imagine a less anxious life. Picture reaching dry land and finally resting. Here on the solid ground is everything you value, without the demand to run and run and run just to stay afloat. How does that feel?

Try to get in touch with the actual peaceful emotion, just for an instant.

For now, allow yourself to believe that there is an edge. That, if you look for it and consciously move, you can make it to shore and rest on solid ground.

It may not be that reading this book gets you to that ground, although I hope to give you enough clues to step in the right direction.

At least, let me tell you that the shore exists, and that it is within your power to get there.

Inner critic: *clap* *clap* You're basically the heir to Shakespeare. I have tears in my eyes.

Really?!

Inner critic: No. That was terrible. Get on with the next chapter so we can get this farce over with.

PERSONAL CUSTARD
And Making It Visible

"The first time a river goes down a mountain, it can only do it randomly; but from then on... it has been down once." - Thom Tuck

Let me first apologise for the mildly worrying term "personal custard". As long as you don't think about it too closely, it conveniently communicates the idea that we all have our own individual custard traps. We're going to begin identifying these now.

One way these traps hide is that we can feel anxious, stressed, or empty for so long that we forget that it is possible to feel otherwise.

Imagine somebody who has an unrealistic belief about how productive they ought to be. They hammer themselves every day for not getting as much done as they 'should', berating themselves harshly for procrastinating, never being satisfied with what they've actually achieved, and seeing the success of other people as a stick to beat themselves with.

After years of this, they believe that this negative self-talk is normal, or even helpful. It is just part of the backdrop of existence. If they could spy inside someone else's brain they might be surprised that this constant stream of inner negativity isn't present. They may also be shocked at the negative habits this other brain has collected, which - from outside - are glaringly apparent.

Our brains quickly stop noticing things that haven't changed in a while. Any messiness in our home fades into the background to us. For a few days after rearranging furniture, or painting a wall, we notice the change whenever we enter the room. But our brains soon adjust to the new normal and we stop being surprised.

Familiarity makes our inner custard traps similarly invisible to us. "But isn't *everyone* anxious all the time..?"

When I was twelve I found out I needed glasses. The moment I put them on I could see detail I didn't know existed. Previously I couldn't understand how everyone else at school could read the faraway writing on the blackboard. I assumed they all saw the same bunch of wavy squiggles as I did, and that they were somehow just better at reading them.

It was an astonishing, freeing realisation that there wasn't anything fundamentally wrong with me: I just needed to wear glasses.

We assume everybody else sees the way we do, when, in fact, we're all wearing unique glasses that colour everything.

We can have the same epiphany about our mental habits. To stretch and mix metaphors, it's as if we wear glasses that camouflage our custard traps to appear like solid ground. To take off the glasses and make the traps visible we need to open ourselves to fresh perspectives.

To this end, in a moment, I am going to invite you to do some things that are outwardly pointless, and possibly even embarrassing.

Inner critic: You should listen to him. He's an expert on pointless and embarrassing.

The aim is to break out of our usual patterns. It is commonly quoted that as much as 98% of our thoughts are identical from one day to the next. This may be an urban myth, but we are generally not surprised to hear it, so I suspect it hints at some truth. Deep down, we know we are creatures of habit. It seems plausible that our thoughts are extremely habitual too.

Habits are incredibly powerful. Very often - maybe even several times a week - I suddenly realise that I'm brushing my teeth without having consciously made a decision to do so.

A routine bathroom trip gets somehow mixed up with my morning/evening routine and I pick up the toothbrush and toothpaste automatically. Usually halfway through I become aware of what's happening and feel a little embarrassed. Luckily, this habit probably has a positive impact for my dental health, at least.

Most of our habits are harmless, like accidentally brushing our teeth during the day, or taking a certain route to work, or the way we answer the phone.

Although, if you brush your teeth with bleach, travel to work across an electrified train track or answer the phone by saying "Hello, this is All Of The Terrorists, how can we help you?" then I suppose even these could be harmful habits. Context matters!

I'm guessing, from the fact that you're reading this book at all, that the habitual grooves you've built for yourself aren't working exactly the way you'd like.

Perhaps this manifests itself for you as anxiety, perhaps as feeling overwhelmed, perhaps as a subtle sense that something is wrong, or any of the countless unique ways we experience the exhaustion of running on custard.

Whatever your personal experience, your habits are not working for you. But they can change.

If it helps, repeat this aloud:

"Right now, my habits aren't working for me. But they can be changed."

Inner critic: How would they know if that would help? For that matter, is saying it aloud at all useful?

Probably not. But I got the feeling I'd just said something good, so I wanted an excuse to say it again for emphasis.

For some of us, the idea that we can change may itself be a freeing notion. We can get hooked by the idea that there's something wrong with us, that we're deficient in some way and that our anxious fate is inevitable. The realisation that we have simply developed some bad habits can be liberating.

There is a famous ancient story in which a Zen master pours tea for a student. As the cup overflows, the master says that space must be made for more tea by removing the old tea. In the same way, we must make space in our minds for new ideas. Grasping tightly to old ideas prevents us from even seeing new ideas, let alone trying them out.

Acting outside of our usual norms teaches our subconscious several important lessons. One: Change is possible. Two: Change doesn't have to be scary. Three: I value myself enough to attempt to change.

So, right now, I'm going to invite you to break some of your usual thought patterns. Let's begin a habit-breaking habit.

EXERCISE: Breaking Out Of The Groove

Here are some mini-activities to stimulate some novel brain pathways:

- Take your socks off and hang them from your ears. For bonus points, grin at your childishness.

Inner critic: Hold on. Are you serious? You've been building up to this exercise for two pages, and your "grand plan" is to encourage readers to HANG SOCKS from their EARS? What the hell is that supposed to achieve?

Hold on, critic! You'll see. Just get over your cynicism for a moment and try it. All will be explained.

Sorry folks. Here's the rest of the list:

- Pull your arms inside your top, spin your top around, and put your arms back in so you're wearing it backwards.
- Make a harrumphing noise with your lips as loud as you can. Pay attention to the sensation of your lips vibrating.
- Touch your elbows together in front of you (if you can!) and wonder why you've never tried this before. Be curious about what other simple actions you could possibly attempt that you've never considered.
- Tilt your head 90 degrees and look at a familiar object. Notice how your brain makes it appear the same despite it being the wrong way around.
- Look closely at another familiar object (or even the back of your hand). Notice something about it that you've never seen before: some aspect of its shape, texture, colour, condition, history. If you can, be amazed that something you've spent so much time with can have details you haven't noticed until now.

For some people these kinds of activities will be easy (and even fun!). Some people will feel a lot of resistance towards doing them, even alone.

If that's you, it could be interesting to identify the resistance. Is it good, old-fashioned human laziness? Is it that these actions seem childish, or pointless? Or that they make you feel embarrassed?

Maybe it would help to think "I will give this a try despite it being foolish, childish, embarrassing, pointless, too much effort, and only a random idea from some useless stranger", or whatever your particular objection is.

If you're still having trouble, ask yourself how you would convince someone else to try this.

Perhaps you'd say "You're feeling lazy - but don't you want to get to know yourself better?"

Or maybe "Why is it a problem to be childish? Why not feel embarrassment - while alone - just for a moment? What's the problem?"

Inner critic: My problem is I'm trapped in a brain with an idiot who thinks that hanging socks from your ears is at all helpful.

Well, critic, I think you secretly want to try it.

Remember when we were kids? We'd happily try anything and laugh about it, because we hadn't yet deluded ourselves that we know everything that there is to know. If we want to change our habits, we must be less rigid. Sure, hanging socks from your face isn't *in itself* a solution to anything. At least, nothing I can think of.

But think of it as practising being more fluid and opening up to novel experiences. If our current habits aren't ideal, then *by definition* we have to do something we don't normally do to break out of them.

The purpose of the exercise is to experience something new, and to widen your perception of what is possible. If you can find a moment's laughter and joy in doing something unusual with your socks, then maybe there are other possibilities you hadn't noticed.

Maybe the way you currently think about yourself, or your situation, or your worries, isn't the only way you could think.

I hope you've tried some of these silly ideas. Ideally, you managed to let go of old restrictions, and were able to experience a moment of genuine curiosity, or joy, or laughter, or all three.

If so, recognise that YOU generated that curiosity and joy from within yourself, and that you are totally capable of changing your usual patterns, and having fun in the process.

Carving out new paths in our minds - however slight at first - hones our ability to recognise our personal custard traps. Over the coming days and weeks make a conscious effort to observe your thought patterns, and shift them out of established grooves and onto fresh paths whenever you can.

Ideas you can try:

- Brush your teeth with the hand you don't normally use, and notice how fresh the experience feels (and minty, too!).
- Take a different route to some place you regularly go, and consciously pay attention to the environment on the way. For bonus points, notice something on your normal route that you normally tune out.
- Stand on one leg in an empty elevator.
- Eat your food in a different order at mealtimes. If you're like me (and many others) you eat your meals in a set order, often without realising it! Another habit that's become invisible to us.

Fresh experiences are great. But - of course - don't do anything unsafe in a misguided effort to break your habits.

Crossing the street safely is a good habit. There's no reason to mess with it. Travelling to work in a home-built rocket-powered helicopter would be an awesome change to your regular routine (if you could handle the lack of parking), but I doubt it's a good idea.

Similarly, don't mindfully eat a brick.[8]

For now, let's play with neutral habits: little ones that we can safely change with minimal resistance, like the examples above.

Practising looking at our situation with new glasses will help overcome our natural inertia, and start to make visible these painful thought patterns that have faded into the background.

---

[8] They taste awful.

CHAPTER THREE
Both Growth Oaths, and Sloths

"You can have no dominion greater or less than that over yourself."
Leonardo da Vinci

Part of me can't stand the word "self-growth".

Thinking further, I'm not so sure that there's *any* "self-" word that I like.

Self-discipline? Sounds like unpleasant, guilt-inducing hard work. Nearly as bad as self-control.

Self-incrimination? To be avoided.

Self-righteous? Not a positive attitude.

Self-fertilisation? A filthy habit for plants and trees.

Inner critic: Trees ARE plants. And I'm not convinced that self-growth is a real word, so this whole rant is somehow even more pointless than your usual drivel.

I suppose, honestly, I don't care if "self-growth" is in the dictionary. I just need a flimsy excuse to talk about the part of me that cringes at the mere mention of self-growth.

Inner critic: I have cringed at most words you've mentioned so far, if that helps.

It doesn't. In any way. But thanks for the reminder!

So, a part of me cringes at self-improvement, self-help, self-growth, or whatever you want to call it. It wants to ask sarcastic questions like "what's so 'self', exactly, about this growth? What exactly is growing? I'm not physically expanding."

Inner critic: You are, actually. I've been telling you for years.

Please stop interrupting! Anyway, I'm sure I'll get around to doing something about that soon. Definitely.

My instinctive reaction to self-growth has always been scepticism that it actually means anything. You can't measure self-growth, unlike proper measurements such as height, weight, the speed of light, beard length or nipple ratio.

Inner critic: Nipple... ratio?

Yeah, sorry. I was on a roll, and made that one up.

But, despite my reservations, I have concluded that self-growth is undoubtedly real. It may not be physically measurable, but the effect of personal growth is nevertheless visible in our lives.

Problems that once nearly knocked us out often seem smaller when we look back at them. We learned to cope, and if the same problem came along again we would now have the resources, ability and experience to handle it more comfortably. This is growth.

Fearing the return of a problem therefore suggests we may have more to learn from it. I always dreaded the return of anxiety, until I finally tackled it at its roots. My cynical inner voice would shudder at the phrasing, but the return of a frightening problem is definitely a 'growth opportunity'.

Inner critic: Very buzzword-y, Neil. I'm starting to think you're doing this simply to annoy me.

How very self-centred of you, inner critic!

Inner critic: If I'm self-centred... and I'm part of you... doesn't that make YOU the self-centred one? I mean, you're the one having an actual conversation with yourself in a book.

Damn it, I thought I'd won that one.

The older we are, the more tempting it is to believe we are stuck with ourselves and our habits. Even in my twenties I believed that any problems I'd picked up would be with me forever. As if negative traits were like ticks that burrowed into me and couldn't be removed. They aren't. We can change any of our habits.

There's no need to pessimistically assume that we're stuck as we are forever. We just have to trust that change is possible, and growth is desirable.

Beginner's Advancement

Once we are past any scepticism towards the very existence of growth, the next step is to figure out the best way to achieve it.

This is an easy answer. It turns out that the best way to achieve self-growth is to deepen our self-knowledge.

Inner critic: Ah yes, more self-words. How long did it take for you to hypocritically adopt them after opening this chapter by claiming you didn't like any of them?!

I'd like to argue with you, inner critic, ("No-one calls me a hypocrite: not even ME!") but I'm sensing it's really not worth it. You can have this round, irritating inner voice.

Inner critic: Haha, in your FACE, fool!

Technically it's also your face. Ha.

Anyway, I remain correct when I say: self-knowledge is crucial.

Over two thousand years ago the philosopher Socrates said "the unexamined life is not worth living."

I found this quote inspiring, and for a while I decided to live entirely by the words of Socrates. This worked out well at first; he spoke wisely on death, on knowledge, on wisdom. It seemed I was setting myself up for success if I lived by his maxims.

Then I found out that his last words were "We owe a rooster to Asclepius. Please pay the debt."

This troubled me. Not that he would wait until he was literally on his deathbed to pay back his friend (not cool, Socrates!), but that he *borrowed a chicken* in the first place.

This must mean that at some point Socrates went to his friend's house, asked to borrow his chicken, and then never gave it back. This is why you should never learn about your heroes. Occasionally they do inexplicable things with poultry.

But, despite his chicken predicament, his quote about examining our lives is insightful. I used to assume that self-growth happened automatically as we got older. But there is no automated process that makes us wiser.

Without self-examination we may never notice our weaknesses. And if we don't even know where we are strong and where we are lacking, how could we possibly take action to improve? Growth relies on increasing our self-knowledge.

There is a further reason to actively prioritise self-examination: we have no choice but to spend time in our own company.

Inner critic: Please don't remind me.

Sometimes we can be difficult company even to ourselves, as you can see from the near-constant interruptions from my inner critic in this chapter. At other times we can be the best possible company we could wish for.

We can take time away from most people when they irritate us, and this respite helps to rebuild the relationship later. But we cannot take any time away from ourselves.

Inner critic: Sigh.

For better, or for worse, the only constant presence throughout our entire lives is ourselves. It is clearly in our interest to get to know that presence as well as possible. But...

It *still* seems to me like an inherently silly idea that it requires time and effort to get to know yourself. Even now that I'm literally writing a book about self-growth, there remains a part of me that insists it's embarrassing, pointless or that growth doesn't exist... *despite the fact I know better from my experience.*

I need constant reminding of the benefits of self-examination to keep my motivation up. I have learned that, left to my own devices, I will distract myself and fiddle time away, merrily ignoring whatever I need to do.

I have met people who don't share my natural scepticism in the face of growth and change, and who are baffled that I need convincing that 'growth is good'.

If you are anything like me...

Inner critic: Let's hope for their sake they are not.

Ahem. As I was saying...

If, like me, you are a growth-sceptic, perhaps you'd find it useful to make a 'self-growth oath'.

EXERCISE: Betroth to Self-Growth

Inner critic: Someone's discovered rhyming dictionaries!

Yeah. But I'm loath to push it any further.

Inner critic: Can't clothe it in anything more respectable?

Don't you start, critic. That'd be the *both* of us.

Anyway. Putting tired overuse of rhymes aside, here's the plan:

Resolve to do whatever it takes to be less anxious, to commit to change, to seek out growth. And find a way to remind yourself of that resolution.

Perhaps write "I commit to getting to know myself better" (or even simpler: "GROWTH IS GOOD, HONEST") and place it somewhere you'll see it regularly.

Whether or not you're a growth-sceptic, it's useful to encapsulate your motivation in a few words, whether it's freedom from anxiety, greater self-understanding, feeling less overwhelmed in social situations, or whatever you like.

At this point, I'm not too worried about whether these motivations are realistic or not.

For example, "freedom from *all* anxiety" is an impossible goal: if a radioactive wolf were to suddenly attack in a haunted forest then anxiety would be an appropriate response. As would a rapid change of trousers. And sacking your travel agent.

For the moment, our motivations provide a direction to travel in, not necessarily a destination.

Later, from more solid ground, it may be easier to accept that some anxiety is a necessary - and positive - part of being alive. In the meantime, "eliminate anxiety" is a reasonable initial direction to aim towards, even if it ends up not being our final destination.

If you haven't already, take a moment to reflect on and identify a self-growth goal. What characteristic would you like to borrow from the ideal you? If it's useful to you, write it down. Sometimes written reminders are useful for me; sometimes they only act as sources of guilt, and I'm better off without. Do what works for you.

I know it's tempting to read on without doing this reflection, and your mind will give all kinds of excuses in favour of temporary laziness, or justifications for why you shouldn't bother:

"I don't need to write this down, of COURSE I'll remember my overriding motivation. Does this fellow take me for a fool?!"

Regardless of these excuses, without action nothing can ever change. Taking just a minute to reflect is helpful, both for the reflection itself, and - more importantly - for the fact that we are overcoming our inertia by acting at all.

Next, we'll take our first step towards shore: getting to know ourselves.

Inner critic: (sarcastically) I cannot wait.

CUSTARD
A Sweet Summary

I'm addicted to summarising.

At my most extreme, I even summarise conversations with my friends; highlighting the various points we discussed, and perhaps reminding everyone involved of any promises made during the conversation. This might be something like:

"So, we're all agreed that the government are making a terrible job of education, everybody likes those new shoes you bought - well done! - and you'll text me tomorrow about cinema times, right?"

Luckily I only do this with friends who have learned to tolerate my little quirks.

Anyway, this means that I'll occasionally pause to squeeze the essentials from a topic and re-present them in simplified form.

Inner critic: Did you just summarise the bit about summaries?!

At least I'm consistent, I guess.

So Far:

We all run on custard, in the form of habitual, exhausting patterns: repetitive, difficult thoughts that cause further repetitive, difficult thoughts.

We have to keep running just to stay afloat, causing anxiety, stress and other difficult feelings.

We can choose to continue to live like this. Or we can make an effort to reach solid ground.

First, we need to open up to new thinking, to make the invisible custard traps come out of the background and into view.

Believing that growth is both desirable and possible is a necessary precursor to action.

Next, we will work on increasing our self-knowledge, as advised by notorious ancient chicken-borrower, Socrates.

PART TWO
SELF

"The mind is its own place, and in itself
Can make a heaven of hell, a hell of heaven."
Milton

THE CHRONICLES OF McBIGGS
Hero-At-Large

CRASH CRASH SMASH CRASH

The metallic grill flew away from the air vent, hitting the opposing wall with a satisfying clatter.

McBiggs charged headlong (but legs first) out of the vent, barely noticing the sharp pain that was his reward for the masterful karate kicking he'd given the grate. He expertly reloaded his weapon mid-manoeuvre. All those hours practising weapon maintenance using only his perfectly aligned heroic teeth were paying off more than usual today.

He heard a slither from around the corner and waited in silence. *Another one. Probably attracted by the noise of the grate after I awesomely kicked it to bits.*

He silently raised his gun.

The Thing oozed into the corridor. McBiggs didn't hesitate for even a second.

BLAM. BLAM.

His Serious Space Laser carved two holes right through where its eyes would be if it were human. McBiggs didn't know much about the Things, biologically speaking. He didn't care much either. Not after what they'd done to his crewmates since the Incident.

He automatically glanced down at his laser to check the remaining charge. 97%.

This fuel cell was his last. When the indicator reached zero that was it. He'd be out of options, unless he could somehow reach the armoury and resupply.

But that meant crossing the entire ship. He had no idea how many Things slithered between him and the stash of fuel cells that represented his final hope.

Not to mention the possibility that the Things might already have found and eaten the fuel cells. Assuming they even ate fuel cells. Maybe they absorbed them. Or married them.

McBiggs shook his head. This was no time to get distracted by thoughts of possible relationships between aliens and fuel cells. Unfortunately, this raised the question of when *was* a good time to be distracted by such thoughts. But this was no time to get distracted by such questions...

McBiggs escaped his thoughts. *Better make this cell count,* he thought, confidently, as he stepped over the still-smoking corpse of the Thing. *Good job I'm super-awesome.*

McBigg's Inner Critic: I'm sorry, who are you talking to?

What was that?! Confused by the unfamiliar sensation of uncertainty, he hesitated mid-step, accidentally dragging his foot in goop.

McBigg's Inner Critic: You always talk to yourself in these moments. I bet a real hero wouldn't do that.

Was that right? Didn't other people talk to themselves in these moments? McBiggs didn't normally consider such things, relying instead on his natural heroism to carry him through the day.

McBigg's Inner Critic: That's not your worst problem, though. You wasted a whole fuel cell already. Imagine if you had just flushed the airlock instead of firing all those shots. You could probably make it to the armoury with TWO fuel cells. You don't deserve to survive.

He fought against a wave of despair. There was no time for this. But the unfamiliar voice was right. He had made some mistakes. His first ever mistakes. Still, wasn't 'worrying' something *normals* did?

McBiggs dipped into his heroic reserves and resolved once more that he would see his family again. He resumed his stride, grasping his determination hard, and his Serious Space Laser even harder.

McBigg's Inner Critic: You want to see the family again?! Better hope they never find out you let Johnson die like that. What a coward. Imagine the shame of everybody knowing what happened! The "great" McBiggs MESSED UP.

This thought was like a knife in his impressive barrel-chest. Well, not much like a knife. He'd shrugged those off before without a problem. This was worse. *Is this what... sad... feels like?*

McBiggs closed his eyes tight shut, and, in desolation, covered his face. Automatically, he flicked his gun into safety mode, in unconscious deference to his Health & Safety training teacher.

Never hold a loaded gun to your face, even in moments of despair, he remembered. At the time he'd wondered how he'd know what despair felt like. But now he was grateful for the advice.

McBigg's Inner Critic: Like it matters what you do with a loaded weapon! It's been pure LUCK you've survived this long. Any second now, that luck is going to run out. You're hopeless.

McBiggs moaned aloud. *Why is creeping through a stranded spaceship filled with ravenous Things from an alternate dimension SO HARD...*

McBiggs didn't know the answer to his own question. He no longer knew anything. But he did know he was the only one left. He had to get to the armoury.

McBigg's Inner Critic: So you DO know something.

What?! McBiggs was confused. Again. He clawed at his face, biting back tears with his eyes.

McBigg's Inner Critic: You said you didn't know anything. Then you immediately said you knew something. How hard is it to maintain a consistent approach to reality? If you're the last hope for humanity, then we're all doomed. I mean, how do you even bite tears with your eyes?! What is WRONG with you? Give up!

McBiggs was getting angry now. Or possibly sad. He wasn't sure. But he didn't like it. He shook his head in a desperate attempt to empty it out, and listened.

Silence. Blissful silence. No voices, not even in his head.

He grinned and opened his eyes.

NO! There was a Thing immediately in front of him. Instinctively, he pulled the trigger. But instead of a *BLAM* there was only a *K-CLICK.* He'd left the safety on!

Damn that safety training! I'M SAFELY GOING TO HELL!

McBiggs desperately, frantically, vainly looked around. But there was no escape. None. He was doomed. The Thing reached out...

Slither... slither... slither...

McBigg's Inner Critic: Now look what you've done!

It was a bad day to be McBiggs.

CHAPTER FOUR
Mea Culpa?

"RESPONSIBILITY, n. A detachable burden easily shifted to the shoulders of God, Fate, Fortune, Luck or one's neighbor"
Ambrose Bierce

Responsibility is bothersome.

I mean, I *know* it's important, and that, honestly, it's a topic I *ought* to discuss before we go any further. Taking responsibility for ourselves is crucial to every part of this adventure in self-growth, blah blah blah.

But... it's boring to think about, and I'm not sure I'll do a good job, and I'm hungry as I write this, and my desk is distractingly untidy, and there are so many more fun ways I could be consuming my time than by writing a chapter on *responsibility*.

So I've decided to pay a student I found on the internet a couple of dollars to write it for me instead.

I haven't bothered checking their work. I'm sure it's fine. Here it is:

Why Responsibility Is Important, an essay by ~~Nigel Harness~~ Neil Hughes

It is totally important to be totally responsible because responsibility is really important. For example I am responsible for this essay on responsibility. If I wasn't responsible for it then it would never get done and therefore the world would be worse, a bit.

Sometimes we make excuses, and that is bad because making excuses is blaming others for your problems, even when it is actually their fault like when I got fired even though my flatmate locked me in a toilet so he could steal the chain from my bike so there was NO WAY I could get to work on time. HOW IS THAT MY FAULT?

According to the online research I am doing for this essay for that guy who's too lazy to write his own book I should take responsibility for everything that happens to me even when it's definitely someone else's fault.

So in some way everything is my responsibility, even if it's just that I am only responsible for my emotions and not my actions like punching my flatmate in the neck.

I think that's two hundred words, especially if we include this sentence. Did I get it right? If you actually read this can you pay me soon - I really need to eat.

Responsibility Is Like Offence: Taken, Not Given

I'm not sure that's really true, but it makes for a catchy subtitle. And I'm sure someone will come along and fact-check it later.

...

Okay, okay. Nobody is going to come along and write this chapter for me.

Nobody is going to rescue me from the custard. Nobody can face my issues but me. If I'm going to be less anxious, I have to take action myself. No-one is going to fulfil my dreams on my behalf.

Sometimes we mistake a genuine desire to help us for an offer to save us. We'd love it if another person - a therapist, friend, partner or stranger - came along and whisked us off the custard to solid ground, without us having to put in any effort. But it's impossible. This excursion through life is one that only we can do for ourselves.

Of course, we don't have to do anything alone: there's *always* support available. But receiving support is not the same as having somebody live our lives on our behalf. It's simply not possible for anyone but ourselves to carry us off the custard.

Imagine running along on your sea of custard. Picture it turning solid beneath your feet with every step. Could you do that while carrying a whole other person? Of course not, and neither could anybody else.

We can cheer people on their journeys, and lend helping hands to pull them back above the surface when they're feeling overwhelmed. We can even lean on each other as we travel together. But nobody has the strength to pick you up and run you all the way to solid ground.

I'd like to generalise this further: to live a fully contented life, we must take responsibility for *everything* ourselves.

Inner critic: Everything? So... the conflict in the Middle East, climate change and the global economic crisis are all YOUR fault then. Ha! I KNEW it!

Well, no, obviously not.

When I say "everything" I don't mean literally everything that exists in the universe. I may be a fool, but I'm not a total fool. I mean "everything we could reasonably take responsibility for".

Inner critic: That's a big climbdown. Is it a record that it only took you two sentences to contradict yourself?

It's not a contradiction. Often, our default attitude is to minimise our responsibility: taking as little as possible, and only grudgingly accepting it when we have no alternative.

In this mindset, responsibility is seen as a scary external imposition, something we'd rather not have if we can avoid it. If we could palm our responsibilities onto someone else we'd happily do so. Perhaps this admission reveals a little too much about myself, but I think I'm normal: with rare exception, we fear responsibility.

However, we can benefit by reversing that attitude and aiming to take the maximum *appropriate responsibility* over our lives.

Responsibility is appropriate if it's over anything in our direct influence, including our inner world of thoughts and emotions. And it's inappropriate if it's over anything else.

Clearly, we are not directly responsible for everything that happens in our lives. If a meteor hit our house it would be perverse to believe we were somehow responsible for the physical event. Similarly, we are not responsible for accidents, crimes or abuses that come our way. Events occur every day that are outside of our control. And we are never responsible for the actions or words of anybody else.

However, we are always responsible for our response to any of these events. This distinction is often lost. We tend to conflate the event with our response to it, as if they were inseparable. But our emotional response isn't inevitable: we always have a choice.

For example, when somebody acts against our wishes we can fly into a fury. Maybe we could have chosen to see the situation differently, and therefore the existence of the anger is our responsibility. Or perhaps not: maybe the situation is such that it would be impossible not to feel angry.

But whether or not we're responsible for the *existence* of the anger, we cannot evade responsibility for our actions afterwards.

The event, our emotional response, and our actions based on that response are all separate entities. In any given event, we may be responsible for all three. We are always responsible for at least one.

Blame versus Control

These attitudes - of minimising and maximising responsibility - differ in their understanding of responsibility.

Minimising responsibility sees it as *blame*. In this mindset, being responsible for something opens you to possible blame; something which we all - quite reasonably - try to avoid at all costs. If responsibility is blame, it makes sense to dodge as much of it as possible.

The opposite attitude - that of maximising responsibility - views responsibility as *control*. This is the healthier attitude to take. In this mindset, avoiding responsibility limits our options, while seeking it multiplies them.

This doesn't mean we should take responsibility over everything. We obviously can't - and shouldn't - seek to control everything around us. The optimal level is control over all of our actions, thoughts and emotions... and as little as is necessary over anything else.

This link between control and responsibility implies that to control our anxiety (and our emotional state more generally) we must first take responsibility over it.

We must acknowledge that nobody is going to fix our anxiety, find our life goals, or bring us happiness, if we do not do it ourselves.

The realisation that "I have to do this for myself" is always frightening, no matter the topic. Given that I even find my laundry an upsetting burden, something major - like facing up to anxiety - can be paralysing.

When I began to truly look at my anxiety I wanted someone to make it all better. I felt frustration at therapists, that they didn't 'just cure me'. I wanted them to take the problems away, not keep making me face them.

But these problems couldn't be solved without my taking ownership of them.

It's always so tempting to hide from responsibility. We may lack belief in our ability to cope. We may fear making mistakes. Part of us may equate responsibility with blame.

We may even fear the freedom of responsibility. Acknowledging that we're in control of our own lives means acknowledging that we're free to make a mess of them. But making a mess is always a possibility; the only alternative is to make nothing of them.

Hiding is not a worthwhile option. When we choose to avoid responsibility, we choose to deny our own control over our lives. We have to trust ourselves.

Delightfully, trusting ourselves already makes us worthy of that trust. Admitting our responsibility automatically makes us more responsible.

But what does taking maximum responsibility mean for our anxiety, our stress, and our battle to stay afloat on a seemingly endless sea of custard? Are we responsible for anxiety too?

This question only makes sense if we see responsibility as blame. Of course we are not to blame for our anxiety. Looking for someone, or something, to blame is the wrong question. It doesn't help. Instead, we simply want to take control over it.

It's common to feel weak in the face of anxiety and our other problems. We can counter that weakness by taking ownership. I found a paradoxical strength in looking at my inner mess and saying "Yes, that's a wreck covered in mayhem. But it's *my* wreck!" This gave me the ability to step in and start cleaning it up.

It helps to separate out the anxiety into parts, and take as much responsibility over those parts as possible. When something triggers our anxiety we have automated responses: perhaps a racing heart, a tense feeling in the chest, a sickly feeling in the stomach. We can't control those. But we can control our response to them. And we are not constrained to act in a certain way merely because our heart is racing.

If we believe that we are incapable of control when we are anxious then we are giving our power away to the anxiety. We are saying "I feel anxious and therefore I have no choice in any of my actions." Afterwards, when we're feeling strong again, it seems obvious that this was never true. We always had a choice.

But at the time, even tiny obstacles can feel utterly impassable. So it's okay to take only small amounts of responsibility at first.

If this applies to you, maybe next time you feel overwhelmed you could choose a small part of your experience to take responsibility over. Perhaps you could choose just your lungs: "Next time I feel anxious I will choose to control my breath", and concentrate only on that.

Or maybe "next time I feel angry I will control my hands and not hit anything" would be more relevant to you. If you have an emotional state that causes you to lose control (or, looked at another way, dodge responsibility), what small action could you take to regain it?

We can't immediately take responsibility over all of our behaviour in every circumstance, but we can increase the amount bit-by-bit. Each time we take more responsibility we gain a little more control over our lives. Eventually, we can make big changes.

To solve our problems, we first have to take ownership of them.

Matters of Context

The extent to which we create our own reality is surprising.

I often find it easier to meet people when I am abroad. For a while, I thought people in foreign countries were just naturally friendlier. But when visitors came to my country I was surprised to discover that they thought the same about everybody here.

Eventually, I realised it's not that people abroad are friendly and people at home are less so. It's me that's different. When outside of my usual circumstances, I become more open to new experiences, more willing to step out of my comfort zone and chat to strangers.

By being more cautious at home, and by being more open abroad, I was creating my own circumstances. But this is always true: my attitude always affects my experience. This realisation allows me to always choose the reality that I want.

In every circumstance, we choose our attitudes, which affect the way we see everything. So, to some degree, *everything* we experience is our responsibility.

Even so, it's not always clear how much we are - or should be - responsible for any given thing.

It's easy enough in situations we have no control over: they're not our responsibility. Conversely, we are always responsible for our attitudes.

But how can we tell when our actions are dodging responsibility, and when we are reacting appropriately to our circumstances?

I am annoyed at the universe that there isn't a clear answer to this question. I would prefer to live in a world where we could divide all actions into neat lists of 'dodging responsibility' and 'appropriate reaction to circumstances'.

Sadly, due to what I can only assume is a massive oversight, it seems that context is everything, and we have to put effort into interpreting each situation as it comes.

Imagine if I took to my bed and refused to leave it. In my current circumstances that would be - I believe - dodging my responsibility to myself. Sure, the world is an occasionally frightening place, and I'm tired and would like to sleep until the world has sorted it out. But I would be avoiding it purely for the sake of avoidance. I'd be denying myself control over my life for no good reason.

On the other hand, remaining in bed seems like a totally appropriate reaction to many circumstances. Perhaps there are perfectly good medical reasons to rest. Or maybe some time is needed to heal emotionally from a trauma.

The *action* is neither good nor bad. And this is true of nearly all actions: the context determines whether the action is appropriate.

The lack of clear, universal rules means that we must decide for ourselves where we are failing to take responsibility, and where we are taking too much.

In fact, we must *take responsibility for finding this answer.* Could it have been any other way?!

EXERCISE: Whose Monkeys Are These?!

Maximising our responsibility comes with an important flip-side: taking too much responsibility onto ourselves. We must recognise which problems belong to us, and which problems don't.

There's an old Polish saying which translates as "Not my circus, not my monkeys" - in other words, "that's not my problem."

We must know which monkeys are ours and which belong to other people. If we're holding onto other people's monkeys then, well, things get scratchy and flea-bitten and violent and nasty and covered in bananas and poop. We have enough trouble managing our own monkeys.

We need to see where we're not taking enough responsibility, and where we're taking too much. Or - if you prefer to discuss things in terms of animals - we need to give everybody back their monkeys and spend some time rounding up our own.

Once you've taken all possible appropriate action, anything further is holding onto somebody else's monkey against its will. For example, after you've given advice to a friend in a tough situation you have done all you reasonably can. You can't force them to actually act on your advice. For now, you can let go of their monkey.

Let's identify the monkeys in our lives.

This exercise will take no more than five minutes. Don't let your brain talk you into not doing it. If you think "I'll do this later" you won't!

Grab some paper. (Or a stone tablet and chisel, if you prefer.)

Make a list of a few worries you have at the moment. Nothing comprehensive, just jot down some things that are causing you anxiety or suffering.

When you're done, go down the list and mark off anything that is your responsibility. Write next to it *MY MONKEY*.

Say to yourself "I am responsible for this monkey."

Be careful in your thinking: you're not blaming yourself for the state of the problem, or saying that it's your fault. You're saying "from now on, I'm going to work on sorting this problem out. I will round up and take care of this monkey."

It's not your *fault* if the monkey escapes and causes a bit of monkey chaos - but it's your responsibility to catch him and bring him back to his little monkey house. And to clean up afterwards.

Remember that while a particular worry may not be your responsibility, your reaction to it always is. For example, "What if there's a nuclear war?" isn't your monkey (most likely you're not the one with the big red button), but your reaction to the idea is.

Some worries may need two or three items: one for the worry itself, one for your emotional reaction, and one for any actions you take. Sometimes, only one of them is your monkey.

Inner critic: That would be a monkey off their back, am I right?!

Er, yes, I guess so. I'm not used to you jumping in with jokes. But even dodgy puns are better than abuse. Thanks.

Inner critic: I couldn't resist a bad joke. It's probably your fault, somehow.

Ah. That's more like it. Though... take responsibility for yourself, inner critic!

Once you have identified your monkeys, next to every other item on the list write in big capital letters: *THIS IS NOT MY MONKEY*, and mentally release responsibility for that particular problem.

A Plan for Responsibility, A Short Summary, Which I am Writing MYSELF

Responsibility is such a dreary topic that I longed to cut it out, but it is too important to ignore. If we don't take control over our lives - and especially our internal world - we cannot make any progress. Without this step I might as well not have written the rest of the book.

Inner critic: That would have been kinder to the readers.

We want to maximise responsibility over our lives, which makes it essential to view responsibility as *control* rather than *blame*.

We accept ownership over our life circumstances. Those that we can change: it's our job to change them. Those that we can't: it's our job to manage our reactions to them.

We let go of the problems that don't belong to us and do not waste our energy on them.

There. Writing this chapter wasn't so hard in the end.

CHAPTER FIVE
Brains. Braaaaiiiiiiiiiiiiins!

"It may not be attractive, but my mind's over-active"
from 'I'm Intense' by Luke Smith

I have a complicated relationship with my brain.

At first, it seemed that we were destined to be great friends. My brain would help me out with school, exams and work, and in return I would keep it alive and healthy by eating (reasonably) well, exercising (a bit) and not falling over and hitting my head (much).

I suppose the first hint that all wasn't perfect in this relationship was noticing that my brain often betrays me in social situations, tripping me up and embarrassing me for its own dark amusement. For example, during a recent conversation with a friend about our life plans:

Them: Choosing a career is tough. Have you tried asking yourself "What gets you excited?"

Brain: Say sexy leopards! Say sexy leopards!

This is the kind of nonsense that the writers' department in my brain suggests while I'm trying to talk. My mind occasionally - okay, frequently - behaves like an excited child that thinks it's hilarious, but is actually just being silly and showing off. I generally have to reject the first idea my brain suggests for what to say.

Now, I don't claim this is normal. In fact, after asking around I haven't found anyone else who relates to this exact problem. It seems that most people are happily able to get their mind to behave during a conversation without extra cajoling.

But this is just one of a number of ways my relationship to my mind is less than ideal.

Inner critic: Ahaha, you have a RELATIONSHIP with your MIND! That's the most pathetic thing I've ever heard!

Mr. Inner Critic, you do realise that it's partly you I'm talking about?

Inner critic: Ahhahahaha, and now you're TALKING to YOURSELF! What a sad case.

I'm hopeless, apparently. But there may still be hope for you, reader.

It's probably not a new idea to you that our thoughts can cause problems. When we examine difficult situations in our lives - those that trigger anxiety, stress, depression or other problems - we often find that the root cause of the unpleasant feelings was a thought.

This link from thought to feeling happens automatically. A thought can stealthily pass through our minds, evading conscious notice, yet still set off an unpleasant chain reaction of emotion.

Before we explore this further, let's ensure we are talking the same language. What are *thoughts* as opposed to *feelings?* A broad definition might be something like:

Thoughts are 'words in our heads' and feelings are 'sensations in our body'.

We associate feelings with a bodily sensation (hence the word 'feeling'?), be it tension in the chest when anxious, buzzing in our skull when angry, or tingling down the spine when happy.

In contrast, we experience our thoughts as an inner monologue just behind the eyes, an unceasing parade of words in the brain.

This difference may seem so obvious that pointing it out verges on being disrespectful to you. If so, sorry. But the distinction is not always so clear, particularly in everyday conversation, where we conflate thought and feeling so frequently that it requires effort to notice the mix-up is happening.

Take this snippet of incredibly realistic everyday conversation:

Speaker One: What are your thoughts on that obscure author Neil something-or-other winning the election to be President of the World last week?

Speaker Two: It makes me so angry! I'm furious that that bumbling moron was even allowed to vote, never mind somehow actually be elected to Supreme Leader of Earth. I'm going to go punch a hole in a wall.

We can see here that the second speaker (who, in my entirely unbiased opinion, appears to be a judgemental fool who will someday get his comeuppance) responding to Speaker One's request for THOUGHTS by venting his FEELINGS. If you weren't specifically watching for this you probably wouldn't notice. Even if you were watching for a swap between thoughts and feelings, it comes so naturally to us that you may still miss it!

This careless lack of precision is just one reason I expect Speaker Two to be summarily executed by a wise, noble and benevolent leader in the nearish future.

Similarly:

Speaker Two: Why, what are your feelings on the matter?

Speaker One: Personally, I think he was the best choice. He is definitely a man of vision and clarity, who is well-poised to lead humanity into a Golden Age of some sort.

In this conversational highlight the delightful Speaker One appears to have accidentally committed a similar error by responding to a request for FEELINGS with her THOUGHTS (albeit in this case her thoughts are extremely well-reasoned and sensible, so we can forgive Speaker One for this tiny and understandable lapse).

Once again, this answer feels natural: we don't notice the substitution of thoughts for feelings, or vice versa.

It would be a robotic and inhuman world if we precisely responded with *only* thoughts or feelings, depending on the exact question we are asked. There's a reason people rarely say "Hey, you're telling me what you FEEL, I only asked what you THINK!"

In our internal world, thoughts and feelings are strongly linked. We experience them together, as something of a 'lump'. Moreover, we identify with this lump of thoughts and feelings. We call it "us", saying "I *am* angry" and not "I am currently experiencing anger" or "I have anger".[9]

If we wanted, we could take time to sift through the lump of experience and label the different bits: this bit is a thought, that bit is a feeling. But why would we go to that effort? It's natural to assume that this lump is reality; inside us lives a confusing mess of thoughts and emotions.

---

[9] In English, anyway. Other languages may vary.

However, it turns out that making the effort to distinguish thoughts from feelings can bring clarity and understanding to our inner lives.

Imagine walking down a street, and meeting eyes with a stranger. A look of disgust crosses their face, and - without a word - you pass each other by. How do you feel?

I'd like to suggest that your emotional reaction depends on what you *think* about what happened. Your interpretation of the event determines your emotional state. This interpretation is affected by all the thoughts about similar experiences built up over your lifetime, plus whatever occurred to you in the moment.

Some examples include:

If your main interpretation of the disgusted look was "They think I'm hideous" (or similar), then you will feel bad about yourself.

If it was "I wonder what that look meant. Maybe they remembered something unpleasant they have to do today", then you will feel reasonably neutral.

And if your thought was along the lines of "They seem like a nasty, judgemental person", then you might feel angry at them. Unless perhaps you have an extra thought afterwards: "But I should be kind to nasty people because they may have had some awful experiences that made them so nasty", and you end up pitying them.

There are infinitely many possible interpretations. Everybody has different feelings in the same situation because our interpretation is different. This interpretation is based on our thoughts, which arise out of our past experiences.

The leap from thought to emotion develops so rapidly that we rarely notice it happening. From inside, it seems that someone gives us a strange look and we instantly feel anxious (or neutral, angry, pity or whatever). The emotional reaction is so instantaneous that the intervening interpretation gets missed.

Human minds are fast analytical machines. They are also designed in a way which makes them incredibly lazy.[10] Once they reach a conclusion they like to re-use their work over and over to

---

[10] Another word for lazy is "efficient", right? My fellow lazy people might recognise this argument. It never works.

save the effort next time around. So each time we interpret a situation in a particular way it becomes more likely that our mind will re-use the same conclusion in similar circumstances.

It follows that changing our thoughts will change our emotions. And, therefore, *failing* to change our thoughts gives up any control we could have over our emotions.

Returning to our example of the funny look on the street, imagine we thought "They think I'm hideous." If, moments later, further down the street somebody else looked at us oddly, what do you expect our interpretation to be?

The second time around, the look doesn't even have to be disgusted; just a slight lingering glance will be enough for our mind to confirm its earlier conclusion: "They're looking at us too! Oh god, I'm a monster!"

It could be that the second person is just staring into space. Or maybe you look like someone they know. But our minds love to spot patterns, so they confirm prior conclusions whenever possible.

Eventually, this interpretation becomes second nature. We internalise the belief that "I am hideous".

The leap from event to thought to emotion becomes faster and ever more natural, as the mind becomes ever more efficient at serving up the same unpleasant conclusions. Once a thought becomes sufficiently ingrained we stop even needing events to trigger it; our brain obediently trots out the "I am hideous" or "Everything is awful" litany without prompting.

Finally, we stop noticing - if we ever did - that our negative emotions have thoughts underlying them. And so it never occurs to us to change or challenge the underlying thoughts. The cycle repeats until our emotion is ingrained.

Unless we do something about it.

Hidden Thoughts

It can be very difficult to root out the thoughts which underlie our emotions. Often, I have no explanation for how I feel.

But this is usually because I don't pay attention to all my thoughts. I start paying attention *after* I feel anxious (or whatever). This means "I feel anxious...why?" is the first thought I notice, and I miss the initial thought that generated the anxiety.

This is frustrating. It seems as if our emotions spontaneously appear, and we are powerless against them.

Sometimes it appears as if external events directly drive our emotions, such as when someone is rude, or ignores us. We blame the event for the feeling: "He made me so angry." But, as we saw earlier, it is our interpretation of events which drives our emotions.

We are not obliged to be angry when somebody acts a certain way. In response to their behaviour, we think thoughts, and those thoughts *may* make us feel angry.

On close inspection, we find that most emotions arise in response to our thoughts, whether or not we consciously noticed them at the time.

I first absorbed this idea during a particularly anxious time. I was especially afraid of being trapped, in traffic jams or on underground trains. Sadly, both were unavoidable daily risks. I couldn't even think about leaving the house without becoming agitated and afraid. I even began to resent my friends for inviting me out. I knew any invite meant I'd get locked into a cycle of wanting to go, yet not wanting to experience the associated anxiety, and hating myself for the whole thing.

I usually went out anyway, but felt awful for even having this dilemma when it seemed like such a non-issue to everybody else.

Anxiety would arise 'out of nowhere', and I'd think to myself "I shouldn't be feeling so anxious: I'm only in a traffic jam", or "everyone else can cope, why can't I?"

These thoughts would generate yet more anxiety, and I would feel even worse.

And so, I turned to the internet (this is not always a terrible idea) where I learned that beneath each 'spontaneous' arising of anxiety there is a hidden thought.

It's easy to see that the thoughts I had *after* becoming anxious - such as "I shouldn't feel this way, I suck compared to everyone else" - cause a negative emotional reaction, usually a combination of guilt, frustration, self-hatred and hopelessness.

More subtly, I missed how my thoughts were responsible for the *initial* emotion that I was wishing away. The sudden anxiety on being invited to a social occasion wasn't without reason. It was because - without realising it - my automatic thought was something like "I have to cross the city to get there, what if something terrible happens on the way? I might get trapped underground if the train breaks down."

Understandably, I had an anxious reaction to such thoughts.

It took me a long time to even notice I was thinking like this. It was such a standard part of my background thought process that these imaginary worst-case scenarios were literally invisible to me. I simply noticed the anxiety and immediately began a critical inquest of why I was such a useless person for feeling this way.

Interestingly, despite knowing that - of course - I still liked my friends, at one point I actually questioned whether I had somehow become unsociable. Before I understood what was happening, I feared that I'd simply lost interest in people. I value my friendships highly and it terrified me that I'd lose them due to some imaginary subconscious wish to drive them away.

In reality, this was me *thinking the thought* "I wonder if I've suddenly become unsociable for no reason?" and reacting with panic to that thought as well! This is why it's so important to patiently observe what's happening inside ourselves. Otherwise we can invent any number of explanations that may make things worse.

With hindsight it's easy to understand, but at the time I was so tied up in anxious knots that it wasn't clear where any emotion was coming from. I was too anxious to spot the thoughts responsible.

I had to learn to notice my automatic thoughts, and to control my response to them, before I could understand and describe the process as clearly as this:

- Some event occurs.
- An automatic thought goes unnoticed:
  "Something bad may happen" [11]
- The automatic thought makes me feel anxious.
- I consciously react to this uncomfortable feeling. As I never noticed the automatic thought, I can't understand why I feel anxious. So I think:
  "I shouldn't feel anxious, there's no reason for it."

---

[11] This automatic thought can even be "This normally makes me anxious; what if I become anxious?" After a while, we don't even require an external event; fear of anxiety works just as well.

- I react to the 'shouldn't' thought by feeling even worse. The cycle continues.

This all happens more or less instantaneously. For me, it feels like a sickening gut punch and a creeping, fizzing terror.

I've underlined the two thoughts in this example: one automatic, one conscious.

Surprisingly, I think the second thought - the conscious one - is the most dangerous. These thoughts begin the cycle that allows these situations to spiral out of control. Breaking the habit of responding to anxiety with anxiety-increasing thoughts prevents us from slipping beneath the custard in crisis.

Once we can prevent the cycle from escalating, it's easier to notice the habitual, automatic thoughts that cause the initial unpleasant feelings.

To do this, we first need to get better at recognising automatic thoughts when they show up.

EXERCISE: What Will I Think?

We have two types of thought. Some are conscious and effortful, and some are automatic, offered up by our chatty subconscious. Usually, we fail to distinguish these automatic thoughts from those we deliberately choose. Accepting our automated thoughts unquestioningly can lead to problems, as they may breed unwanted emotions.

If controlling automated thoughts were possible we could turn off the tap at the source, stopping the mental monologue of "I am useless, I am ugly, I am doomed" or whatever our personal recurring themes may be. Yours may be more fun than these.[12]

I have always loved thinking, and so I was resistant to the idea that I can't control all of my thoughts. It seemed to take away something I loved.

But there's an easy way to prove that subconscious thoughts are beyond our immediate control, and that there was never anything to be taken away in the first place. Let me demonstrate it to you with the following exercise:

---

[12] Though I guess even "I am awesome, I am awesome, I am awesome" might get tiring after a while.

Sit comfortably, and take a deep, slow breath to get into an appropriately peaceful, chilled-out mood. If you like, you can sit on a big cushion, light a scented candle, and think cosmic thoughts.[13]

Inner critic: Get on with it!

Sorry. Here's the real part of the exercise:

Predict the next thought you're going to have.

That's it.

Seriously, sit and observe your mind, keeping your conscious thoughts as quiet as possible. Imagine what the next thought that arises is going to be, and wait for it to see if you are correct.

You'll find that you can't. Your mind will randomly wander, serving up chatter and observations. It's likely you'll find yourself debating the pointlessness of this exercise. Possibly you'll worry about what you're going to cook for dinner later, or remember a conversation from the other day, or fantasise about winning a talent contest.

Whatever it is, you *cannot* predict it. You cannot stop it. Your mind just does what it does: serves up observations and analyses, without stopping.

Thoughts just arise, with or without our conscious input.

If you still don't believe me, then you haven't tried it. Predicting your thoughts is not possible.

The implications of this are significant. Many of us are wrapped up and identified with our internal monologue, to the point that we believe that we *are* the stream of thoughts. We believe that the voice that chatters in our heads *is us*. But if we have no idea what we're going to think next, how can the automatic thought-stream be us in any meaningful way?

We can answer that by repeating the exercise with a twist:

Sit, get comfortable, and watch your mind carefully to see what the next thought is. This time, while you watch, ask yourself *who is it that is watching?* If you are watching your own thoughts, who is doing the thinking? And who is doing the watching?

This may surprise you if you've never considered it before. If you're anything like as sceptical as I am, it may also sound like

---

[13] None of this is strictly necessary, but honestly it gives this exercise a little more substance. It's VERY short! Plus don't you think cushions and cosmic thoughts create a useful atmosphere for this kind of thing?

meaningless nonsense. The immediate answer I would give is "Well, I'm doing the thinking, and I'm doing the watching. What kind of stupid question is that?!"

If your reaction is similar then I ask you to give the question a little more time, and allow yourself to consider the possibility that *whatever-you-is* is separate from that stream of thought that arises without your direct bidding.

It's possible to see the stream of thought for what it is: simply a tool offered by your mind.

Look at it another way. When you hold your breath, you don't stop being you. It would be ridiculous to believe otherwise. Breathing is not crucial to your ongoing identity.[14]

You don't stop existing during a pause between breaths. Because you are not your breath.

It's the same when you pause between thoughts. When you experience a small gap in the monologue you don't stop being you. You are neither your breath, nor your automatic thoughts. These thoughts are merely a feature of being human; an incessant, automated commentary on what's happening. We can tune into it, or ignore it, whenever we choose.

This was a revelation to me. A freeing realisation: I am not my thoughts.

---

[14] Well, okay, admittedly, if you stopped breathing entirely then your identity would be compromised quite rapidly.

IT'S ONLY A THOUGHT
"Only"

He smacked himself in the face.

"It's only a thought!"

He slapped himself again and checked how he felt. *Mostly the same, except now my face hurts. Maybe I'm not doing this right.*

He tried it a little harder. *SLAP.*

"It's only a thought! I don't have to be anxious, because it's only a thought. I am not my thoughts."

The more he thought this, the worse he felt. Freeing himself from the prison of his thoughts was supposed to be liberating.

But now, all he could think about was how his thoughts were only thoughts, and the more he thought about that the more confused and worse he felt. Or thought he felt. Or did he feel that he thought? He couldn't think.

He tried slapping himself to give his mind something else to focus on, but that just made him think about how much it hurt and how stupid he felt for not being able to do this right.

He tried writing his thoughts down.

All my thoughts are terrible. I feel terrible. Is there a connection?

If there was, he couldn't see it. But then, he had no time *between* thoughts to think about it properly.

He thought about how everyone would think of him if they could read his mind. *They'd laugh at me if they could hear these thoughts,* he thought, miserably. He managed to feel worse after this thought.

It's impossible to feel better! I keep trying, but all I think about is how bad I feel!

This thought wasn't helping either.

But maybe this is one of the thoughts he shouldn't listen to. That thought made him think.

What thoughts SHOULD I listen to? If they're all "just thoughts", do I ignore all of them? Should I be ignoring THIS thought?

He looked once more at the writing pad. At the single line he had written.

All my thoughts are terrible. I feel terrible. Is there a connection?

He underlined 'thoughts', and then - after some thought - underlined 'feel'. He chewed his pen, and then underlined 'terrible'. Twice. He looked at it again.

All my thoughts are terrible. I feel terrible. Is there a connection?

It seemed that there might be.

But he needed to think about it some more to be sure.

CHAPTER SIX
The Unbearable Lightness of Bananas

"For after all, the best thing one can do when it is raining, is to let it rain."
Henry Wadsworth Longfellow

"Are you an idiot?! Go buy an umbrella!"
Henry Wadsworth Longfellow's Fictional Wife

Years ago, I went through a phase of masochistically joining amateur theatre productions, out of a confused desire to try activities I'm not good at. Like acting.

I ended up going to the Edinburgh festival, to perform in a sequence of short plays. In one, I played an eccentric madman.

Inner critic: "Played"

Yes, PLAYED, thank you very much.

My costume suggested plenty about my character: a waterproof top, summer shorts, knee-high socks with sandals, and two bulging plastic bags full of miscellaneous objects. Each night, I sat on a park bench and delivered a rambling monologue about nothing in particular. For the rest of the show, my instructions from the director were to "sit in the corner and do weird things".

This was a fun directive. Each show I attempted a new activity my eccentric alter-ego might conceivably do in the park. One night, I ate raw spaghetti while reading the phone book. Another night, I became incredibly fascinated by my shoes, tying my laces together into such an enormous knot that I had to shuffle off stage and spend nearly an hour untying them afterwards.

The stage was basic; just an area of floor surrounded by the audience, so I sat directly at the feet of some of the crowd. Those closest to me were usually the ones who paid the most attention to my bizarre activities.

I never planned specifically what I was going to do each night. The fun of the challenge was taking something ordinary and interacting with it in an unusual way.

My favourite show was the night I brought a banana as my prop. I took it out of my bag and looked at it thoughtfully. There are only so many activities you can perform with a banana. Surely I wouldn't be able to come up with anything truly new.

After all, "There's nothing new under the sun" as the wise writer of Ecclesiastes once said.

(Although he also said "He who digs a pit may fall into it; and whoever breaks through a wall may be bitten by a snake," so not everything he said was true. Or even makes sense.)

As I peeled the banana, it occurred to me that normally we peel fruit to access the inside. Maybe I could seek originality by being more interested in the skin.

I removed the fruit from the skin and discarded it without much interest, getting a small laugh from the portion of the audience that was still watching me instead of the actual play. I always enjoyed seeing how many people I could keep interested in my messing about in this scene, instead of paying attention to the plot playing out a few metres away.

I looked at the banana skin, and realised that if I held onto one tendril I could spin the rest of it around like a fan. *Whum-whum-whum-whum*. This was fun!

I soon found the right frequency and was happily whirling my fruity propeller. *Whup-whup-whup-whup*. It span faster and faster, creating a satisfying blurry, yellow circle.

I was fully focused, lost in childish curiosity and joy at doing something so silly in public. Several audience members were laughing, some probably wondering what on earth any of this had to do with the play (the answer, of course, being absolutely nothing).

Suddenly, something unforeseen - but, with hindsight, inevitable - occurred. The banana skin snapped, leaving me holding just one thin tendril. The rest zoomed off, like a streaky yellow missile ... *SLAP*... right into the face of a woman sat in the front row.

I had accidentally assaulted a woman with a banana.

Immediately, I did the only thing I could. I hid behind a local phone directory,[15] blushing bright red. This was both entirely in character and probably what I'd have actually done if this had happened in real life.

Luckily, the audience - and the woman whose face had been walloped with the banana skin - loved it. She laughed hysterically, and - a little later - grinned at me as I mouthed "sorry" to her.

I want to pause this story at the exact moment that the banana skin struck her face. Not (only) because I'm easily amused by such images, but because I had an interesting choice in that moment. I could berate myself for my lack of foresight, and wish I'd been more careful. Or I could *accept* that what's done is done, and react to reality as it is, and not as I wish it was.

Of course, this was an easy situation to accept. I was on stage in the middle of a play: there was no choice. The only option was acceptance; running offstage in panic would have ruined the play.

Life would be simpler if only there were always enough pressure to force us into an attitude of acceptance.

Accepting Acceptance

Acceptance is essential to facing and solving our problems, from tiny examples - like my inadvertent banana onslaught - through to crippling panic attacks that knock us out for days at a time.

This is because fighting negative feelings generates even more negative feelings. When we are anxious about our anxiety, we feed it.

From the outside, this is obvious. Wishing away our anxiety creates frustration (that it won't leave) and dread (that it may never leave).

But in the midst of anxiety, it's not so obvious. We instinctively resist: this is horrible, why would we accept it?! We fight unpleasant feelings, without realising we are strengthening them in the process.

Quicksand and Chinese finger traps are similarly paradoxical, both requiring you to stop fighting to successfully escape.

Admittedly, I've never encountered either quicksand or a Chinese finger trap... outside of cartoons, anyway. But I am led to

---

[15] My character always carried one for just this sort of emergency.

believe that the solution to both is to adopt an acceptance strategy: stop fighting and stay still.

It's the same with custard traps. The custard is a creation of negative thoughts. Having negative thoughts towards the custard therefore only makes it harder to escape.

It's not until we stop fighting that we can win the fight.

This seems counter-intuitive. It sounds like "give up trying in order to succeed" or something else equally mysterious. And irritating. But sometimes good advice is counter-intuitive.

For example, I don't live in a country that has wild bears, so I was never taught how to survive an encounter with one. Luckily, a number of friendly locals at a bar in bear country told me exactly what to do.

At first, I found it strange that bears respond so well to rapidly undressing and running at them screaming, but once my new friends explained how bears find clothing repulsive and are relaxed by high-pitched loud noises it made much more sense. People are so friendly abroad![16]

So, to change a situation we must first accept it. However, our minds resist this by equating acceptance with giving up.

But accepting the existence of something doesn't mean we have to like it, or to give up hope of making it better. It means turning off our resistance. Instead of wishing the anxiety were gone, we accept that it exists, and figure out the next step from there.

This idea seems almost an insult: here's this anxiety I've been struggling with for years, and you're telling me I need to *accept* it? But I HATE it! I hate feeling anxious. I hate feeling ill. I hate feeling depressed. I don't want to accept any of this.

Let me say it again: acceptance is NOT the same as giving up.

Acceptance is not declaring that anxiety has won and now we quit. If anything, it's the opposite. Acceptance takes the fight back against our problems in a way that they cannot defeat. Other strategies make anxiety stronger, acceptance can only weaken it.

---

[16] My fictional lawyer tells me to highlight that this paragraph is a joke, in case anybody actually strips and screams at a bear, and gets eaten to death. Of course, you should be appropriately sceptical of everything (everywhere), and particularly check thrice before acting on any of my ramblings, but I want to break character to unequivocally say: Please DO NOT undress near bears. Thank you!

Countless stories illustrate the power of acceptance. In these stories, it's common for little old men to calmly face the prospect of death without blinking an eye, or for some character to nobly sacrifice themselves without a second thought.

Given my current blubbering reaction to minor setbacks (like accidentally dropping something I was about to eat), I'm not sure if I could ever master acceptance to the point where imminent death wouldn't dismay me.[17] But at the very least, if I could drop an ice cream without throwing a tantrum that would be progress.

Dr Russ Harris, in his book *The Happiness Trap*, demonstrates the power of acceptance in difficult emotional situations via the metaphor of The Struggle Switch. This switch exists in our mind and can be set to ON or OFF. When we turn the switch ON, we fight against and resist unpleasant emotions; when it's OFF, we accept however we feel, and continue come what may.

When the Struggle Switch is ON we battle against reality. We say things like "I shouldn't feel like this" and "It's not fair!" and "If only things had been different" and "This feeling is intolerable."

This attitude turns our single problem into two problems: anxiety, plus our feelings about the anxiety. Resisting anxiety only makes us more anxious about it, or angry about it, or depressed by it.

Believing we ought to be able to control our feelings is the essence of non-acceptance. Recognising that we cannot - and should not - battle our own emotions switches off the struggle.

When we turn the switch OFF and embrace acceptance, we are left with only our original emotion. We respond to reality alone, not to the conjurations of our minds.

This saves energy that would otherwise be wasted in pointless resistance. Perhaps we could spend it on relaxation, to deal with the anxiety directly.

Or maybe removing all the extra emotion lays bare the original anxiety, and it no longer seems so bad. Acceptance stops us from magnifying our problems out of all proportion. It makes them appear more manageable.

---

[17] Is that even a good idea in the first place: isn't imminent death worth reacting to?! Stupid ancient wisdom.

Or perhaps we use the saved energy on something else entirely: doing something we enjoy, or being productive. Acceptance provides us this choice.

I find it helpful to think "Oh, it's anxiety again. I've felt this a million times before, and survived it every time. Hello, old friend."

This doesn't immediately get rid of the anxiety, but it does prevent me from spiralling out of control in a feedback loop of anxiety-about-anxiety. It's my way of turning off that particular Struggle Switch.

EXERCISE: Accepting a Tough Spot

Let's practise turning off our Struggle Switch in an unpleasant scenario. As you read, take some time to visualise the images as vividly as possible.

Imagine waiting to board a plane. Perhaps this normally stresses you out, but not today. You feel great.[18] You're sat in the departure lounge, excited about getting on the plane when, unfortunately, an unpleasant fellow passenger sits next to you. I don't mean to be judgemental, but... you don't want this person to be there. Perhaps they're noisy, or smelly, or whatever attribute you find the most aggravating on public transport.

Imagine them sitting right next to you and doing that annoying thing. Actually *feel* annoyance at their behaviour as they sit there.

You can't move; there are no free seats. You can't ask them to move. You're stuck with this. It is ruining your good mood. You were so excited for this trip, and now this person is annoying the heck out of you. By the time you board the plane you're feeling furious and despondent. But it gets worse: they're sitting next to you on the plane too!

As you sit next to them for the long flight, imagine yourself accepting their presence. They don't change; they're still as annoying as ever. They don't leave; you're stuck with them until it's time to land. But instead of mentally wishing bad things towards them for the entire journey, just focus on your own trip.

---

[18] If it's too difficult to imagine ever enjoying a plane journey, then substitute a bus, train, or just waiting in a local library. Anywhere you feel happy and confident will do.

Perhaps you like to read, or to daydream, or to listen to music. You can still do those things even with that passenger next to you. Stay with this visualisation until you've managed to enjoy your journey with the unpleasant passenger sat next to you.

Just as we recognise that we shouldn't let a situation like this ruin our entire trip, we have to not let unwanted emotions drag us down.

Our difficult feelings and unpleasant thoughts are like this passenger. As much as we'd like to have them ejected from the plane (we'd get to spread onto two seats - living the dream!), that's not our decision to make. It's up to the pilot. Or, in real life, it's up to everything that is outside of our direct control. Which is nearly everything, including our own brains.

Our only choice is whether we fret, wishing reality were different - a pointless waste of our energy and emotions - or whether we calmly accept their presence, and allow ourselves to enjoy the journey anyway.

Acceptance is a skill we can develop. The ability to let go isn't some cosmic gift only some people have. We can all acquire it.

Important: What Acceptance Is Not

Accepting everything doesn't mean the exact same as "everything is acceptable."

In this context, acceptance simply means not resisting reality by wishing it were different. Things can still be "unacceptable" in the sense of "not okay".

If somebody behaves inappropriately we should take appropriate action to remove ourselves from the situation, or to stop them, or to seek help. The role of acceptance is to accept that our emotional response has a right to exist in every situation, whether it's anxiety, anger, joy or whatever.

We mentally accept that the situation is what it is, and, if necessary, we take steps to change it.

Acceptance & Avoidance

The flip-side of acceptance isn't non-acceptance.

Inner critic: Well, yes, it is. It's pretty obvious that non-acceptance is the flip-side of acceptance.

Yes, okay, true. I shall accept this petty criticism, from my own annoying fellow passenger. Fine. The flip-side of acceptance IS non-acceptance.

Inner critic: So what's your point?

Well, I was about to make a point before you interrupted me the first time.

Inner critic: Get on with it then!

* through gritted teeth * ... Sure. I accept this too. Thanks for the practice, inner critic.

Another way of looking at acceptance is that it is the opposite of avoidance.

When we accept reality our world grows. The alternative is to only accept parts of reality, and to wish away the rest. This shrinks our world down to only the parts we find acceptable: the rest is made up of things that we deny or resist. Any time we refuse to accept a feeling or situation we diminish the amount of life we are willing to experience.

For example, if I am unwilling to accept any feeling of anxiety at all, then my world shrinks to only those parts that don't make me anxious. Since I can worry about pretty much anything, this makes my world extremely limited.

In contrast, accepting everything makes our world as big as it can be, as well as bringing greater emotional peace. It's easier said than done, I know. But it's worth the effort to remove our self-imposed restrictions, and to live a full life.

Can I Tolerate Acceptance?

If we want to live on solid ground, we have to not allow small setbacks to knock us back onto the custard.

Every day we're beset by petty frustrations. Each time we have a choice: do we battle reality and wish it were different, thus adding to our inner reservoir of furious rage and negative emotion? Or do we accept reality, and make the best of it?

Fully achieving equanimity - being calm and composed in the face of every possible setback - would be impossible even for the most patient saint. Accepting the inevitability of failure is the first challenge.

We have to practise accepting everything, even seemingly insignificant setbacks. If we resist reality in small things, we develop a habit of non-acceptance for bigger things. Accepting and letting go of the frustration of a missed train builds the same acceptance muscles as accepting our anxiety during a panic attack - a much harder challenge.

Here are some ways to build the acceptance muscles up so they're ready for those tougher moments:

A consistent practice of meditation. This is the classic method to develop equanimity. We will explore how to do this very soon.

Recognising what we do and don't control. We can only be responsible for our own thoughts, feelings and actions.

Acknowledge that it's okay to feel whatever feelings arise. Sometimes we forget that it's normal to feel tired, stressed or anxious. Would you reasonably expect someone else to feel anxious in your current situation? Then it's okay if you feel anxious right now! Remind yourself that your emotions are valid.

Forget that the phrase "if only" exists. When you find yourself wishing things were different, just acknowledge that whatever has happened has happened. Focus on what you can do now instead.

Consciously practise acceptance in everyday situations. The next time someone walks too slowly in front of you, cuts you up in traffic or irritates you in the office, make a solid effort to accept it.

At first, you may just grit your teeth and remind yourself you're doing this to improve your overall emotional health.

Eventually you might reach the point where you realise things you used to find annoying don't matter as much as you thought.

If you can choose calm in the face of bad weather, misbehaving kids, or not getting a compliment at work, then you'll be better prepared next time you feel an anxiety attack approaching.

In my experience, nothing eases anxiety more effectively than accepting its presence.

PERPETUALLY INDECISIVE

CHAPTER SEVEN
Are Thoughts Good, Or Are They Bad?

"There is nothing either good or bad, but thinking makes it so"
William Shakespeare, 'Hamlet'

In any book like this, it's traditional for exercises to appear near the end of a chapter, to reinforce all the imparted wisdom[19] with a call to action.

However! Prepare your mind for *maximum opening*, because I'm blowing that tradition into tiny, confused smithereens by *starting* this chapter with an exercise.

I know, right? This kind of craziness should be illegal! Confounding your expectations so powerfully will jolt your comfortable routine and establish dynamic and vigorous new pathways in your brain.

Well... not really.

It just seemed like a good idea to do this particular exercise before we get to the subject of this chapter. Any mind-blowing you experience as a result of the placement of this exercise is purely coincidental.

EXERCISE: Observing The Thought Habit

As we have seen, we are normally unaware of our habitual identification with our thoughts. We want to begin noticing the hidden thoughts that trigger our difficulties, so let's replace our unawareness with a habitual awareness.

The best method humanity has developed to observe our thoughts is *meditation*.

Don't be put off by the 'M' word; perhaps you have images of bearded gurus sitting in awkward positions on a frayed cushion of

---

[19] Or rambling stories about bananas.

some kind. None of that is necessary. Though if you can grow a cool beard, and would like a nice frayed cushion, then be my guest.

All that is required for basic meditation is this:

Observe your thoughts as they arise. Don't hook onto them, don't follow them down any particular path. Just allow thoughts to arise and pass by, watching them as they go.

This sounds fine in theory, but is very difficult in practice, which is why there are so many visualisations to help get you started. Mostly these involve nature, such as imagining your thoughts as debris floating down a river, or birds flying through the air. But the basic premise is always the same: watch thoughts turn up, and watch them leave, without interacting with them.

You can visualise your thoughts as anything, as long as it makes two things clear: you are not the thing you are visualising, and you cannot control whatever it is.

So you could use meteorites orbiting a black hole, rocks rolling down a mountain, or the aforementioned drifting river debris.

I'm going to use shooting stars, for their pleasing combination of modern and natural. Feel free to substitute your own visualisation, as you please.

Practitioners of meditation often advise to meditate for at least ten minutes a day. I can attest to noticeable benefits from twenty minutes of meditation in the mornings. But when starting out, *any* meditation is preferable to none, so if you can only manage a few minutes, then that's fine. Try to increase it little-by-little to find your own sweet spot.

Let's give it a try.

Sit comfortably (in accordance with Ancient Tradition) and picture yourself lying in a comfortable, warm field at night.[20]

Every time a thought is offered up by your chattering mind, mentally picture the thought as a star shooting across the sky. The shooting star appeared from nowhere. Soon it will disappear again. Your goal is to remain where you are, and not to follow the thought through space. Just remain in the field, and calmly wait for the next thought.

---

[20] Yes, I know... why would you lie in a field at night? And are fields ever truly comfortable? Just imagine there's an excellent reason to lie in a nice field, even though there hardly ever is.

You don't want to *resist* the thought. Arguing with it, willing it to disappear, purposefully ignoring it... all of these are forms of engagement. Instead, just observe it and wait for the next one.

This is difficult, and you will be distracted. When this happens, gently place yourself back in the field, and resume watching for the next thought.

Don't worry: distraction happens to everybody when they try this. The habit of engaging with our thoughts is incredibly powerful. Some thoughts are so tempting that you may as well visualise the shooting star crashing directly into your relaxing spot in the field, rather than passing peacefully above.

When distraction inevitably occurs, simply be patient, don't berate yourself, and try again.

It can be hard to know if you're succeeding. The good news is that trying is succeeding. By attempting to watch your mind you are automatically developing greater self-awareness.

Regular meditation helps to spot automatic chattering thoughts as they arise in real-life situations. Perhaps a habitual thought will arise during the day: "I could go out tonight, but what if nobody wants to talk to me and I look stupid."

After all your practice of watching your thoughts you catch this one before you hook onto it, preventing the anxious reaction. Now you can choose how to engage with it, instead of instinctively reacting.

You can say to yourself "Well, maybe nobody will talk to me. But maybe they will. I won't know unless I try!"

Alternatively, of course, you may choose to believe the thought and stay home. It's up to you. But either way, you are making a choice. We want to take control of our feelings, and therefore our actions, instead of reacting without question to an automated thought.

Sitting quietly and meditating for five minutes a day doesn't have magic healing powers, but it can help with noticing and controlling these reactions. Think of it like a coaching drill: Athletes practise repeatedly so that at the competition their instincts take over.

We practise observation of our thoughts for much the same reason, except our 'competition' takes place *constantly* in our minds, and we can't choose not to take part.

Unless...

Thoughts: Evil, or Not?

We have seen that thoughts can be a major source of difficult emotions, negativity and lack of self-belief.

So it's time to declare a War on Thoughts, right? If we can destroy all of our thoughts before the treacherous little bastards cause us any harm then victory is assured! Bring on the lobotomy! *Electro-shock and awe!*[21]

Needless to say, carpet bombing our own brains isn't a great strategy for creating a happier and more secure life. As tempting as it may occasionally be.

Inner critic: *gulp*

We're practising noticing our thoughts as they happen, but so far we have dodged the issue of whether our thoughts are actually true. Surely truth is important? Well, while I would normally agree that truth is extremely important, in this context, it isn't.

At least, truth isn't the be-all-and-end-all.

Proving a thought wrong is a war we could never win; we'd be going to war against our minds, using our minds. Remember, our brains are analytical machines. They love any excuse to argue, to examine evidence, to come up with theories, and ruminate endlessly.

Caring exclusively about the truth of our thoughts leads us to obsess over them. Back and forth, no escape, exhausting us each time... rumination is a custard trap. Getting stuck on whether or not a difficult thought is true helps nobody and only ratchets up our anxiety.

Of course, if we know that a thought *is* true, we have no choice but to accept it. There's no sense battling reality.

---

[21] A snide observer of reality television and internet comments might think that the War on Thoughts must have already happened and been decisively won. But I suspect that if television or the internet had existed for all of human history they'd have been pretty much the same as they are now. Humans are human.

It's when we *can't be sure* if a thought is true or not that we get stuck on it. In these instances, a better way to judge a thought is: *is this thought helpful?*

Often, our unhelpful thoughts developed for a good initial reason, but became harmful once we began applying them too widely. Our thinking patterns are a double-edged sword.

Let's take, for example, the fictional Bob:

Inner critic: Really, Bob? Can't you come up with a more original fake name than that? I mean, there's a whole world of interesting possible names, from Arthurian legend to all the cultures of the world... and you pick... "Bob".

I think you may be inadvertently insulting any readers named Bob, inner critic. But sure, since it bothers you so much, let's pick a name from Arthurian legend. How about... Excalibob.

Inner critic: Excalibob.

Yes. Let's look at the life of our fictional Excalibob.

Excalibob - The Bad

Excalibob is constantly afraid of the worst-case scenario. As a result, he turns down new opportunities due to fear of what could go wrong. Secretly, he'd like to travel the world but he is too frightened of possible disaster. He remains in his comfortable safe spot instead.

Deep down, he is uncomfortable. The part of him that wants to go adventuring feels stifled and suffocated. He's unaware of the source of this tension, and he's baffled when it occasionally bubbles out in physical symptoms such as panic attacks. This confusion only makes him even more afraid of leaving his comfort zone. His world shrinks in response to this constant terror of what may happen.

Excalibob - The Good

Excalibob's brain developed this habit because his job is carrying out safety checks for dangerous workplaces. He spends his days searching for potential disasters. His mind has been honed through daily practice at spotting problems before they happen. This makes him excellent at his job.

But his well-trained brain doesn't properly distinguish between work and the rest of Excalibob's life. Without observing his thoughts, he doesn't realise he has conditioned himself to overreact to the worst-case scenario, instead of what is actually likely. He has become inappropriately afraid of remote possibilities, so he remains anxiously stuck and resists fulfilling his own dreams.

This pattern that Excalibob has developed is a source of help and a source of problems. The thoughts themselves are neither good nor bad; they are simply occasionally applied in the wrong context.

We all take thoughts that are helpful in one context and apply them elsewhere. It's normal; our brains love re-using their work. If we don't perceive when they do this, we open ourselves up to trouble.

Some thoughts are always unhelpful, no matter what the context. For example, falsely believing that invisible aliens are chasing me is never a helpful thought. Short of an actual invasion, there's no context in which that thought is useful for me.

Other thoughts are helpful in some situations, and unhelpful in another. Imagine a scary thought, such as "everyone's probably talking about me behind my back." Is this helpful?

I would guess that, usually, it's not helpful to believe that everyone is talking about us behind our backs, and we can probably safely disengage from that thought without negative consequences (we will see how to do this in a moment).

However, Julius Caesar may have benefited from wondering if people were talking about him behind *his* back!

Remember: there are no good or bad thoughts: only thoughts that are helpful in our current context, and those that aren't.

Making Thoughts Unhelpful

In most cases, it's apparent whether a thought is helpful or unhelpful. But perhaps it would be useful to recognise some common types of disagreeable thought.

Here are some foolproof ways of turning your thoughts into unhelpful inner enemies. Do you do any of these?

- Imagining and fixating on what could go wrong.
- Ignoring all the good in a situation, exclusively dwelling on any imperfections.
- Assuming that because a bad thing happened once, it will happen again and again.

- Thinking in a binary fashion: "I can't do this perfectly, so it's not worth trying at all" or "I'm slightly tired, so everything is awful."
- Believing that there are rules: the universe ought to be a certain way, or that you must do something, otherwise bad things will happen.
- Assuming everything is always about you. Whatever people do, imagine that it reflects on you, usually negatively.
- Believing that emotions are everything. Everything that makes us feel bad has to be bad, right?

It's interesting that these so clearly appear to be terrible ideas. I suspect that if we were advised to try any of these, we'd reject them like a tiger rejects lemon meringue.[22]

But despite these obviously being awful, we all think this way at least some of the time. At least, I do. I'm particularly great at imagining the worst that could happen, and obsessing over comparatively tiny imperfections.

If you are already able to identify any of these unhelpful thought patterns in your own thinking, then that's fantastic.

Of course, the hard bit isn't noticing that a particular thought is unhelpful; reading the list, it's obvious that these are damaging modes of thinking. The trick is noticing the thoughts at all.

Defusing from Thoughts

As we practise observing our thoughts we will naturally begin to spot the regular offenders that show up.

But once we've caught an unhelpful thought, we need a strategy for neutralising it.

The advice "just don't think about it" is some of the worst advice that exists. If you've ever tried to 'just not think about something' you'll know that it is impossible. The act of not-thinking is the SAME as the act of thinking, so the second you remind yourself "don't think about it", you've thought about it!

If I told you to not think about an aardvark drinking milk through a straw made of bees... well, it's too late. You've thought about it. You might even have gone so far as to mentally criticise

---

[22] Tigers famously prefer Black Forest Gateau.

the aardvark for his choice of a straw. *Bees will leave gaps, so your milk will spray everywhere, you foolish aardvark!*

Or maybe you wondered about the aardvark's choice of milk at all. Can aardvarks even digest milk? Is this going to lead to stomach problems? Where did he get the milk? Wait, maybe it wasn't cow's milk. Is it aardvark milk? Does aardvark milk *exist?*

Or maybe it's only me who over-thinks things to this extent.

Either way, I'm sure we can agree that simply suppressing thoughts isn't just hard, it's impossible, and counter-productive. It simply adds a layer of guilt, due to the inevitable failure of an impossible task.

We need a proper strategy for engaging with our unhelpful thoughts. Time to wheel in an expert, or two.

Inner critic: Thank heavens for that.

Popular authors (and various combinations of therapist, doctor and professor between them) Steven Hayes and Russ Harris both suggest a technique known as *defusion* for disengaging ourselves from unhelpful thoughts.[23]

It took me a while to understand the name of this technique. I kept picturing defusing a bomb, which is not a helpfully positive image when applied to the inside of your head. Instead, it refers to the other meaning of being 'fused': to be joined together with our thoughts.

Defusing undoes this join with our thoughts. We step back to recognise what they are: just thoughts, which we can take or leave as we choose. This distancing technique allows us to evaluate the helpfulness of the thought, and to react accordingly.

Defusion takes a variety of forms, so it's best explained by demonstration. Once you get the basic idea, you can come up with your own defusion techniques and build a repertoire of favourites for whenever an unhelpful thought pops up.

For my example, I'll imagine somebody panicking that they can't cope with the demands of their workplace, who is fused with the thought "I am useless and a fraud and when everyone finds out I'll be fired."

---

[23] See 'Further Reading' for details.

If you can, pick an unhelpful thought of your own, and try each of the following techniques on it, to show yourself how it disengages you from the thought.

Defusion Techniques

These are partly inspired by defusion techniques found in *The Happiness Trap* by Dr Russ Harris.

1) Consciously remind yourself it is only a thought, by thinking to yourself "I'm having the thought that..."

   E.g. *"I'm having the thought that if everyone knew how useless I was I'd lose my job."*

2) Imagine your thought as breaking news.

   E.g. *"This just in - Simon is worried that if everyone knew how useless he was he would be FIRED! More at ten."*

3) Be grateful for the thought.

   E.g. *"Thanks brain! I appreciate you suggesting that if everyone knew how terrible I was I would lose my job!"*

4) Imagine your thought in a funny voice, or a cartoon voice, or speaking super fast, or super slow, or in an accent.

   E.g. Errrrrrrrr... honestly, this isn't easy to put in writing. I'm sure you're familiar with the concept of funny voices, so I won't insult you by attempting to convey a 'hilarious' accent via text.

5) Name the thought:

   E.g. *"Oh, it's the old I Suck And I'm Going To Be Fired Story. I love this one."*

6) Laugh at the thought.

   E.g. *"Haahahahahahahaaha."* (Your laughter may vary.)

7) Imagine your thought as a headline, or as an old-fashioned telegram, or as a computer error message.

   E.g. *"ERROR 501: SIMON IS USELESS. PRESS ANY KEY TO FIRE HIM."* or *"HELLO STOP SIMON IS USELESS STOP HE WILL BE FIRED SOON STOP"*

All of these techniques create a separation between us and our thoughts. Once you understand that this separation is what makes it work, you can come up with defusion techniques of your own. As we practise observing our thoughts occurring in daily life we can make it a habit to defuse from those we find unhelpful.

These defusion techniques aren't a cure for difficult feelings. That said, it is possible that they will reduce unpleasant emotions, and as defusion becomes habitual the anxious feelings may reduce altogether.

However, this is just a happy side effect to the main aim of creating a separation between yourself and your thoughts.

Why is the main aim not to reduce our difficult feelings directly? Because, as we've seen, resisting our negative emotions only feeds them. For maximum serenity, we must defuse from the thought, but accept its right to exist, along with any emotion that's floating about. Fighting either the thought or the emotion achieves nothing.

It is possible that defusing from an unpleasant thought will somewhat reduce the associated feeling. But even if not, defusing allows you to choose your reaction, rather than responding on emotional autopilot.

It may be that Simon still feels awful after defusing from his thoughts of getting fired. But with the freedom gained by defusion he can choose to work effectively anyway.

If he unthinkingly fuses with the thought "I am terrible at my job", he may well go into panic mode and paralyse himself, thus creating a neat self-fulfilling prophecy as the paralysis causes him to fail and be fired.

You can imagine how his mind would then think "I told you so", further strengthening the power of this thought pattern next time his chatty subconscious offers it up.

"Hey, remember how you panicked the other day? Wouldn't it be awful if that happened again..?!"

Now we can recognise that trap as it occurs in our own lives, and we have the tools of observation, defusion and acceptance to rescue ourselves from it.

It's Not Quite So Simple

Naturally, people are complex, and so it's not quite true to say thoughts always precede our emotions.

Inner critic: Wait, what? Didn't you spend two chapters already saying that's what happens?

In reality, we are a complex interlocking set of layers. Our thoughts influence our feelings - and vice versa - and our behaviour influences both. And both thoughts and feelings influence our behaviour. We are complex.

But this complexity makes life interesting. I imagine it'd be pretty dull if we could choose any emotion we wished to feel merely by thinking the appropriate trigger thought.

So, my inner critic is correct, I have been over-simplifying the picture. But that's because the leap from thoughts to feelings is the bit that's easiest to miss, and learning to master it has a significant payoff.

It's also worth remembering that we are inherently puzzling animals, so there's no need to be frustrated if we can't get it right immediately. If we had iron control over ourselves, life would be a bit boring. Probably.

Inner critic: I knew you loved having me around, really.

Go away, inner critic.

*Inner critic: *blows a kiss**

Thoughts In Brief

Our emotions are often reactions to our thoughts, which can be conscious, or the automatic chatter of our subconscious.

We must develop awareness of this automatic mind chatter. Otherwise we are on shaky ground, as we unquestioningly accept every automatic thought that pops into our heads.

After practising noticing our automatic thoughts we can judge whether they are helpful or unhelpful.

Distancing ourselves from unhelpful thoughts via defusion provides a worthwhile payoff for the effort: the ability to choose our response.

We don't have to believe everything we think.

HOLD IT RIGHT THERE
A Critical Interlude

You realise this is pointless, don't you? This won't help anyone at all.

Sigh. Must I argue with myself? I'm busy.

Don't be disrespectful. Aren't you supposed to be all enlightened and wise, if you've written a book like this? You don't sound like a legitimate purported guru.

Guru, really? And I'm not purporting to be *anything*. Can't you just let me write this book without beating me up for it?

Well, yeah, sure. I suppose. As long as you know it's pointless and won't help anybody.

... what makes you say that?

It's impossible! You can't possibly help everyone. I mean, to advise someone in real life you have to tailor what you say specifically to them. You have to frame concepts in different ways because everyone thinks differently. Everyone has their own personal barriers. You can't possibly handle that via a static medium like a book, so you are wasting your time.

Oh I see. You're claiming that I shouldn't bother at all, because there's no way I can foresee every conceivable circumstance in which someone may read this?

Yes! It's futile. Nobody will benefit.

Nobody will benefit... Wait, wouldn't that mean that nobody could ever find help in *any* book? I've read helpful books, so they must exist.

(stubbornly) It won't help everyone.

That's not what you said a moment ago! You said "nobody". Don't change the rules mid-conversation.

You can't tailor what you're saying to everyone.

So, I should just give up?

What you're saying is a recipe for total inactivity, as if I should never try *anything* because I can't possibly do *everything*...

Ah, wait a minute. This is my Inner Perfectionist talking, isn't it? Hello Perfectionist.

I'm sure you could come up with a better nickname for me, you know.

Well, you would think that, wouldn't you?

Anyway, now I know who's talking I think I can move on without abandoning the whole project.

Nooo! It could be better. Like I was saying, you should give up. What if you miss a vital sentence and somehow cause the end of the world?

Wow. I can't worry about sentences I haven't even written. Particularly not ones with such ludicrous consequences. All I can reasonably do is my best. Unless you have a better idea?

You could fix every problem in the world and make everybody happy?

No. No, I can't. It's not my job. Remember the Polish saying: "That's not my circus, and those aren't my monkeys." I can't save the world and everybody in it!

Did you just call everyone in the world a monkey? By extension you insulted everyone reading this.

Uh-oh.

"How to Instantly Become The Bad Guy: A Self-Hindrance Book by Neil Hughes".

Aren't you meant to be my sense of perfectionism? Abusing me like this doesn't seem like it should be your thing.

I'm helping out Self-Mockery. He's taking a break. Said something about how now that you're writing a book you're basically doing his job for him.

Ouch.

That was before the 'Monkey Incident' too.

Hey! Listen! That was just a metaphor about knowing the limits of my responsibility. Don't blame me for that - it's a Polish expression!

Let's not bring racism into this.

Good god. Why do these discussions with myself always get so out of control?! You *know* I love the expression. And Poland.

Yeah. I know. I'm just enjoying watching you squirm now.

Thanks a lot. Can I go now?

I think you'd better.

CHAPTER EIGHT
Crisis

"The most fortunate of us frequently meet with calamities; to fortify our minds against these should be one of the principal endeavours of our lives."
Thomas Jefferson (abridged)

Up to now, we've been gradually transforming the custard beneath our feet into solid ground. Or - depending on how you prefer to flavour your metaphors - journeying on our giant pool of custard towards shore.

Most of the labour lies in replacing our everyday habits. But I want to spend some time discussing those terrifying moments when we become exhausted and overwhelmed and we plunge under the custard. The sensation of drowning in our own lives is awful, whether it lasts minutes, hours, or even days.

During crisis moments we stop aiming for solid ground. Instead, we give ourselves permission to forget long-term goals, only to focus on one thing: getting back on top of the custard and returning to a steady maintainable rhythm. Afterwards, we can resume the journey to somewhere more permanently restful.

In other words, in an acute crisis our needs become simple: we want the crisis to end.

You can think of a crisis state as a simple mathematical inequality, which I have skilfully and artistically illustrated below:

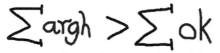

A crisis occurs when we have more 'ARGH' than 'OK'.

The Σ sign is a symbol used to mean 'the sum' and you may remember from school that '$>$' is the 'greater than' sign. So, this translates as "the total amount of ARGH is greater than the total amount of OK".

In other words, a crisis moment occurs when our total difficulties (at this moment) exceeds our total coping mechanisms (at this moment).

I mention "at this moment" twice because both our difficulties and our ability to cope change, all the time. Put mathematically, they're both functions of time. Let's update the equation to illustrate this:

$$\sum argh_t > \sum ok_t$$

Both 'OK' and 'ARGH' values change over time, so we only care about how much we have at any particular moment.

There. The 't' symbols indicate our feelings at a particular moment in time. Since both sides are always changing, the balance of this equation also changes with time.

Inner critic: Are you sure this mathematics stuff is useful?

Leave me alone, I'm having fun making pictures! But, yes, this is useful, because we often forget that one side of this equation[24] exists. It's clear that our problems change over time.

But it's less clear that our coping ability changes too. If you're in a stressful situation, and you're hungry and tired, then you're less able to cope with any difficulties. This is easily forgotten when under pressure.

We can draw two conclusions from this equation.

Firstly, a crisis is a temporary state (though it often doesn't feel like it at the time). It is encouraging to remind ourselves that this feeling will end, particularly if we've been through a similar experience before.

Secondly, there are *two* ways to rebalance the equation so that we escape the crisis. A strong strategy for crisis would be working on both sides at once: removing some of the difficulties, and increasing our coping abilities.

---

[24] I know it's not technically an equation, my fellow mathematical pedants. I'm sorry.

As problem-solving animals we instinctively leap at removing the things that make us go ARGH. But sometimes we can't, or it's not even obvious what the problems are. Luckily, we can always change the other side of the equation by increasing our current ability to cope.

For example, talking to a friend, going for a walk, putting on a relaxing video, having a lie-down, tidying your room, a cup of tea, thinking about kittens... anything. If those examples seem overwhelming at the time, aim for the smallest possible thing. Even thinking a deliberate thought can be enough. Sometimes I think "My ARGH vs OK equation is imbalanced right now", and it makes me laugh that I'm describing an awful situation in such absurd terms. Laughter helps increase the OK side of the equation.

Anything that distracts from thinking about the problem has the same effect. When we're absorbed in thinking about the ARGH, we magnify it. Distracting ourselves therefore reduces the ARGH as well as increases the OK.

The Birth of Fear

This is a good moment to briefly explore how fear works.

(Warning: My understanding of neuroscience is mostly absorbed from television hospital dramas and the back of cereal packets. You should probably consider this more as a useful way to visualise it than as an accurate description of scientific truth.)

Our brains constantly create links. Following a panic attack they link the circumstances and the horrific feeling. Next time we are - even subconsciously - reminded of those circumstances the link re-activates, and we feel afraid. This fear is a warning from the brain: *"Last time this thing was horrible!"*

Such fearful warnings are, in theory, a good thing. They come from a chunk of the brain known as the amygdala, which is responsible for keeping us alive by warning us of threats.

The amygdala evolved to scream in the presence of danger: predators, sudden falling rocks, giant scary jungle-beasts, drowning, or anything that it deems a threat. This is fantastic for avoiding predators in prairies, but when it starts linking to something everyday or harmless we may have a problem. The amygdala is one of the most primitive and fundamental parts of the brain, so it has a powerful effect.

If it develops a strong association with something we encounter regularly, such as public transport, going outside, or talking to people, then we either severely shrink our world by avoiding the object of our fear, or we live in the shadow of anxiety.

These links may begin extremely innocuously. We don't need some huge traumatic experience to generate a phobic link, though, of course, such a trauma gives a considerable head start. Perhaps it starts with unease, or a single negative thought that becomes associated with an experience. We can repeatedly strengthen that association until it becomes uncomfortable to even imagine whatever it is we're now scared of.

Rationally, I should be able to step back from my fears, and realise "this little spider can't hurt me", or "nothing bad will happen to me on this train just because something once did on another train." But these links in our mind are incredibly powerful.

The good news is that the brain appears to be remarkably flexible, and these links can be unlearned. Neatly, the solution uses the same mechanism as the problem: we take advantage of the fact that the brain just can't stop creating links.

By creating positive, peaceful associations with the objects of our fear we generate new brain pathways alongside the scary, unpleasant links to the amygdala. Eventually these positive links will outnumber the fearful links and we will be less afraid.

Feedback Loops

Let's look at a common crisis: a panic attack.

If you have ever experienced a panic attack you will know how crippling they are. They can roll in without warning, with the intensity, subtlety and fun factor of a thunderstorm in a bathtub.

During a panic attack, we can be so gripped by terror that we believe that we're dying, that we're going to shame ourselves beyond repair, that the world is falling apart. The exact experience varies but there is often a feeling of helplessness, usually accompanied by physical symptoms such as tightness in the chest, nausea, difficulty breathing and a racing heart.

This is often so awful that we go to great lengths to avoid ever experiencing anything like it again. Unfortunately, our brain can't stop categorising and linking. So it creates a new category: "panic attack".

It didn't like the panic attack, so it helpfully links this new category up to the amygdala, so we know to be afraid of them. Now fear of panic attacks is a thing too.

This fear of panic can be nearly as crippling as the panic attack itself, as we go out of our way to avoid anything that might set us off. Someone invites us on holiday, and we worry that we might have a panic attack on the plane. Imagining the event is enough to strengthen the association between panic attack and fear. Eventually, anything that even remotely feels like a panic attack - a raised heartbeat, a slight tension in the body, a fizzing sensation in the mind - is enough to cause a panic attack.

Even if you never experience these extremes, it is useful self-knowledge to see that feedback loops like this exist, and that they are due to multiple levels operating in our emotional world at once.

The root level of any crisis is *our initial problem*. This may be an experience, a fear, an event, or it may simply be a negative thought. This thought may not even be based in reality: we react emotionally whether or not a thought is true.

The next level is our emotional reaction to whatever this problem is. This comprises the fear we have of it, the sensation of stress, the frustration, the depression, or however we react. This is called the *primary emotion*.

For example, my problem is that I've seen an absolutely huge spider. My reaction, my *primary emotion*, is - quite understandably - gibbering fear.

The next level is our reaction to the primary emotion. This is the fear-of-fear, the dread-of-dread, the self-criticism which complains we are not feeling how we "should" be feeling. These are *secondary emotions*, or 'feelings about our feelings'. Secondary emotions can cause emotional feedback loops that rapidly spiral out of control:

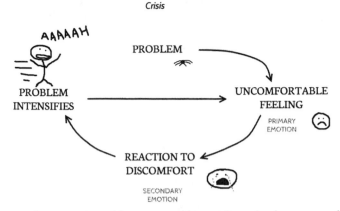

The secondary emotion adds to our problems. After a few loops around the cycle, we are exponentially worse off.

Please don't be disappointed by my artistic skills, which you should be getting used to by now.

(I genuinely used to get detention at school for being bad at art. I was so bad that the teacher assumed I wasn't trying, and so regular detention became an unpleasant Tuesday tradition. I'm hardly bitter about it at all, honest.)

When we have an uncomfortable feeling, such as anxiety, we inevitably react to that feeling. If we get anxious about the anxiety, then we have *more* anxiety to feel anxious about.

It's clear that going around that loop, each time pouring more fuel on the fire, leads to a feedback effect. It doesn't take long to reach a full-blown panic.

This is why in a crisis we should ignore the idea of solving our root problem at all. Let me repeat that slightly differently: *In a crisis, we only care about stopping the secondary emotions.* Or, as mentioned earlier, when we're drowning under the custard, forget heading for shore, just get back on the surface. Our priority must be breaking these feedback loops.

How? We know this already. Emotions are reactions to thoughts. We need to find the thoughts that generate our *secondary* emotions. They may drag us deeper into depression ("I'm so depressed that I'm depressed") or into a full-fledged panic attack ("Oh god, I can't stand feeling anxious!"), but whatever they do, they are bad.

Once we learn to control these thoughts, we can prevent these crises from spiralling out of control.

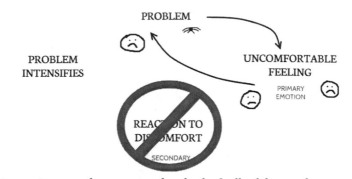

Preventing secondary emotions breaks the feedback loop and stops our emotions from getting out of control.

If we stop our secondary emotions then the loop gets cut off at the source. The primary emotion remains, but is not repeatedly multiplied. This may still be unpleasant... but it's considerably better than a runaway panic spiral.

The key skill is recognising this process when it is happening. When it feels like the bottom is dropping out of our world, we have to recognise the potential for a feedback loop.

Acceptance is our most powerful ally for preventing secondary emotions. Simply accepting our primary emotions cuts off any possible source of feedback. We don't fear our anxiety. We aren't depressed by our depression. Sure, it sucks that we're anxious, but we don't resist it, we allow it to exist.

Our minds sometimes wail in protest about this tactic: *"If we accept it then we're giving in! We have to solve the initial problem, whatever it is! This person preaching acceptance is an IDIOT!"*

Remember: we're in a crisis. This means our only aim is avoiding inflaming the situation further. Once we're safely out of crisis mode we'll get to working on our root problems, so for now, just take care of yourself and prevent the panic from getting out of control.

It takes practice to identify which emotions are due to the root problem, and which are secondary. Step back any way you can, then try and unpick the different levels. Perhaps notice the primary level: "Oh, I'm feeling anxious because I saw a spider." After that, try to identify the link to the secondary emotion: do you fear feeling fear? Finally, try and break that link. Allowing the primary emotion to exist can break the feedback loop.

Sometimes, only small steps are necessary. For example, your heart may be thudding, and this may occasionally trigger you into believing something is wrong, which itself sets you off to further worry - thus raising your pulse even more. A baby step may be to concentrate simply on breathing, ignoring everything else. This takes the focus away from potentially anxiety-inducing thoughts.

Once you feel calmer, maybe you can identify the next small step to take back control. Perhaps going outside and sitting down, or even going for a walk. Or doing anything that you can achieve with your current level of energy. Afterwards, set another tiny goal. Chaining together enough little steps gets us slowly back above the custard and out of the crisis.

EXERCISE: Breathing From the Diaphragm

This is a useful exercise to practise for crisis moments.

As ever, tradition decrees you get comfortable first, so why not first make yourself as comfortable as possible? Book a six-week cruise on a yacht, somewhere sunny.

Or, more realistically, sit somewhere you can relax whilst keeping your back straight and your feet on the ground.

Bear in mind that - if you're anything like me - you might feel like a bit of a lemon sitting around doing insultingly simple things like breathing. My reaction on hearing about the importance of breathing exercises was to be aggrieved that apparently I was *breathing wrong*. Honestly, how can something as simple and everyday as *breathing* be difficult?!

My inner critic naturally leaps onto this kind of thinking: *"You can't even BREATHE PROPERLY! What kind of a useless human are you?"*

In this case he's wrong: it's common for people to breathe non-optimally.

Once you're comfortable, notice your own breathing without judgement. Is it fast, slow, deep, or shallow? Take a few breaths without changing the way you naturally breathe. Be aware of the air as it rushes in, as it fills your lungs, and as it leaves. Take a moment to do this now.

No, really. Did you do it? No? Do it now then. Just breathe and observe for a few seconds. How fast do you breathe? How long do you pause between breaths?

Don't label your current breathing as good or bad. Thoughts such as "I'm breathing too fast!" are unhelpful, so put them aside. This is simply to get you used to noticing your breath.

Next, take a conscious effort to breathe in a particular way. You want to perform what is known as a 'belly breath'. Place one hand on your stomach, and the other on your chest. Notice how both hands move when you breathe naturally. Perhaps the lower hand moves first, or perhaps it's the upper hand.

To breathe from the belly you want your lower hand to move first. In other words, breathe using the diaphragm muscle at the base of your stomach, rather than the muscles between your ribs that many of us use without realising.

Let your stomach rise as you breathe so your lower hand moves away from your body. Don't worry about the speed. Just let yourself breathe at your natural rate, ensuring you use your stomach instead of your chest. You'll know you are doing it correctly if the hand on your stomach is moving back and forth, and the hand on your chest is mostly staying still.

Take a few breaths from the diaphragm. You want to fill your lungs most of the way with a comfortable breath; you don't need to breathe too deeply or fill your lungs ALL the way to the top. Shallow but steady is fine. Each time, inhale to a comfortable point and stop, and exhale even more slowly than you breathe in.

If you've followed along you may be wondering what the point of all this is.

Belly-breathing has some handy effects. Firstly, it naturally calms you down.

Secondly, it's impossible to focus on this, and simultaneously create secondary emotions. This is therefore a useful technique in a moment of crisis.

Lastly, it's a helpful way into the meditation exercises we've already explored. Try combining the two by making a habit of belly-breathing during your regular meditation practice.

EXERCISE: Eternal Diaphragmatic Breathing

This exercise is partly about improving our overall breathing habits, and partly just an excuse to use the fun-to-type word 'diaphragmatic'.

Inner critic: Sigh. At least everyone else is getting to see what sort of pointless idiocy I have to put up with.

If you're one of the many people who forgets to breathe from the diaphragm, then it may be useful to make a habit of it.

Try some of the following:

- Set a timer to go off every hour (only when you're awake, obviously. I'm not evil!). Whenever you hear it, consciously use your diaphragm to take a few breaths.
- First thing in the morning, and last thing at night, do a few deliberate belly-breaths. This is a nice easy routine to remember, and has the extra advantage of not sparking much argument from our change-resistant monkey-brains: even they can't freak out too much at a few breaths twice a day!
- Reward yourself whenever you naturally notice your breath throughout the day. Take a few belly-breaths to celebrate.
- Write the word 'diaphragm' on your face with permanent marker. Then, whenever anyone asks you "why the hell do you have 'diaphragm' written on your face?" you'll be reminded to belly-breathe. This is a plan with no flaws whatsoever. (Except for the many easily apparent flaws. Obviously, don't actually do this last one, unless you live in a world without consequences.)

SUMMARY: A Simple Plan for Crisis

Mainly, don't fear fear. Accept all emotions as they arise. Recognise we can't perfectly control our emotions, and don't waste any energy on fruitless attempts to do so. If we allow our emotions to be, runaway feedback loops *cannot* take place.

Politely reject any complaints from your mind about embracing acceptance. For now, it's just about feeling better. This lack of resistance ought to break any feedback loops and maintain control.

If you can, do something to increase the OK side of your equation. Maybe a breathing exercise, emergency chocolate, or talk to someone you can phone anytime who'll cheer you up. Anything that increases your ability to cope is helpful.

As an optional bonus: afterwards, if possible, we identify and then defuse from the thoughts that produced the primary difficult feelings. Making this habitual will help us avoid the difficult emotions in the first place.

My approach is often something like this:

Oh hello anxiety, old friend. This immediately ends the feedback loop of anxiety-about-being-anxious.

My subconscious sees that I'm *not* anxious about being anxious, so it doesn't pour more anxiety fuel on my panic fire.

I identify the thought that produced the initial anxiety and let it pass me by without reacting to it. Perhaps I defuse from the thought by telling myself "ah, I'm having the thought that I will fail at everything I try", or whatever it may be.

I accept any anxious feelings that remain. Defusing from the thought doesn't - and isn't supposed to - remove the anxious feelings entirely. But I am able to continue with what I'm doing no matter how I feel.

This weakens the link in my brain between the anxiety trigger and panic, as I demonstrate to myself that I'm capable of continuing work in the presence of a spider (or imaginary brain cancer, or whatever triggered the initial fear response).

Sometimes, simply understanding this process is enough to give us confidence that we can handle a panic attack if one comes along.

I laughed when I was first told that it was an easy task to prevent this sort of anxiety. I had felt anxious more or less all my life. I saw anxiety as an eternal enemy. But learning to remove the feelings-about-feelings kills feedback loops, and makes the size of the actual problem seem much more manageable.

Some people say that learning to break these feedback loops completely cures their fear of panic attacks, which can even prevent them from occurring in the first place.

You may have realised that this is because fear of panic attacks is a secondary emotion. No longer fearing panic attacks can therefore make them less likely to happen at all.

Crises are horrible. But there is a way out. Once we get adept at escaping them, they come along less frequently, and we have much more energy to put into heading for solid ground.

CHAPTER NINE
The Inner Cuddle Dilemma

"Self-love, my liege, is not so vile a sin, as self-neglecting"
William Shakespeare

A friend of mine said recently: "I would hate to 'do unto others as I do unto myself', because it would make me a terrible person!"

If she acted as unkindly towards her friends as she does to herself she would soon have none left. It's strange. Anyone meeting her, even only briefly, would see her as kind, open and generous. Yet the person she spends all of her time with - herself - doesn't experience that loving side of her.

I expect many of us experience the same double standard, of harshness towards ourselves that we would never unleash on anybody else.

Self-compassion is the topic I dreaded writing about the most. Simply because it's easily the most embarrassing part for me personally.

By now, you no doubt have an impression of me as some kind of superman. A superior being, heroic in thought and deed, dashing and courageous. And I'd hate to shatter that positive impression by being overly vulnerable.

Inner critic: Am I needed here? I sense that I'm needed, as if someone - somewhere close by - is saying something utterly stupid that needs pointing out. Anyone?

Sure, I've scattered some embarrassing stories throughout the book, along with the occasional reveal that makes me cringe, and I fear the vulnerability of being so open about myself. But generally I don't feel obliged to hide.

However, what I'm about to tell you makes me feel scorching embarrassment and blistering vulnerability. Maybe this terror is partly cultural: we British aren't exactly famous for heartfelt emotional outpourings. Maybe there's a bit of gender pressure too: some internalised idea that it's not 'manly' to talk about love and compassion.

But while I don't mind sharing emotional situations if I can hide behind a defence of humour, this upcoming story leaves me nowhere to shelter. There's nothing particularly amusing to it. It's just me being vulnerable. And very, very cheesy.

Quite honestly, I'd rather not mention any of this at all, except I think it's pretty important.

Okay, I'm going to stop avoiding it now. Any second now.

Then again, I'm tempted to ramble for a while and hope we all forget that I'm supposed to be telling you a cheesy, embarrassing story about self-compassion. But no amount of time-wasting introductions will help, so I'm just going to bite the bullet and go for it.

Wait, that's a weird expression, isn't it? Bite the bullet? Do people really bite bullets? I wonder where that came from...

Okay, okay, okay. No more distractions.

Here's the story.

November

It's November. It's cold. It's dreary. It's grey. And it's miserable.

I am cold, dreary, not-yet-grey, but definitely extremely miserable.

I'm in the midst of a slow, excruciating breakup with someone I loved. I'm terrified at my lack of direction, having finally quit my job in the hope that it would force me to find fulfilment. I've moved far away for a new start, but the new start hasn't materialised yet and instead I'm just lonely. I feel far from all my friends. And this ongoing heartbreak looks unavoidable. It's going to hurt. Even more than it does already, which is a lot. And I can't see anything in the future that looks better than the present.

Every day I wake up with anxious knives stabbing in my chest. I suffer through an empty day without attempting to improve my situation, and at night I lie wondering if everything will be like this forever now.

I know I ought to force myself to do something. Anything. Even though it feels like there's no reason to even get out of bed, and everything in me just wants to stare into space and hope the pain goes away, I make myself do something every day. I go out for walks, my mind muttering about how pointless it is.

I feel pathetic. I know people have it worse, and this is just a break-up and relocation and unemployment all at once. I feel I ought to deal with it better, and the guilt that I'm failing to cope makes me feel even worse.

I try not to text my friends too much. I don't want them to know what a dark place I'm in. I know they wouldn't mind, but I don't want to because I have nothing else to talk about. I don't want to push them away by only talking about how miserable I am. So I don't talk to them much either.

I feel trapped. In my circumstances, in my feelings, and, most of all, in myself.

One day I woke up in an especially bad mood, after a dream in which I was playing the piano. Normally this is one of my favourite activities. It has the right balance of mindlessness and concentration to be both relaxing and rewarding. All those years of dreading piano lessons and getting into regular trouble for my lack of practice were worth it in the end.

But in this dream I didn't enjoy playing. I was playing a song for my just-about-still-girlfriend. It was an obscure love song I hadn't heard for years called *You're Beautiful.*[25] In my dream I sang passionately, putting my heart fully into it, but she didn't care. She was cold and just wanted me to stop.

The symbolism was pretty clear. At times, my subconscious is inventive with dreams, and will set me a puzzle to solve using all kinds of intriguing symbols for what's happening in my life. Recently, I had an especially disturbing dream involving laxatives, a green garden sack and some wellington boots. This piano dream was nowhere near as inventive or opaque.

I woke up feeling intensely sad, and that turbulent feeling stuck with me all day. Worse, the love song kept echoing around and around and around in my head, tightening the pain each time.

---

[25] In fact, it was originally a song I'd heard at church as a teenager. The lyrics are more like a typical love song than a religious one but I'm still unsure exactly why my subconscious picked it.

Finally I gave in. The only way I was going to get rid of the annoyance of the song, and perhaps that violent stabbing feeling in my chest, was to play it.

I sat at the piano and began to play.

Instantly I burst into tears.

I don't cry often. I've gone years without crying, though sometimes I cry frequently between droughts. I'm not the best piano player, but the sound of it isn't usually so bad that it drives me to tears.

I needed to release some emotion, and figured a cry was probably helpful, so I didn't stop playing. At the end of the song I looped back to the beginning, each time singing along in my head.

After what must have been ten playthroughs I was finally done crying (thankfully - even though I was alone there's only so much emotional release I can manage before I become embarrassed).

But I wasn't finished. I found myself thinking of all the people I'd have enjoyed playing this song to. My current-soon-to-be-ex girlfriend, past girlfriends, past loves, past unrequited loves. Suddenly the weight of all those loves felt crushing.

A thought came to my mind.

It's not about them. It's never been about them...

I tried to ignore the thought, rightly suspecting it was going to lead me to an embarrassing place. A little cry was surely enough for now, thank you very much.

The thought was insistent.

It's not about them. This is about ME.

Uh-oh. My brain had an idea. I wasn't sure I liked where it was going.

I have to sing this song to myself.

Oh bloody hell. Part of me wants me to sing a love song to myself. I don't know how to react.

Seriously. All these relationships have been about them. I put them before me at every opportunity. I was trying to use them to fill a hole inside myself that they CANNOT fill. I have to fill this hole myself.

I considered this idea for a moment. Sure. That sounds reasonable. But... is the way to fill an internal hole - if such a thing even exists - really to sing a love song to yourself? I mean, isn't there an easier way? Maybe there's an article online somewhere that has a better idea on how to do this sort of thing. Or, in fact, can't we just NOT fill it? This doesn't sound like a thing that normal people do. To be honest, it doesn't sound like a problem normal people have. Let's just not do this. I'm going to go now.

Now you're just making excuses. Sing it. To yourself.

During this internal debate my hands kept playing, repeating the song over and over. There was nobody around. Nobody would know, unless I decided to tell them. Which, obviously, I NEVER would, especially not publicly.

Eventually I came to a decision. I was going to do it.

To sing a love song... to myself.... for reasons I wasn't sure made any sense whatsoever.

I steeled myself and played the song through once more. And, on the next repetition, I opened my mouth and began to sing aloud.

I'm not going to lie. It was tentative. I had to concentrate on playing the music, on singing, and also on making a serious mental effort to imagine myself as the object of the song. Not to mention a *large* part of my awareness was checking nobody was around to witness my mortifying display.

"You're beautiful, you're beautiful... I've never met anyone quite like you at all..." [26]

After a bit, I somewhat got over the embarrassment. *Somewhat.* Though had there been anyone nearby I doubt this would have been possible. Still, I continued to feel highly embarrassed while completely alone and with only limited threat of discovery.

But as I played, and sang, and listened, I started to feel strong. It felt good. Powerful, even.

I finished the song and went round again one final time. This time I sang louder, much more strongly and confidently, allowing myself to actually enjoy doing something so silly, purely for myself.

I found myself really feeling love as I sang, loving the stupid things I'd done in the past, loving the way I'd tried in those past relationships, loving the way I was still trying, even as hope faded with this person who was breaking my heart at the time. I forgave

---

[26] "You're Beautiful" © Kelly, Johnston, Emmausongs/IMRO 1999, recorded by Emmaus from the album "Closer Nearer", excerpt quoted with kind permission.

myself for all those things, and loved myself anyway. It felt fantastic.

After the final go around I sat and laughed for a moment. I've done some ridiculous things, but that whole experience was new. And more than a little embarrassing.

Still, it felt good. I felt like a heavy weight had lifted, and - to crack out a cliché - like I'd healed some major inner pain.

I think this shows how hard it is for sceptical, emotionally-repressed types like me to get into personal development at all.[27] It's so airy-fairy, so individual, so strange, and with so much potential for humiliating vulnerability and confusing emotional happenings.

This was a transformative experience that remains powerful for me even today. For months afterwards I returned to this moment, each time feeling a comforting peace.

And a thin layer of cringing humiliation, of course.

I don't offer this as a template to copy. I *really* don't believe that everyone has to have a cheesy emotional event while singing a song to themselves. The crucial part was that I was willing to try such a ludicrous idea, and the very act of doing it - despite my great reluctance - proved to me that I did, in fact, love myself.

Before this, I would certainly have *said* that I loved myself. If pressed further, I would have acknowledged self-love as a generally important concept. I would then have shuffled uncomfortably and hoped we could talk about something else.

But this experience made it clear that my thoughts and beliefs about self-love hadn't translated into action until that moment. I had recognised the theoretical importance of it, but hadn't done anything to make it real.

This was clear from the harsh way I was treating myself at the time. I blamed myself for the failure of this relationship, for my lack of direction, even for the emotional pit I'd fallen into. I gave myself no generosity or understanding whatsoever, and the self-criticism only made me feel worse.

---

[27] Maybe I'm projecting, and it's not so hard for anyone else. Or, maybe I'm overgeneralising and it's hard for the less sceptical too. I guess we all have our individual struggles.

Instead of offering myself time to heal and a gentle reassurance that everything would improve, I lashed out inwardly for being in a tough situation in the first place. This blame created extra pain, and a spiralling feeling of impossibility. Because I felt I must be a worthless moron to have gotten into such a deep hole, I had no belief in my ability to get out... which simply deepened the hole.

On the other hand, when we love ourselves despite our shortcomings and mistakes, we allow ourselves room to grow. Instead of adding to our emotional burden with self-criticism, we lighten it with self-compassion.

Why are we so self-critical? Well, sometimes, when we catch ourselves lacking compassion, our minds will justify their behaviour: *"I'm just saying this for our own good. I'm only pushing us for motivation."*

This inner critic is fearing for its very existence. It only has a stick to beat you with, and if you stop responding to the stick it won't have anything to do. Instead, we need to teach it to use a carrot.[28]

The critic's justification is wrong. We don't need criticism to perform. Generally when we're motivated by fear of failure - the stick - we don't perform to our potential. We're stressed, uptight, more likely to fail. If we succeed it's *despite* the fact we were being whacked with a stick at the time.

Loving ourselves doesn't necessitate abandoning our goals. We simply don't hit ourselves as we work towards them. Beating ourselves up is the worst possible way to get what we want - we waste all our energy on a pointless internal battle.

Perhaps it began with a part of our mind honestly trying to motivate us. But we can recognise now that the harsh self-criticism is unhelpful, and replace it with a positive encouraging voice instead.

As usual, the trickiest part is recognising when we are lacking in self-compassion. It's so easy to immediately accept criticism from our inner monologues without question. Even when we're on the lookout they often slip beneath our notice. We are too affected by

---

[28] Not to beat you with, of course, but to offer to you as a reward. Assuming you like carrots. If not, you can substitute a more suitable treat into the metaphor.

the emotional impact of their words to stop and question if we need to listen to them at all.

Inner critic: Speak for yourself, I'm fine. It's you that apparently has this "abusive inner voice" problem. Personally, I've never noticed one. I expect this is because you suck.

This is part of the reason I highlight my inner critic so often...

Inner critic: I assumed it was because I'm the only one here that talks sense.

...even when he's merely annoying or abusive. Often I fuse with destructive thoughts as soon as they appear, and I take on unnecessary negativity for the rest of the day.

You may feel that you don't deserve positive self-talk. Perhaps you hear a voice saying "Easy for you to say I should love myself, but I AM a failure."

That voice *right there* is your inner critic talking. That's the voice you want to disengage from and replace with a compassionate encourager.

Even if, right now, you're fused with that voice and don't believe it's possible not to listen to it, imagine how it would feel to have a loving voice inside, instead of one that beats you up. Do you think you'd feel better? Happier? More encouraged? More grounded? Less likely to suddenly slip beneath ground you wrongly thought was solid and have to struggle your way back up?

You might not think it's true that you are worth loving. You might have fused with your inner critic so often that even the idea of loving yourself seems impossible. I can say with confidence that you are worth loving. But we all know that it's not enough to be told so; words from outside just bounce off.

You might think it'd be easier to feel self-loving if we could outsource the work to other people. It's tempting to think that if only someone else told us they loved us, we could love ourselves more. But love received from others must pass through our internal filter. If that filter doesn't believe we are worthy of love we deflect it when it is offered. We have to do the work of fixing the filter.

This is exactly why this love has to come from within. It's why I had to have a weird and embarrassing experience with a piano. And it's why I'm telling you about it: so you can find your own way to fix that filter and stop those words from bouncing off.

Our minds hate this. They would prefer to debate the pros and cons, the arguments for and against the idea that we're worth loving. Logically, I'm sure you could agree that everyone has something to love about them, and that therefore you are probably lovable in some abstract logical way. But logic doesn't help. You can't logic yourself into loving anybody, not even yourself.

Forget the idea of deserving love. Whether you believe you deserve it or not, I'm sure you agree it would be more helpful to have a self-compassionate, forgiving, encouraging voice in your head than one that berates you and makes you feel bad.

If you can commit to that idea then you're halfway there. Remember, it doesn't depend on logic, so if you start thinking of *reasons* why you should (or shouldn't) be loving, you've already lost. You're right back in inner critic home territory. Instead, once you've decided compassion would be helpful, simply give the same treatment to yourself that you would to someone you care about. In other words: if you wouldn't say it to a good friend, don't think it to yourself.

We're getting plenty of practice at observing our thoughts. As we tune into our inner radio, apply a new filter: *Would I say this to someone I care for, in this exact situation?* If not, then this is our cue to be compassionate to ourselves.

What *would* we say to a friend beating themselves up over a mistake? We might say "everyone makes mistakes" or "you were tired - you were up all night with the kids" or "in a few months this won't matter." We'd likely give them a hug or cheer them up with a treat: a coffee, a glass of wine, or a listening ear.[29]

When you catch yourself being critical, replace the thought with whatever you'd say to a friend. If we catch harsh thoughts and transform them to compassionate ones, over time self-compassion becomes just as habitual as our previous harshness.

Eventually it becomes natural to love and forgive ourselves, even if we didn't believe we were worthy of love when we started. Taking the action - even cheesily singing a song - is what makes it true.

---

[29] If any of my friends are reading, I also accept Mediterranean holiday villas, cars, or simply cash.

Being Nice

I know I've said this about many things already, but self-compassion is seriously important. It underpins everything else.

When we fail to take responsibility, fuse with a thought, or get sucked into a feedback loop, then the way we respond to the failure is crucial. If we respond hatefully, we only hurt ourselves further.

We're right back on the custard: our response just makes us feel worse. Left. Right. Left. Right. No escape.

We have to respond compassionately, to solidify the ground under us.

It may help to schedule time to actively work on cultivating an attitude of self-compassion, perhaps by performing cheesy mental exercises like hugging yourself, thinking positive affirmations, or whatever works for you. Maybe you'd prefer to practise catching and replacing the negative self-talk as it happens.

Catching yourself in the act of self-criticism offers an additional opportunity to cultivate self-love. For most of us, the first thought immediately after recognising some self-criticism will be something else self-critical, like:

Oh god, there's another negative thought. Damn it, I can't stop beating myself up. I suck at self-compassion. I'm such an idiot.

At which point you are beating yourself up for beating yourself up! The only possible response is to laugh at the absurdity, forgive yourself for it, smile, and move on.

Compassionately.

> *"To love oneself is the beginning of a lifelong romance."*
> *Oscar Wilde*

SELF-LOVE IS ALL WELL AND GOOD
But What if I Actually... Kinda... Hate Myself?

(also I'm not sure how to capitalise that title, and I hate myself for that too)

Honestly, my main advice is just not to worry about capital letters too much. As long as your meaning is clear people generally don't mind. English has fairly loose rules when it comes to capitalisation, and it's obvious what you meant, so just relax! Does that help?

Er, fine. But what about, you know... the self-hatred?

Oh. I guess that's important too.

I expect we all experience self-hatred from time to time. Maybe at times of weakness - failing to keep to a diet, giving in to temptation, not sticking to an exercise plan -

Inner critic: Failing to write for an entire day because you were wasting time watching other people play videogames on the internet..?

Ouch. Yes, hypothetically, I can imagine that *might* induce someone to have negative thoughts about themselves.

The lucky few of us only experience such powerful self-loathing occasionally, during momentary failures, stressful times, or perhaps at 3am when our psychological defences are lowered.

But some of us are stuck with that self-hating feeling more often. Self-compassion can seem like a laughable idea. And not a fun kind of laughability. Why should we love ourselves?

This is incredibly hard, especially as we have to solve it ourselves. I'm afraid all I can offer is a few thoughts of support.

First, don't give up! You are worth loving. It is absolutely worth the effort of learning to love yourself more. It may require a painful amount of effort to do so, but it *will* improve your quality of life. Believe that loving yourself is worthwhile, and believe that it is possible.

I *know* that this is easier to say than enact, and that when we feel like this we will ignore even our best friend or soul mate telling us how worthwhile we are. Breaking out of that defensive shell is as hard as breaking in.

Here is a mildly cheesy exercise which may help.

EXERCISE: Loving When You're Not Sure How

Imagine meeting somebody who feels about themselves the same way you feel about yourself.

Imagine listening as they express their feelings of disliking, liking, loving, or hating themselves. What words do they use?

Imagine how they act as they tell you. Are they calm and businesslike, describing their feelings mechanically? Or are they emotional, passionate, or volatile?

Imagine how it feels to hear them tell you this. Do you feel sympathy? What would you say to them? Would you want to offer advice? Or to give them a hug?

How do they feel that you're listening so attentively? How would it feel to receive such emotional support from someone?

If it helps, try imagining that this person is you. Maybe at an earlier time in your life, maybe you now. If they're younger, how do you feel about this more naive, less able-to-cope version of yourself?

If you can cope with the cheesiness (and believe me, my inner *fromage-o-phobe* is screaming hard about this exercise!) then imagine giving yourself a hug. Imagine receiving this hug, too.

If you managed to feel compassion for this other person, then recognise you generated that compassion for yourself. You do care. It may hurt, but you do care.

Hopefully, this helped you get in touch with a part of you that already thinks you're pretty great. If so, tap into that feeling as often as possible. If not, then please don't give up. You are worth loving. Even the fact you *want* to believe it proves it, does it not?

A GIRL STUCK IN THE FUTURE
And Her Brother Stuck In The Past

"Yes please," she replied.

Her mother passed her some ketchup.

"Would you like some ketchup, dear?"

She spurted the ketchup generously over the plate.

Her brother finished his meal and slid the plate away. Then he started to cry at how hungry he had been hours earlier.

Aggrieved, the girl stuck in the future paused with her spoon in the air, exclaiming:

"Mum! We've been over this! You know it doesn't work like that."

"I was thinking, maybe we could get you to listen to the lottery broadcast tonight?" her mother wondered, hopefully.

"Even if we were AT the stand buying lottery tickets, at the exact moment they make the draw, you wouldn't be able to get the ticket in time. Last time you nearly crashed the car trying to -"

The girl paused. Her mother waited awkwardly, before realising she was supposed to interrupt. Or have interrupted. She'd never quite got to grips with how the whole stuck-in-the-future thing was meant to function. She tried talking, hoping it was the right thing.

"That was your dad's fault, love. I TOLD him we'd better just listen to the draw from the car outside the shop, but he said he likes seeing the little coloured balls getting chosen. Anyway, maybe - "

"Well that would just spoil the whole purpose!"

Her mother hated when her daughter interrupted *her*. It was always confusing, especially if she hadn't yet thought of the question her daughter had already answered.

This time she couldn't figure out what she might be about to say that would have elicited that response. Or would have been about to elicit that response. Or something.

She thought furiously. Her daughter hated it when people never said the words she'd already responded to.

Some moments passed. Her daughter looked expectant, then anxious, then disappointed.

The girl stuck in the future finished her cereal in silence. She would have regretted her disappointing decision to put ketchup on her breakfast, but she was already regretting her choice of tomorrow's lunch.

Her brother continued to cry. The girl stuck in the future didn't know what had happened - or when - but the two of them had long since given up attempting to communicate except through their mother, who at least had a fighting chance at being near the same time they were currently inhabiting. Anyway, she already knew how the attempt would go, so why bother?

Her mother returned for the empty plates, and waited for an instant, in case either of her children showed any sign of wanting to go outside today. But they were both preoccupied with their own worlds, so she left them to it.

She dumped the dishes into the sink and looked out of the window.

It was a beautiful day.

CHAPTER TEN
The Gift of Presents

"Strive to live only what is really thy life, that is, the present"
Marcus Aurelius

"Sure thing, Aurelius"

Sometimes I feel like the most ungrateful moaner in the universe. I don't mean that in a self-pitying way. I just mean that no matter how great my situation may be, I *still* manage to find something to worry about.

Even if all seems well, I chew over some imagined problem that may come up. The solution, of course, is to "stay in the present moment"...

... which is a bloody irritating command, because it sounds impossible to disobey: *How can I NOT be living in the present? What other option is there?!*

Actually, we spend the majority of our lives being anywhere but the present moment.

This is a bold claim, so rather than waffle about it, let's prove it by observation.

EXERCISE: What time is it in my mind?

This exercise is adapted from one found in *Get Out of Your Mind and into Your Life* by Steven Hayes.

If you have one, set a timer to go off in three minutes. Then rest both hands on your lap. Allow one hand to rest on your thigh, halfway to your knee. This spot on your leg represents *the present moment.*

Become aware of your body, and of your surroundings. Now, consciously hold your awareness in the present moment *only.* Notice what is happening right now.

Until the timer goes off, observe any thoughts arising in your mind. When you inevitably notice yourself thinking, move your hand to where in time the thought is located. If it's about *anything* in the future, move your hand up your thigh and think to yourself 'Future'. If it's about *anything* to do with the past, move your hand down your thigh and think to yourself 'Past'.

Aim to keep your hand still, remaining at the spot representing the present moment. When you find yourself moving away, bring yourself back to the present by noticing that *right now* you are thinking about the past or the future.

Try it now. If you're like me, you'll be surprised by how often your thoughts are anywhere but the present; how little you engage with your experience right now. We naturally relive replays of conversations from earlier, imagine conversations for later, wonder about tasks we ought to be doing - anything but recognising what is actually real, right at this moment.

It is too easy to dwell on autopilot, engaging more with our imagination than with the real world.

Of course, autopilot is a necessary tool, allowing our brains to automate the easier parts of whatever we're doing. I *like* not having to consciously recall how to move my muscles each time I pick up an object. Forgetting would be pretty embarrassing. But, like all of our mind's tools, autopilot shouldn't be used indiscriminately.

We must be present to appreciate any experience. We have thousands of conversations every year, and so it's effortless to slip into autopilot and hardly be present to the other person. Time flies, and we spend it worrying about what's to come, or regretting what has been, instead of interacting with our actual lives.

While there are benefits to imagining, fantasising and reminiscing, the ease with which we slip into these makes it tempting to live more in our inner world than in the real world.

Even if our inner worlds were purely beneficial places to visit, we'd be missing out on reality. But, as is all too familiar, our inner worlds can be actively harmful when we go there to batter ourselves over mistakes, or to fret about possible difficulties. Dwelling in the past can make us depressed, and getting stuck in the future can make us anxious.

Engaging with the current moment frees us from such painful rumination, and immerses us with the reality around us.

Of course, it's not a cure-all. It doesn't mean we magically enjoy ourselves more. A boring conversation or tedious task isn't always transformed by consciously engaging. But deliberately involving ourselves gives us a chance to enjoy it, whereas autopilot gives none at all. Perhaps we are missing out when we lose touch with the present moment.

At first, I was deeply sceptical of this. It sounds suspiciously like hearing 'if only you'd open your eyes there is joy and beauty everywhere', as if I ought to spend my days skipping around like a cartoon character in love, gazing at flowers and exclaiming inane statements about how wonderful the world is every five minutes. My inner cynic cringes at the thought.

Even so, mindful presence genuinely helps, and doesn't have to be so cheesy.

While it is useful even for mild worry, it is most powerful in times of crisis. Panic attacks are rarely about what is happening *right now*. Any suffering we experience is rarely in the present moment, but more often in a relived past or an imagined future. Coming back to the present helps prevent the exponential anxiety that characterises a panic attack.

Past Dangers

"Do not disturb thyself by thinking of the whole of thy life"
Marcus Aurelius
"Stop telling me what to do, Aurelius"

Let's rapidly tour a few ways we can get stuck in the past.

I often ruminate on missed opportunities. One of my regular fantasies is inventing a time machine; not for a noble goal such as preventing wars or witnessing historical events, but simply to pop back a few years and slap myself in the mouth for being such an idiot. I suspect I'm not alone in wishing to smack some sense into my past self.

Inner critic: I feel that way about your present self.

Ruminating on past failures only hurts us in the present.

Of course, it's good to learn from our mistakes and do better in future. But we can't do better in the past. So, resist the urge to dwell there.

One way to escape dwelling on mistakes is to acknowledge that if I *could* have done better in the past then I *would* have. This is a difficult idea to accept at first. We're accustomed to imagining ways we might have acted differently. And it seems like a simple leap from *imagining* a different possibility to *believing* that it could have happened. In truth, it couldn't have happened, because it didn't. Reality is what it is. Imagining otherwise is meaningless.

Another way the past haunts us is believing we are condemned to eternally repeat some inescapable pattern of failure.

I get rejected a lot, so I'll never get a boyfriend. I get fired from every job, so I'll never succeed at this one. Two people have cheated on me, so why start a relationship? Everything I buy breaks, so why buy anything? Whenever I eat a peach, a pigeon defecates on me. I hate peaches.

That last example is exactly as ridiculous as the first few. We are not doomed to repeat the past! Our pattern-addicted brains immediately leap on a perceived sequence of failure, and convince us to give up all hope.

We would tell anyone else claiming these things that the future can always be different. Yet we deny ourselves the freedom to change that we so easily grant to others.

There's no law of physics that forces the past to repeat. Sure, if we do the exact same thing, nothing will change. But no situation is ever the same. We grow, things change. The next time we ask someone out we are not the same person. The outcome is never constrained by past failures, only by what we have done to make it different this time.

Another hazard in our relationship with the past is pain. Whether due to trauma, disappointment or regret, this is something we all have to deal with.

I hate feeling pain, obviously, so repression is always a tempting tactic. But, unfortunately, repression isn't a great strategy. It causes pain to leak out in other ways; like a game of Sad Whack-a-Mole, it just pops up elsewhere.

We have to release regret, let go of pain, give up missed opportunities and grieve the person or circumstance we have lost. This comes with an emotional load: it hurts. But that's normal, and healthy.

A handy approach to past pain is *non-attachment*.

Inner critic: Do you mean 'detachment'?

Er. Yes, I guess so. But *non-attachment* sounds wiser, somehow.

Inner critic: How about you write a chapter on that? I'll give you the opening sentence: "Sometimes when people don't know what they're talking about they make up words to sound clever."

Alright, alright. Point taken.

All I meant was that we shouldn't attach ourselves to our pain. We want to face the past without repression, handle any emotions appropriately, learn what we can from it, and move on.

I suspect that we all instinctively know how to do this, and that it involves allowing ourselves to feel the hurt. Sometimes we need help to face it, and that's fine too. This may involve talking to friends or therapists, listening to music, punching pillows, crying, writing: whatever it takes to healthily let it out.

Even interpretive dance, if you like. Though please don't invite me. Inner demons are fine and all, but emotional dancing is *terrifying*.

Handling past pain is highly personal, and I wouldn't presume to tell you how to do it. The important thing is that you choose for yourself your relationship to it; finding a way to deal with any hurts, while seeking not to be defined or limited by them.

A healthy relationship with the past relies on plenty of self-compassion, and on being fully in the present even while visiting time gone by.[30]

Living from the Future

> *"Let not future things disturb thee"*
> Marcus Aurelius
> *"Getting seriously pushy, Aurelius."*

Any sufferer of anxiety is intimately familiar with the future. We live there most of the time.

---

[30] Or 'days of yore'. I wish I had days of yore, they sound so much better than the boring old past.

Our minds are excellent predictors of what could go wrong. Without prompting, they conjure doomsday scenarios of loneliness, failure and desperation. They are skilled at rationalising, so if we wonder "Do we need to be panicking about these possibilities?" they object strongly:

"Of course we need to ceaselessly worry, or we'll never get anything done. I'm just helping you out! Incidentally, have you considered recently how you'd feel if everybody you love died?"

This justification is a lie. Addiction to worry is not necessary. It is perfectly possible to live a well-planned life without fearing the future.

At this point the worry-addict will normally object with the same defence: *"I can't just blunder randomly through life. SOMEONE has to think ahead!"*

And I would agree with them. Living in the present moment does not mean never planning ahead. It simply means doing whatever action is appropriate in the present moment, including thinking ahead.

Perhaps I'm planning a trip abroad. I need to book transport and accommodation and to contact the people I'll be visiting there. These actions concern the future, and take place in the present moment.

The alternative, anxiety-based method involves *worrying* about the trip, and allowing imaginary future difficulties to rob me of joy, excitement and ability to plan.

What if I have an accident, what if I get lost?

This is a common mode for the anxiety-prone. Instead of calmly planning in the present, I'm in some imagined future feeling the negative consequences of a disaster that hasn't happened. Not that that helps; our bodies don't distinguish between stress due to real or imagined events. Both affect our hormone levels, tire us out, and can cause health problems. Worrying is bad for us.

And, before you start, worrying about 'worrying being bad for us' is also bad for us. Laugh, and let go!

Like visiting the past without dwelling there, we want to operate out of calm action in the present moment, rather than a fearful anxiety of the future.

Planning takes place in the present. Worrying takes place in an imagined future. We need one, but not the other.

Sometimes I get so entwined in dire fantasy that I begin living as if it's already true. My doomsday scenarios are so convincing that it seems I'd cope better after receiving the actual bad news than how I cope with merely imagining it happening.

This isn't to demean the anxious as having imaginary concerns. Anxious fantasies are very real problems. But it's never a good idea to trade imaginary future possibilities for genuine anxiety in the present. This is the trade we make when we live in the future.

Even having a concrete reason to worry is not a good reason to fantasise about it. Perhaps we know, for certain, that circumstances are going to degenerate. It still remains a waste of energy to fear how we might feel when the change comes. Worse, it needlessly damages our enjoyment of the less-bad circumstances that we live in right now. We can plan for the change, but good planning takes place in the present moment, not in the future.

Our future selves will undoubtedly wish we'd lived as fully as possible right now, whether we're worrying about the inevitable or the unlikely.

But what can I DO to be present?

Like acceptance, mindful presence is a learnable skill.

We want to minimise the depression from the past and anxiety from the future by noting when we've slipped away from the present moment and - gently, compassionately - bringing ourselves back.

It helps to learn how it feels when we slip into the past or future. Practising the exercise from earlier in this chapter helps develop awareness of how much time we spend outside the present moment.

We want to develop a habit of remaining present. As ever, this means doing it in everyday situations.

Inner critic: What a hypocrite. You claim you want to practise these skills in everyday situations but half the time when you're not feeling anxious you don't even remember to do the meditation practice you "committed" to. And now you're writing a book telling people to do what you don't?!

You're right, inner critic. It's hard to stick to a new habit. I start all enthusiastically and get up early every day for a morning run. For a week or two I evangelise to everybody about how "life-changing" it is. But then, the day comes when the alarm clock goes off and I think "I've done well lately. I'll just sleep for thirty more minutes instead of running this morning." And soon I have only the creeping guilt of "I've not run for a while." And the habit is replaced by guilt that we failed.

Inner critic: Wait, what? When did you ever take up running?

Er...

Inner critic: Did you just try to refute an allegation of hypocrisy by pretending to have failed at a running habit?

Maybe. Um. Look. Let's not get caught up on "facts" and "details". I was only illustrating that it's hard to stick to habits. This same difficulty applies to working on our emotional habits.

So, inner critic, I don't claim to be perfect, but I do know that when I put the effort into meditating and dwelling in the present moment I am much more grounded and happy. So I'm sharing that experience and trying to live by it the best I can. You could help out a bit more, you know, but we'll get to you in a later chapter.

Inner critic: Gulp.

We're never alone in finding it hard to do this stuff. Don't feel guilty about it, but do keep trying.

EXERCISE: Workouts for Presence

Let's build on our breathing exercises to practise staying out of autopilot, and in the present.

It may help to think of these as a regular workout. You are building a metaphorical muscle, after all.

Then again, it may not help to think of it as a regular workout, because that sounds disappointingly like hard work, and nobody wants that. You may prefer to think of it as a tour around a chocolate factory that finishes in a giant hot tub with a free bar. Whatever works.

For an easy introduction, you could schedule a few minutes a day to repeat the exercise from earlier, when we used our hands to mark when in time our thoughts are located.

Here are a few more ideas you try:

ONE: The Body Scan

Sadly, this isn't as much fun as the name might imply. Sorry.

Our bodies constantly transmit information to our minds. Each instant, a ludicrous amount of data is beamed along nerves to the brain. Of this, we consciously notice only a tiny percentage. Just as our breath is usually automatic but we can take manual control, we can choose to become aware of this data from our bodies.

I am near-criminally underattentive to my body. I have a habit of sitting uncomfortably and ignoring the messages of pain from my feet and legs until I fall over after trying to get up. This mild public humiliation could be avoided with a habitual sense of self-presence.

Paying attention to these messages automatically grounds us in the present moment, by forcing us to notice what is happening *now*.

To perform a body scan:

Become aware of your feet. Feel the sensations in your soles. How do your socks, shoes, or the floor feel against your skin?

Take a deep belly-breath. Imagine the breath rushing all the way to your feet as you inhale, and then rushing back up and out as you exhale.

Repeat this with each part of your body, from the bottom to the top: your lower legs, then your thighs, your mid-section, your chest, your arms, your neck and finally your head.

For each part, tune into the sensations from that part of your body and concentrate your awareness on each spot for a couple of breaths.

You can do this quickly by taking one breath for each part, or slowly by spending multiple breaths on each. You may choose to focus on every little part of your body: ankles, knees, hands, etc. Or just the main bits: legs, torso, arms, head.

However you do it, you ground yourself in the present by listening to the usually-ignored parts of your body.

If you have read this far without trying it, why not experiment by trying it for one body part? It's hard to see the benefit if you don't attempt it, and a few seconds of enforced presence is always useful.

TWO: Watching Emotions Rise and Fall

This is another form of meditation.

Sit comfortably. Or not, if you like to meditate on hard mode.

Breathing at whatever rate feels natural, focus on one spot in your body. Weirdly, a common suggestion is to use the rim of your nostril. It's a good choice as the sensation changes in a rhythmic fashion, as you feel the air rushing past during each breath. Others prefer to focus on the belly as it rises and falls.

Keep your attention on your chosen spot. When you find yourself distracted by anything, remind yourself that your only job right now is to maintain concentration on that spot, and observe the sensation of breathing. Respond to any distraction by calmly and gently returning your attention to the spot.

It may be that you get distracted for a long time, following thoughts or fantasies for minutes at a time before noticing the distraction. That's fine. Don't dwell on it. Resume the concentration.

You will find emotions arise naturally, just as thoughts do. Quite possibly the first will be frustration that you're wasting your time "doing nothing". Instead of reacting, just observe the emotion. See what happens if you do not respond. Once again, return your attention to the spot you are concentrating on.

You may feel an urgency to move. If so, acknowledge that you feel like acting, but, again, do not respond. If it helps, label it by saying to yourself "urgency", and return your attention back to your breath in your chosen spot. Watch what happens if you simply observe the urgency instead of reacting.

It was surprising to me that nearly every emotion disappears of its own accord if I don't engage with it. Frustration, sadness, anxiety, urgency - positive emotions too - just come and go.

In my everyday life I react to every emotional swing as if it were a huge deal. But observing emotions ebb and flow proves to me that I can choose my response when an emotion arises.

We're not obliged to fly into a rage when we feel angry, or spiral into terror when we feel anxious, or leap into action at every inner prompting. We can take more control.

THREE: (A Few) Everyday Mindful Triggers

Here are some ideas for triggers you could use to remind yourself to be present. As ever, reminding ourselves at intervals can make presence a habit.

1) *Talking.* Challenge yourself to be fully present to each person you meet, without going on 'conversational autopilot'.
2) *Walking.* As you walk, concentrate on each step, and on how it feels. Notice the sensation of the ground beneath you, the temperature of the air, and the speed of the wind. Paying attention to any sensory experience brings you automatically into the present.
3) *Eating.* I am terrible at this. I am a champion inattentive eater. I may as well be a vacuum cleaner. To break this habitual autopilot, it's good to notice the sensory experience of eating: how it tastes, how it feels, etc.

All of these are about practising our awareness, so when we are drawn anxiously into the future, or painfully into the past, we have already practised returning to the present.

This is Where the Concluding Title Would Be If I Had Planned Ahead

Being in the present moment keeps us grounded, and prevents pain from the past and anxiety about the future.

This allows us to focus on improving our circumstances, or to simply *enjoy* them, which is - after all - the point.

Presence isn't a cure-all for past traumas and hurts. We still need to healthily let go, move on, and heal. And end the addiction to worry.

But it's a powerful tool for reducing anxiety, and a helpful step in our quest for dry land.

CHAPTER ELEVEN
The Full Revelation

"...the gecko, and the monitor lizard, the wall lizard, the skink, and the chameleon." - Leviticus 11:30

I have a confession to make.

We are ruled by invisible alien lizards that we cannot sense or interact with, except to receive their instructions.

It's time to apply this new insight to the extremely serious business of self-growth.

...

Not really.

I was just checking you were still paying attention.

Not to mention that, *obviously*, I would never lie about anything so important. Of course there are no invisible alien lizards!

...

...

...

They're llamas.[31]

---

[31] My inner critic thinks this is a pretty irritating joke, so I'm leaving it in out of spite. Technically, this contradicts my own policy on inner critic relations, but sometimes I just like to be annoying. Even, apparently, to myself.

CHAPTER TWELVE
Voices In My Head

"Why have you spent TWO HOURS searching for quotes to put here instead of just writing the chapter? What a WASTE OF TIME." - The Pusher

We have already met one of the regular voices in my head: my inner critic.

Inner critic, shyly: Hello. Also, that was a bad opening sentence.

The phrase "voices in my head" may be a little misleading. I'm not referring to intrusive voices, but to regular patterns of self-talk, which we experience not as sounds, but as streams of thoughts with their own distinct - but limited - personalities.

We have seen that our minds follow established grooves whenever possible. Each time we relive the same pattern, we reinforce a whole system of related thoughts around a particular theme. These systems can be thought of as voices that we've internalised: like simple personalities that surface as part of our self-talk.

We have also seen how easily we identify with these voices, failing to recognise that what they say is not necessarily true, helpful, or what we actually believe.

Learning to recognise our more frequent voices is an important aspect of self-knowledge. Familiarity with when particular voices are likely to speak up encourages us to expect their input, and therefore resist their negativity more easily.

When the voice pipes up we can think "oh, it's that voice again" instead of immediately reacting to its bleating with anxiety, depression or panic. With practice, we can reduce its power altogether.

Some people refer to these sorts of voices as 'bad spirits', though mercifully not in the spooky, demonic sense. Imagining a little cartoon character whispering on your shoulder is a helpful defusing technique to remind us we don't have to believe what they say.

Let's look at a couple of my regular voices as examples.

Inner critic: Real authors have examples that aren't them, you know! Isn't it a bit self-indulgent to constantly go on about yourself? And now you're even writing these words as I say them?! That's disgustingly self-referential. You should delete this whole chapter and start again.

As usual, my inner critic has strong opinions. Although, they are apt; he is certainly one of the more prominent voices I've learned to detect.

Here are two other voices I've identified that are definitely unhelpful for me:

The Pusher

"I'm too old. Time is running out. I can't believe I'm 21 already[32] and I haven't sorted everything out yet. Why is my career not perfect? Why aren't I married? Why haven't I accomplished everything yet?"

The Pusher is a regular companion, whose main obsession is berating me for my 'failures'. He especially loves harping on about relationships and achievement.

If I'm not in a relationship: *I'm wasting time if I'm not actively searching for a relationship right this second.*

If I'm in a relationship: *Why isn't everything perfect?*

If I'm in a relationship, and it's going well: *Why aren't we married already?*

If I have a job: *It's got to be ideal and I've got to perform perfectly or I've failed.*

If I'm not working: *I'm doomed to poverty forever and any second not spent looking for work is wasted time.*

If I'm not in a job OR in a relationship: *I'm hopeless. Also, any time spent looking for one is time wasted looking for the other! Good luck with that.*

If I'm taking a holiday: *I have to fill all the time fully or the holiday is wasted.*

---

[32] Or 25, 27, 31, or whatever... the actual value is irrelevant to the Pusher.

If I'm relaxing: *I AM WASTING TIME. I need to go work, so I can afford to relax.*

For the Pusher, life is always happening somewhere else. How dare I do nothing in particular for a few hours? How dare I visit friends in Australia? Or read books, watch cricket or enjoy the sunshine? Do I not realise there is a life to be lived? Whatever I'm doing has to be *directly* and *immediately* fulfilling *all* my life goals or I am wasting my time. According to the Pusher, I have wasted enough already.

No list of prior accomplishments can sate the Pusher. Sure, he acknowledges that some successes happened, but they were in the past. Which no longer matters. The Pusher is worried - deeply, terrifyingly worried - about the future. A future which *always* requires me to act *right now* to prevent life from becoming non-specifically awful.

Sounds exhausting, right? Honestly, it really is. If I were to believe everything this voice says I'd be constantly drained. It's impossible to reconcile the contradictory demands the Pusher makes on my time. This voice is the source of years of exhausting running on custard.

I never questioned this voice. I listened to it without doubting, never wondering "Who is saying this? Do I have to believe this? Is it even true?" Heeding the Pusher was a major contributing factor to my anxiety.

I don't know how I came to internalise this voice. Sometimes, if we look closely, we can detect other people in these internal voices. Perhaps a cruel classmate, or a critical parent, or some other authority figure. Maybe we once absorbed a harsh comment and built our own pattern around it, like a pearl made of criticism inside the oyster of our minds.

I'm sure it's often possible to find whatever little speck of grit the pearl formed around. But even if we can't, it doesn't matter. Where we are going matters more than where we came from.

Our minds love to delay us by claiming we need to answer the impossible question "but *why* does this voice exist?" Don't let yours trick you. Explaining how a problem began is not the same as solving it, and understanding why we are this way is *not* a prerequisite for change.

I suspect this voice began quite innocently from within, as I pushed myself to be the best I could be. I'll probably never know for sure. But what matters is that I have learned to recognise when the Pusher speaks up to ruin my contentment.

These voices all have simple personalities. The Pusher is motivated solely to improve myself and my situation. However, he isn't equipped to do anything *but* constantly push me to improve. He lacks all compassion or desire to enjoy the present moment; he is simply a drive to keep pushing forward without regard for anything else.

Listening to the Pusher puts me on an endless conveyor belt of compulsory improvement, with no possibility of pausing to enjoy where I'm at: the very definition of walking on custard.

The Comparer

"You suck."

This voice speaks up whenever I hear about anyone else having achieved anything at all. Or even sometimes on seeing happy strangers.

> *"That couple walking down the street look happy. Unlike you."*
> *"They look like they love their job. Why don't you have passion? Don't you care about anything?"*
> *"How come literally everyone else knows how to start a business and you don't?"*
> *"Look at all these pictures of your friends getting great jobs and houses and having kids. What are you doing with your life? Nothing."*

Sometimes it's even about things I don't particularly desire:

> *"She got published in the paper! Why haven't you done that?"*
> *"You'd be an awful doctor. You'd spend all day self-diagnosing yourself with every disease going. Why don't you do anything that helps anybody?"*
> *"He's a successful combat pilot. You could never do that."*

Seriously, I have never wanted to be a combat pilot, or a doctor, or to write for a newspaper. Yet these thoughts still show up to make me feel bad. As do even more ludicrous comparisons:

"You're an awful acrobat"

I actually feel bad after comparing myself to some professional who has been training all their life in a discipline I have no desire to try. I expect my first thought after making extra-terrestrial contact would be "You'd make a crap Space Being From Another Dimension." The Comparer isn't necessarily very nice to other people, either:

"He's getting married, and he's an idiot! Why aren't you married yet? Does everyone love you less than that idiot?"

And sometimes the Pusher even chimes in, so I'm essentially ganging up on myself:

"They ran a 10k race. You used to be able to do that. Now I bet you couldn't. Is hating running just an excuse for your laziness?"

I never come off well to the Comparer.

Although, to be pedantic, in that final case, he's wrong. I only ever ran *one* 10k, at the age of nineteen. I arrogantly turned up having done zero training, naively assuming that 10k didn't sound very far.

Much later, as I pathetically staggered over the finish line, I was cheered by my team mates who had already finished: the middle-aged ladies in the typing pool at my workplace who'd invited me to join their team.

I had *significantly* dragged down their average time.

Recently, I listened to a friend telling me her uncle's life story. I'd been in a good mood before this part of the conversation, enjoying an evening of wine and pleasant company. But as I heard about him marrying three times, earning a load of money and generally living an interesting life I suddenly felt terrified and then sad.

I didn't even want this man's life. The marriages didn't sound much fun, and money for money's sake has never been of interest to me.

Yet something about this story stirred the voice of the Comparer. The mere fact this guy had done some things I hadn't got the Comparer riled up:

"Why don't I run several businesses? How can someone get married three times and I've not even managed it ONCE? Why don't I have a boat?!"

The Comparer whispered to me, I listened and believed, my emotions plummeted, and it spoiled my enjoyment of an otherwise excellent evening. It wasn't until afterwards that I belatedly recognised the handiwork of the Comparer.

It was shocking to realise that he could undermine me so powerfully without my noticing. Particularly since I wasn't even jealous of this man: owning a boat sounds like way more hard work than it's worth![33]

Learning to recognise this voice has helped me defend against these useless mood swings.

Like the Pusher, the Comparer thinks he is helping. He thinks he's providing me with motivation. But, also like the Pusher, this isn't true. If I didn't compare myself with people, would I be a useless lazy lump who never strived for, nor wanted, anything?

Inner critic: ... is... is that supposed to be a hypothetical question?

Of course it is. My inner critic may believe I'm a useless lump who wants nothing, but he is also a one-note personality, existing only to criticise.

Inner critic: I resent that.

You disagree?

Inner critic: Not really. I just resent being criticised by a moron.

I rest my case. Anyway, as I was saying, I lose nothing if I stop listening to the Comparer. Except an unnecessary sense of inferiority. He only pretends to be helpful.

Now, when I'm in a situation that's likely to set him off, I expect him to start squeaking. And that knowledge is enough for me to politely request him to stop.

Characteristics of Inner Voices

These voices tend to have shared features. In particular, they are based around repetitive criticisms on a single note: we have no time, we are no good, we are unattractive, we will fail. They each

---

[33] I'm sure owning a boat is lovely, but I'm a natural land-lubber. I expect I'd sink it in embarrassing fashion within hours, so it's best that I don't get involved with boats... although... is that my Inner Pessimist talking?!

have such an obsession. And they fear for their existence. Their response to challenge is to claim we couldn't get on without them.

The key to handling these voices is, counter-intuitively, self-compassion.

Despite having spent this whole chapter painting them as annoyances, these voices *aren't the enemy.* They're not evil. These voices exist because they love us and they want us to do well. After all, they are part of us.

But each voice only has one strategy to help. They are like carpenters with nothing but a hammer, who see every problem as a nail. They relentlessly bash everything with their single tool in the misguided belief that they're helping. Perhaps the hammer was once helpful, but now we have outgrown the need for that particular tool. We can retire it safely, or choose to use it at the right time only.

Remember my inner critic complaining after I used myself as an example? He isn't some self-hating part of me that wants me to fail.

That part of me is genuinely worried that people might not like what I'm writing, and that therefore they won't like ME, and therefore I'll be rejected from the world and left to die alone.

My inner critic meant well, albeit in a panicky and overblown manner. Of course, he is no more psychic than I am, so I'm not obliged to believe his freaking out. And I certainly don't need to join in with it.

Rather than treat the voices as insurgent enemies, it's helpful to respond compassionately, thanking them for their input, and seeking to understand what they are trying to do.

If I ask them why they are speaking, they say "Because we want you to be happy, and we think that pushing you this way helps". Understanding their good intentions helps resist the temptation to beat ourselves up for "being our own worst enemy" which helps nobody.

Internal wars only have one casualty: ourselves.

EXERCISE: Identifying and Responding to Our Voices

Please don't sit comfortably. This exercise takes time.

For the next few days, when a negative thought arises, identify if it is part of a pattern for you. Can you spot any consistent internal voices that cause you pain?

As I did with the Pusher and the Comparer, can you name that voice? If possible, choose a single word that encapsulates what that voice is about. What is the single tool it uses? What does it tend to say when it shows up?

Can you identify why the voice says what it says? Remember, it certainly has your best interests at heart: it is part of you. What is its intention? Does it want you to be happy? Secure? Safe? Idle?

Next time it shows up, greet it: "Oh hello, the Pusher". You don't need to do anything more than that. Just learn to spot the voice when it shows up, and welcome it. Treat it like a friend-of-a-friend; someone you'd treat respectfully to honour your friend.

Continue with your life, but acknowledge them politely when you spot them. See if that reduces the power these voices have.

In this way, we cease responding emotionally when our regular critics appear. By treating them with compassion we start to replace them with more positive voices. Encourage supportive thoughts in place of their usual fault-finding, and slowly your voices will transform from a team of critics to a team of allies.

This doesn't happen overnight. Keep yourself motivated by reminding yourself of the goal: a contented life on solid ground.

I find work like this to be mildly embarrassing to think about, let alone talk about. It feels silly having to convince parts of my mind to support me instead of undermine me. Yet experience has shown that it's useful and important.

The Pusher: WHY HAVEN'T YOU FINISHED CONVERTING ME TO AN ALLY YET? HURRY UP, THERE'S NO TIME!

A WIZARD DOES IT
An Adventurer Seeks Fulfilment

Mist swirled portentously around the feet of the mighty wizard.

Nobody had ever commented on his mist, but he was pretty sure that it added to his impressive appearance. He hated the idea that a brave adventurer might be disappointed after completing their quest to find a mighty wizard.

In his opinion, it was basic professionalism to use a Big Booming Voice and maintain the mysterious feel of his cave. So, portentous swirling mist it was.

Even if it meant drying out wet socks every evening once the adventurers had left.

He glared balefully at the latest frazzled adventurer, noting with satisfaction that their hair had been gently singed by the new fire spell he'd installed last week. It was soooooo important to make visitors feel deeply threatened on arrival.

He'd heard Brian the 'Potent' had taken to sitting on a cushion - an actual *cushion*, not a bone carved to look like one - while he waited for adventurers to find him.

Thankfully, sense had prevailed. Brian had had an 80 percent drop in adventurous visitors the following month, and the board had insisted he get rid of the foolish indulgence. This was exactly why the mighty wizard had never skimped on the perilous feel of his abode.

Of course, none of the traps would actually kill - or even injure - anybody. There was simply no way he could afford the medical insurance if any of the adventurers *actually* got hurt. But they didn't need to know that.

The adventurer shuffled uncertainly.

Oh yes, I should do the Voice thing.

"WHAT DO YOU SEEK, ADVENTURER?" boomed the wizard. He wondered about releasing a touch more mist, but he could already feel a slight dampness on his feet from the first batch. He didn't want to risk a fungal infection.

Fortunately, this adventurer appeared sufficiently impressed already, and responded in the traditional manner.

"I seek fulfilment."

"Fulfilment it shall be", the wizard said, using his less-booming voice. He had learned to make that switch at a recent seminar on vocal chord management. He planned a long wizardly career, and didn't want to end up sounding raspy. "I shall grant you all you desire, but you must pay the cost."

"And what is the cost, O Mighty Wizard?"

The wizard flinched slightly at the flowery language.

He always felt awkward when the adventurers started with the flattery. It was nice, but all this 'O Mighty Wizard' stuff honestly made him feel uncomfortable. He had never figured out a good way to handle it. You couldn't exactly say "Please, call me Robert." He usually just let it slide and hoped it wouldn't get too over-the-top.

He answered quickly, in case the adventurer tried to get any more poetic.

"To receive your desire, you must only die. This is the cost, adventurer."

There was a silence. Quite a long silence.

"You what?"

The adventurer sounded considerably more reedy.

"I must... die? Are you sure? What's the point in having fulfilment if I have to flipping die?! I didn't wade through stinking monsters for this crap."

Funny how quick the 'mighty wizard' talk disappears, the wizard mused. *Bloody adventurers.*

"Perhaps not, adventurer. But nevertheless this remains the cost. To receive all that you desire, the you that exists must die."

"The... me that exists? You mean, me, right?"

The adventurer sagged, nearly dropping their sword due to the effort of thought. Continuity of personal identity had never been on the curriculum at Hero School.

"Yes, you. You will remain. But the *you-that-exists-now* will die, and be replaced by a new you. This is the only way to gain what you seek."

The wizard watched as the adventurer attempted to contemplate this. He had seen this reaction before. These alleged swashbucklers faced death every day, from fearsome monsters, hidden traps, dangerous spells and bizarre wizards.

They had long ago embraced *that* kind of death. Relished it, even. But death that changed them into a new version of themselves? This was frightening.

A long moment passed before the adventurer spoke again.

"Screw it. I'll stick to fighting goblins."

He turned, and left the wizard's cave.

The wizard watched, until he was sure the adventurer was out of sight.

Well, that's that then.

It wasn't common, but he had seen many an adventurer decide against the cost, and it no longer surprised him.

He loosened his belt, and turned off the mist. That was the last adventurer of the day.

He headed back to his private chambers, squelching slightly as he walked.

I'll dry these socks first. Then I'll finish that knitting.

By the time he was comfortably settled onto his sofa, he'd already forgotten all about the adventurer.

CHAPTER THIRTEEN
Cleave La Resistance

"For I don't know what I am doing.
For I don't practice what I desire to do; but what I hate, that I do."

St. Paul

Soon after I first moved away from home I found myself in a fast-food restaurant with a new friend. As we talked, my mind wandered, exploring the possibilities of my newfound freedom.

I can do anything! I can stay up all night, eat seven tonnes of cheese and then get a train to Norway, and NOBODY can stop me! This is amazing!

I was an adult. A grown-up. I could vote, get a job, travel... I had more freedom than I'd ever had before in my life.

It was time to express my adulthood.

So I blew into my milkshake straw as hard as possible. Yes... I celebrated my maturity by doing what every five-year-old does when confronted with a straw.

Inner critic: My work here is done.

I grinned in delight as the milkshake burbled and popped.

"Stop that!"

My friend issued the command harshly, visibly angered by my childish behaviour. My rebellion was quashed before it had begun.

The world has often resisted my ideas and desires,[34] but it has nothing on the ways in which I resist myself.

Inner critic: With good reason. Imagine how much more stupid stuff you'd have done if I wasn't here to stop you!

It's not only the nagging of my inner critics that prevents me from living up to my ideals. There are many factors, including unwillingness to tolerate discomfort, inertia and fear of change. (And we shouldn't forget good old basic laziness.)

---

[34] As happens to all misunderstood geniuses, right, everyone? Right?!

Often, I support the idea of change, but resist the reality of it.

This resistance surfaces in most areas of my life, but it comes into force when I attempt any significant undertaking, like escaping anxiety, going on a diet, or starting a new productivity regime.

I *want* to change, but I fail to do so. Something talks me out of it.

This resistance is known as *akrasia*, the tendency we have to act against our own judgement. We *want* to go to the gym, to spend time in meditation, or whatever. But we end up frittering time away doing something else.

Inner critic: Like... looking up posh words for simple things to sound smart? "Akrasia", honestly...

Alright, inner critic, you can have that one. We'll stick to "resistance", then.

Just as it helps to see our inner voices as well-intentioned, we should understand that resistance is a natural, reasonable phenomenon. Again, it helps to see it as an ally, rather than as yet another thing to battle.

This is partly a practical decision: we even resist battling resistance, so we *definitely* need a different strategy.

The first step is to notice that there's always some valid reason at the root of resistance.

Perhaps part of us is worried that spending all this energy handling inner pain won't leave enough for anything else. This isn't *true*, but that resistant voice can't be sure of that. Or perhaps the resistance fears experiencing pain at all, even for a long-term benefit.

For me, the most common reason is fear of changing. Growth requires change, and change means death for some part of us. Metaphorically, our current self dies, to be replaced by a new, (hopefully) improved identity. Viewed this way, it makes sense that our current self fears change. We may know better, but those scared little voices within don't.

Resistance is further fuelled by the fact that, at first, self-examination can appear to make everything worse. Actually confronting any problems we've been avoiding can be even more intense than the chronic (but lesser) pain of repressing them.

Unless we overcome our resistance to this short-term pain, we are tempted to quit, scurrying back to comfortable safety.

I can certainly empathise with this. At first, it seemed that exploring my anxiety only created extra problems.

All this over-thinking is only making things worse. We should have just left everything as it was.

My resistance leapt onto this as a "reason" to stop trying to change.

But now I can see I was only unearthing issues that had previously been buried - fears for my health, the death of loved ones, the apparent meaninglessness of life. I wasn't generating issues out of nowhere... I was finally facing those that had been there all the time.

This is how we end up living a whole lifetime stuck on custard. It's tempting to give up when confronted by short-term pain, and so we stick with the familiar custard traps we are used to.

Even positive change can be frightening: *Sure, I'm anxious, but I'm resigned to that now. Better the devil you know...*

Sometimes circumstances become intolerable enough to give us the push we need. A little short-term discomfort no longer seems like such a high price to escape the now intolerable situation. This is why people tend to get into self-growth when things get really rough.

But the price of staying immobile is even higher still: a lifetime of not-quite-intolerable-but-still-unpleasant anxiety.

Our capability to continue despite resistance is a major factor in our growth. Don't wait for an intolerable moment that may never come - escape the custard now, and be better equipped to deal with the tough times before they arrive. Don't just scratch the itch for a whole lifetime; take the unpleasant medicine to remove the cause of it.

Inner critic: That is a LOT of metaphors. Escape the custard! Take the medicine! Scratch the itch! Got any more?

Er, stop carrying the load? Return the overdue library book of life? Manifest your eternal crab of happiness?

Inner critic: Just stop.

Resisting Resistance

Dealing with resistance is difficult. Not least because we resist our efforts to overcome resistance. This is rapidly depressing, so I normally give up pretty easily.

You can probably guess the antidote to resistance: ALL-OUT WAR.

For a while, I ate sandpaper for every meal to teach those pesky inner voices who's boss. Hint: IT'S ME. NEVER SHOW MERCY.

Actually... no. Obviously, I didn't do that.

Not only because eating sandpaper is a self-evidently awful idea, but because, *boringly*, we're better off reasoning compassionately with our resistance, and treating it as a friend to reassure rather than an enemy to quash.

Yawn.

I'm not sure it's possible to come up with resistance-proof ideas. This is why I suggested earlier for you to perform tiny, silly actions, like hanging socks from your ears.

Any action at all diminishes resistance, by proving we are capable of action, and that there's no need for our minds to fear the consequences of change.

Here are some steps we can take to spark action, whether for self-growth, or to aid with procrastination in general.

Firstly - and boringly - we need to compassionately accept resistance, without dwelling on how we have failed already. Feeling guilty and self-critical is always counter-productive. Whipping ourselves for failure only empowers future resistance.[35]

Instead, we recognise that we would like to stop wasting time. We don't feel guilty about any time we have wasted so far, or about any previous failed attempts at whatever it is we want to do.

Next, we take the action we want to perform (say, daily meditation practice), and shrink it to a comically tiny scale:

"I will meditate once for ten seconds" is a much harder goal to resist than "meditate for an hour every day for ten years."

Getting started is normally the hardest part of any action, so after ten seconds you may find you wish to continue. Or maybe

---

[35] As ever, if you're tempted to whip yourself for your tendency to whip yourself...

you'll stop, as you planned. Either way, any action is better than none.

Inner Resistance: No, it isn't. If you can't do it properly it isn't worth doing at all. Definitely not worth doing ten seconds. I'd rather just do zero. Trust me. Don't bother trying.

Don't be put off by these excuses.

Another angle of attack is exploring how the resistance feels. Engaging with our resistance head on can be illuminating. What is the associated emotion? Perhaps you're fearful, imagining that if you look within you'll find something scary. Labelling and experiencing that emotion can help dissolve the resistance.

For example, is part of you angry at the idea of changing yourself, or maybe at the perceived insult that you need to change? Or perhaps there's a sense of injustice that "everyone else seems okay, why aren't I?"

Once you've discovered the emotion, spend a short amount of time (a few seconds is great, and difficult to resist!), and make a concerted effort to *feel* that emotion.

Say aloud "I will now feel scared" and try as strongly as possible to *actually feel scared* about whatever you're resisting.

Actively seeking out an undesirable emotion takes away its power. This goes for other situations too: trying to feel as anxious as possible during a panic attack often reduces the panic. This is confusing, until you remember that this is a form of acceptance, and that it therefore prevents any secondary emotions by validating the primary emotion.

It's important to remember that completely removing resistance is impossible. Believing "I must get rid of all my resistance before I can act" is itself a form of resistance.

In the end, sometimes we have to just act.

Imagine jumping into a cold plunge pool on a hot day - if you thought about it beforehand you'd be less likely to do it. Though, admittedly, I wouldn't jump into the cold pool at all. It sounds horrible; I'd prefer a nice cold drink. But if I *wanted* to do it, for some reason, I'd be better off just doing it.

Acting despite resistance greatly diminishes its power over us.

CHAPTER FOURTEEN
Limited By Belief

"There are more things likely to frighten us than there are to crush us; we suffer more often in imagination than in reality."

Lucius Annaeus Seneca

A thought that goes unquestioned long enough becomes an automatic assumption, part of the framework through which we view the world. The thought is now a *belief.*

When I breathe in I'm making the unquestioned assumption that the air around me hasn't magically disappeared since I last breathed in. This seems to be a reasonable belief. It's so uncontroversial that I don't notice I believe it. But I do.

Other beliefs I never, or rarely, notice: the sun will rise tomorrow. There are no lizards in my underwear drawer. I haven't forgotten how to speak English.

These all seem like reasonably helpful (or, at least, not unhelpful) beliefs. And they all correspond to reality.[36]

Once a belief has taken root it's a real endeavour to shake it. This is a feature, not a bug; we need beliefs to function.

It would be impractical to begin every day by reaffirming our beliefs that a) our limbs are still attached, b) we can still move them, c) we haven't teleported overnight, d) we still breathe oxygen...

To live at all, it's necessary to build a model of the world out of our beliefs.

But if a rogue belief gets into our model we can cause ourselves difficulty. We need to be open to questioning our beliefs to ensure our model of the universe is as true and helpful as it can be.

---

[36] Unless there's been a surprise plague of lizards. Though maybe I ought to question my implicit belief that finding lizards in my underwear drawer would be bad? Even that is an assumed belief...

As usual, the first obstacle we face in updating our model is that most beliefs are transparent to us. Like the fact that air remains in the room, we don't notice this belief. We just believe it.

My uncle likes to play golf. For years, at the end of play his feet would be painful. He didn't complain about it, assuming this discomfort was just something that every golf player experienced. It was a belief of his: playing golf makes your feet hurt. That was just how it is.

Until one day - after years and years of soreness and hobbling - he mentioned to his wife that his feet hurt after playing golf.

"Maybe you're wearing the wrong shoe size?" she queried.

He laughed away her suggestion. "Don't be ridiculous, I know my shoe size! I've always been a size nine in golf shoes." But it gnawed at him, and next time he got new golf shoes he measured his feet.

He was a size ten.

Years of pain, all because of the false belief his mind had pointlessly created from somewhere: *that your feet are supposed to hurt after playing golf.* If he'd questioned that belief at any point in those intervening years he could have saved himself a lot of hobbling. But he hadn't even noticed it was a belief at all.

We rarely question a belief once it has taken root.

For years, every time I visited my mum I was mildly irritated when her house phone rang. It was in another room, so one or other of us had to cross the house just to answer it. Eventually, I cracked and asked why she didn't just move the phone into the room she spends most of her time in.

She looked at me as if I was mad. "But the phone is in the other room", she said.

"Yes. Yes it is. But it could be in *this* room, instead."[37]

She shook her head, and left to answer the phone.

Half an hour later, she got up and unplugged the phone, carried it into the lounge and replaced it next to her armchair. Victory.

Of course, there's nothing wrong with having to walk to answer the phone; arguably it's even a handy way to enforce a little

---

[37] It would be nice to claim I wasn't so sarcastic in real life, but I probably was.

exercise. But it hadn't been *chosen* to be that way. It was simply an unquestioned assumption that the phone exists where it is.

As a child I picked up the belief - for reasons that still escape me - that sleeping with the head of the bed underneath a window would kill me. Yes, that's right. That it would make me *die.*

When I moved to university I was surprised to see that my new room had the head of the bed under a window. I thought it was odd that a university would have such a potentially dangerous system, but it didn't occur to me to question if I would actually die if I slept in that bed. I was just a little uncomfortable, until one day I realised: "Oh. That belief was complete fiction."

These examples of invisible beliefs weren't too harmful, but they can be considerably more harmful.

Perhaps an event at school gave us the belief "I am not as smart as other people, so my opinions don't matter as much as theirs", or somebody accidentally transmitted the idea to us that "I must be successful or nobody will love me."

Some beliefs are insidious. A friend has a deeply-ingrained belief that if she has to do anything involving numbers she'll crumble, and publicly shame herself. She's an intelligent woman, and is easily able to perform well at her technical job. But this belief brings her unnecessary anxiety every single day.

On the surface, her belief isn't helpful at all. However, it contains a little self-justification:

"I'm protecting you! I'm helping you avoid situations you can't cope with! I don't want you to embarrass yourself! It's in your best interest!"[38]

The belief protects itself through this slim self-justification. Maybe it was once true; maybe one day at school something bad happened involving numbers. I have no idea. Nonetheless, I know her as a capable, intelligent woman, and this belief doesn't fit.

I can imagine how her belief avoids getting updated, thanks to our mind's self-selective evidence bias. Because our beliefs form our model of the world, we interpret new facts in the light of our beliefs, instead of updating our beliefs in the light of new facts.

---

[38] I'm not sure why my imagined personification of this belief abuses exclamation marks so much. Maybe it's just a REALLY passionate hatred for numbers.

It takes effort to realise that things might make more sense if we changed our initial assumptions. Often, we don't even see this as an option. But it always is.

This means that if my friend ever does make a mistake involving numbers - which literally everybody does at some point - the belief is confirmed, and strengthens its grip on her.

And whenever she gets something right: *"Well, it was probably just luck"*, or *"I had help."*, or whatever other interpretation keeps the model intact in the face of evidence. Brains are lazy!

Another easily-missed factor is how these beliefs are so often self-fulfilling prophecies. The belief itself makes us act in a way that makes it come true. For example, if I believe I crumble in the face of numbers, I am much more likely to make a mistake when I work with them. The belief isn't objectively true, it only happens because I already believe it. The sneaky belief creates its own 'confirming evidence'.

Beliefs can be extremely painful. For example, imagine that the idea "if I let anyone get close to me I will disappoint them and they'll reject me" formed part of your worldview. One of my friends struggles with this belief, born out of a painful experience in her teen years. Years later, this belief affects all of her relationships, both romantic and with friends.

Most of the time these limiting beliefs remain completely unconscious. It would be rare - if it happened at all - to consciously think something like "I'd better not talk to this person in case we get too close and I disappoint them", or anything so visible.

They are more often experienced as pure emotion; a spike of anxiety, an underlying unease. The leap from belief to painful thought to emotion is so ingrained that we don't notice anything beyond the distress. Lack of recognition is once more the primary obstacle.

When unexplained discomfort emerges, our suspicions should trigger that it's time to use some self-analysis tools to unpick what's happening.

Perhaps after reflecting on a particular belief we decide it is worth keeping. But without noticing and questioning our beliefs we will never realise we are part-controlled by beliefs we never chose.

For our beliefs to reflect reality we must be open-minded, and that requires accepting that some things we believe might be wrong. This isn't a problem. It's great to be wrong!

If we never realised we were wrong, we'd have *carried on being wrong*, so these moments of realisation are to be celebrated. Realising I'm wrong gives me a chance to be right.

We should never be afraid of the effort - or embarrassment - of updating our beliefs. Noticing and checking our beliefs is the only way to make our mental model more true and more helpful.

Assessing Beliefs

Realising that a belief is irrational, incorrect, or even just unhelpful, is costly to our minds. It takes effort, both in self-examination to find the belief, and perhaps in the social cost of changing our behaviour. But it's always worth updating them to be correct, or at least healthier for us.

I have some personal experience with the effort of assessing beliefs and assumptions. For a while, I was a full-time travelling evangelist for the Catholic Church.[39]

Sadly, after a couple of years I had to stop, as I no longer believed in God. Which is a problem for an evangelist. (At least, for an evangelist who wishes to attempt to live with integrity.)

So I moved on, and became a computer programmer.

Incidentally, Catholic evangelist to computer programmer wasn't as jarring a transition as you might expect. Though it did take me a while to get out of the habit of genuflecting and making the *Sign of the Windows Logo* when I arrived to sit at my desk in the mornings.

Before I go on, I want to be very (very) clear that "beliefs" are *not* exclusively spiritual or religious. Usually we reserve the word "belief" for a consciously chosen position, like spiritual or political beliefs. But these are only a small subset of all possible beliefs, which include *anything* that is part of our understanding of the world, e.g. "golf should hurt", "I am bad at conversation" or "my clothes hang in this cupboard, not that one."

---

[39] This is fully 100% true. I know it sounds like the build up to a joke, like a sentence crying out for a punchline. Or possibly just a punch, depending on your own beliefs. But it is a true tale from my life history.

I realise it's potentially confusing for me to use this spiritual example, but it's a good illustration of a time when I had to update a number of my beliefs at once.

As far as spiritual or religious beliefs go, I am not interested *at all* in converting you towards or away from any particular set of beliefs. I'm a little wary of mentioning my religious past, as it has the potential to alienate everybody; some people might dislike my prior religious association, some might be saddened at my traitorous move away from the fold. Hopefully, most won't care.

Anyway, for the curious amongst you I will be dropping in a few fun stories from my travelling evangelist days later. But, as this book isn't about religion, please believe whatever makes you happiest.[40]

Updating a complex set of interlocking beliefs about ourselves or the universe can take months. But since there is a base cost to assessing and updating beliefs, even updating a small belief like "the phone lives there" requires the not-insubstantial effort of noticing the belief and considering alternatives.

But it's exhausting to constantly question everything. We don't want to overcompensate and become overly sceptical. This mentality undermines our foundations by demanding proof for every little thing. And then proof for the proof... and then for that proof... and finally you've got no basis to believe in reality itself. And what if *that* is a trick, and we're all fish just dreaming we're human? Clearly, this is not a fruitful approach.

We can't question everything, so we need to direct our energy into finding beliefs which cause us pain. Our practice at observing our thoughts will have developed our ability to understand what's happening inside. We can explore to find the hidden beliefs at the root of our difficult thoughts.

Once we have found these beliefs, we assess them by asking "how *helpful* and how *true* is this belief?"[41]

Of course, we should always aim for our beliefs to be as true as possible. But sometimes we can't know the truth of a belief. For

---

[40] For me, I want to believe whatever is true. So if it turns out God (or gods) is (or are) real you can count me in. Equally if he/she/they isn't (or aren't) real, you can count me out. Bring on whatever reality is!

[41] Hopefully this refrain is getting familiar by now!

example, a belief I occasionally encounter right now is "if people read this book they'll think I've got nothing useful to say and I'll be shown as an impostor and everyone will hate me and I'll die in a ditch."[42] It's not clear whether this belief is true. It might be; I can't see the future. But it is certainly unhelpful.

To assess the helpfulness of a belief, look at what it inspires you to *do*. Could it conceivably inspire you to take a positive action?

It's not just about how it makes you feel. Even a helpful belief may make you fearful; as we've seen, our inner resistance often opposes good ideas. In contrast, my scary belief about ditches inspires me to do nothing but hide. Its solitary effect is to paralyse me.

A belief can be both helpful and unhelpful. For example, if I were to listen to the Pusher I might identify a belief he holds to be something like "I must keep striving endlessly to live a good life". On the surface, this might appear to be motivating.

But, as we've seen, if I subscribe whole-heartedly to it, it leads to an unhappy existence where I am unable to appreciate what I have. I'd be better off reframing it to remove the unhelpful parts; perhaps something like "I can balance working hard along with appreciating the good things in life."

We want to find the beliefs that cause us pain, and update them to both better reflect reality, and to be more helpful. In general, there's no contradiction; beliefs that reflect reality are the most helpful. But that's just my belief...

EXERCISE: Updating Limiting Beliefs

As we have seen, our beliefs hide by pretending to describe reality.

Perhaps we think that everyone shares the same painful belief and they somehow just cope better. (This can be a stick to beat ourselves with, so don't forget the importance of self-compassion.)

---

[42] I'm not sure why a ditch. Obviously, some part of my subconscious thinks that after being driven out of society by an angry mob for whatever crimes against humanity I've apparently committed, I'll seek out the refuge of a ditch. I wouldn't even know where to find a ditch. And I can't imagine I'd prefer to get in one, rather than, say, a nearby field, or under a tree. Or a hotel. Then again, I probably shouldn't read too much into the details of my subconscious disaster fantasies.

I discovered another limiting belief of mine by exploring uncomfortable feelings. For a time, all kinds of situations made me anxious. I couldn't fathom the link between them. In fact, it seemed that there was no link - just an ever-multiplying number of things I feared. Perhaps I'd be feeling slightly ill, perhaps I'd have to sleep in a different room from usual, perhaps I had to change my plans at the last minute. At seemingly random times I'd feel that slippery slide into the black pit of anxiety, panic and discomfort.

Finally, I decided to delve into it deeper. I mentally put myself into those situations over and over, seeking to feel and understand what was happening. Why couldn't I let these little things go? Why did they bother me? Suddenly, the link came to me: I'm not in control. Whenever I felt out of control I instinctively reacted anxiously, without recognising the underlying problem.

Now I had a belief to work with: *I have to be in control, or something indefinably bad will happen.*

In some cases, merely identifying the belief is enough to limit its power. We can expect it to show up in situations where it typically applies. Expecting a difficult emotion is only a short hop from accepting it, and hence reducing its grip.

Now when I'm in a situation I can't control, like being stuck in traffic, I can greet the expected anxiety confidently: I don't actually *need* to be in control of this. It feels different, like I can cope. Almost as if I could have coped all along, if only I hadn't been holding onto this belief that I hadn't even known existed.

Of course, it's only rarely so easy. In most cases, after we've identified our beliefs we need to work on loosening their hold over us.

The first step is to encapsulate the belief as perfectly as possible in a sentence. Here are some examples:

If I let anyone get close, I will disappoint them; If I make a decision on my own, I will get it wrong; If I have to work with numbers, I will crumble; I must always be in control, or something bad will happen.

Be as specific as possible. Try and pin down the negative consequences too. "Something bad will happen" is often left to our own imagination, which can be scarily good at filling in the blanks. Describing the 'bad thing' can sometimes take the sting out of it.

Once we have the belief trapped in its purest form we can get to work on it. We're aiming to do anything that reduces the power of the belief. If it's part of our worldview, then we've been carrying it for a long time, possibly our whole lives. It has carved a groove in our mind. Anything we can do to weaken the pattern and escape the groove is helpful.

TACTIC #1: Boring Questions

Investigate the belief:

If I didn't already believe this, would I begin believing it today?

If someone else believed this, what would I say to them?

What would I do differently if I didn't believe this?

TACTIC #2: Repetition and Satiation

Spend some time defusing from the belief. Repeat it aloud. Repeat it ten times. Repeat it fifty times, until the words no longer sound like words, but a jumble of sounds that have no meaning. That little moment of meaninglessness helps us to defuse, and to recognise that there is no Law of the Universe that corresponds to our belief.[43] If they're just thoughts in our head, we're free to tweak them as we wish.

TACTIC #3: Baffle Your Mind

Try believing the opposite of what you originally believed. This reduces the power of the belief by showing your mind that you can directly contradict it. For example, "I crumble when I have to work with numbers" becomes "I never crumble when I have to work with numbers."

Or substitute other people, or alternative objects, or actions, into the belief:

"I crumble when I have to work with cutlery"

"Everybody crumbles when they have to work with numbers"

"I sing with joy when I have to work with numbers"

Make it a laughable belief: "I crumble when I have to work with seafood."

Accept the truth of the new form each time you alter it. Convince yourself of a way in which the alteration is true; perhaps

---

[43] Unless you're attempting this with, say, belief in General Relativity, but I can't imagine why you'd be trying that in the first place.

remember a time you burned some squid. Each altered belief is just as true as the original, if you look closely enough.

TACTIC #4: Fantasy And Action

Imagine yourself acting differently because you no longer hold this belief. How does it feel? Imagine every detail of how you behave differently. Your mind doesn't distinguish perfectly between imagination and reality, so when you picture the mundane details of acting without the belief you dislodge its hold.

If you can, physically *do* whatever you would do differently if you didn't hold this belief. Prove to your unconscious mind that you are not limited by these thoughts as much as it thinks you are.

Of course, this is assuming the action is a good idea: obviously don't do this with a helpful belief like "I shouldn't jump down the stairs." We want to work with unhelpful, painful beliefs like "Nobody likes me", where, for example, a sensible action could involve talking to somebody new at a party. Or even just going to a party.

The great thing is that fantasy can work just as well, if you can feel comfortable during the fantasy. Mentally link the details of your fantasy with peaceful parts of your brain, and it becomes easier to take action.

TACTIC #5: View It From A Distance

Return to the original belief. If you've been playing with it, switching it around, twisting it, and laughing at variations of it, then I bet that it feels less frightening and less real than it once did.

This won't be a one-off process. Perhaps you feel more able to cope with numbers - or seafood! - but next time you're actually faced with them your mind will rush down the old fearful channel once more. Don't be discouraged. Keep picking away at these beliefs and their power over you will fade.

The edge of the vast swimming pool of custard - with a comfortable chair on solid ground - gets a little closer with every limiting belief we identify and free ourselves from.

SELF
Being Ourselves

*"If you have built castles in the air, your work need not be lost;
that is where they should be. Now put the foundations under them."*
Henry David Thoreau

We have reached the end of the most important section of the book, and effortlessly achieved self-mastery. Congratulations! Your inner world is now clear.

Well, perhaps it isn't quite so definite, and self-mastery is some way off. But at least we're going in the right direction.

Here's what we've talked about so far:

- Taking responsibility increases our control over our lives. We are responsible for any circumstances that we can change, and for our reaction to any circumstances that we can't.
- We practise self-awareness through meditation and similar exercises.
- We catch, and defuse from, the thoughts that lead to difficult feelings.
- We prevent these painful feelings from getting out of control by accepting that they have a right to exist.
- We practise staying in the present moment, mindfully appreciating reality as it is, noticing the good parts and experiencing them as fully as possible.
- We don't get drawn into dwelling in the past or future; we happily go there to visit when we need to, but we don't make a home in either.
- We love ourselves, and are compassionate and forgiving towards our quirks, failings and imperfections.
- We thank our inner critics (and other voices) for their contributions, but recognise that they are only thoughts. We don't have to listen to, or believe, them. Over time we transform

them into positive supporters, by recognising that they are trying to help, and finding ways for them to contribute constructively.

- We discover our limiting beliefs and gradually remove their power over us.
- All of this is resisted by our own *akrasia* - sorry, resistance - for completely understandable, but quite frustrating, reasons. We dissolve this resistance by accepting it and taking action no matter how we feel.

Easy, right?!

I'm exhausted just thinking about it.

Although, remember that we're aiming to stop wasting energy merely staying afloat, so this investment can benefit us greatly in the long-term.

So far, I've deliberately avoided discussing in detail the external things we blame anxiety on: relationships, careers, ambitions, and questions like "what's it all about?" We couldn't do anything about those before getting the relationship with ourselves right.

From now on, though, we'll be concentrating less on the direct experience of anxiety, and more on finding contentment.

If you like, we're going to spend less time on ARGH, and more on OK.

Let's look at the rest of the universe now, starting with Other People.

ONE OR TWO
Questions That Occur To Me At This Point

Wait! Won't doing all this lovey-dovey nonsense turn me into a facsimile of everyone else? Do you want to create an army of tedious, meditating, granola-eating clones preaching love and avoiding stepping on insects?

Hell no. I *hate* granola. It tastes of misery.

Also, none of this will turn you into *anyone,* except a truer version of yourself.

It sounds like you're listening to your inner resistance and fusing with their fear of change: "what might I become?!"

Freeing ourselves from thought traps can only help to discover what we really want. If anything, you will become more individual, not less, as you discover your true self.

Well, how do I know if I'm being true to my True Self (whatever that is) or not?

I worried about that for a while too. There's a lot of talk about being true to your true self. I was frustrated.

Worse, I couldn't pinpoint the source of this frustration. Was it because I was being true to my True Self but failing to live up to the ideals my True Self believed in?

Or was it because I *wasn't* being true to my True Self, and my True Self was desperately trying to tell me that I had to change something important?

This meant that the frustration was either a signal that something was deeply wrong in my life, or a signal that things were fine but I should do more of what I was already doing.

So. I should either speed up in the direction I was going, or change direction entirely.

In the end, I decided it was impossible to tell the difference, so I went to the pub instead.

I felt better then, so I guess my True Self didn't care either and we both just wanted to go to the pub.

So, sometimes you've got to undertake a Jungian journey into the abyss of your mind, discovering your true core through the painful process of stripping away your sense of self.

And sometimes you've got to just do something you enjoy?

Exactly.

PART THREE
OTHERS

"Human relations were so utterly beyond all understanding that when one thought about it one felt uncanny and one's heart sank"
Chekhov

CHAPTER FIFTEEN
A Small Thing That Happened To Me Once

*"Thus do we fear more what our neighbours will
think of us, than what we ourselves."*
Marcus Aurelius

"What we ourselves... what? Hello..? Get a grip, Aurelius!"

I awake in a student college in Melbourne, Australia. This is no surprise, because - at the time when this happened - I lived there.

I groggily stagger to the shared bathroom on my floor, to perform my morning washing routine. There's nothing surprising about my lavatory procedure so I'll omit the details, for all of our benefits.

So far, so good. Already I'm full of optimism for today.

As I wash my hands, I glimpse myself in the mirror, and notice my majestic messy bed-head.

I don't want you to imagine that I'm describing the fashionable bed-head that some strive so hard to effortlessly achieve. Please don't picture that "my hair is ever-so-slightly messy, and it just falls this way naturally, honest" bed-head of male catalogue models and beard-sporting cool kids.

Side-note: I wondered if male catalogue models actually look anything like I assume they do. A cursory image search for "male catalogue model" shows that yes, that's *exactly* what I looked nothing like.

As a bonus, if you would enjoy picturing my hairy failure more vividly, an image search for "terrible man hair" will point you in plenty of appropriately awful directions.[44] Have fun!

I often sport this motley look for entire days, as I forget to check in the morning that I look sufficiently normal to go outside. When this happens, I tend to see myself in a mirror for the first time just

---

[44] Even though the internet changes constantly, this seems likely to remain true.

before I go to bed. Invariably, I feel a little ashamed that I've had tufts of hair beaming in assorted directions since I woke up.[45]

On this day, however, I notice my unconventional tufty hair, and take immediate action, slapping the top of my head with my wet hands to encourage my mane into an acceptable shape.

I stride out of the bathroom feeling satisfied. Universe 0 - Neil 1. One triumph already: *not appearing for the entire day as if I have just fallen out of bed.* What an excellent start to the day.

Sadly, I had only gone a few steps before the soapy water I had unthinkingly applied to my head poured into my eyes, burning them immediately with painful chemicals.

Still, no need to panic. I'm an adult, I can handle a little soapy water. I am aware of the process for fixing a foamy intrusion into the eyes. As per the plan, I don't even break stride, simply rubbing my eyes to remove the water.

Unfortunately, this only makes things worse. It feels like I dislodged my contact lenses and got the soap in *behind* them. Now everything really burns.

Okay. There's no need for alarm. I simply need a new plan. I'm already most of the way to my bedroom, so I can slip in there, find the sink, wash my eyes out, replace my contacts with chemical-free fresh lenses, and then we're all sorted. I'm still destined for victory today.

I take another step towards my bedroom door, eyes screwed tightly shut.

I fumble for my keys, and pull them hurriedly out of my trouser pocket. Sadly, in my haste they slip out of my hand and fly somewhere into the dark void in front of me.

Damn.

I squint my eyes open slightly, and shut them immediately. I can't see a thing through the caustic chemical tears. *What the hell is in this soap,* I probably would have wondered if I hadn't been so distracted by the agony behind my eyelids.

Right. Time for a new 'new plan'. The corridor is small, so it can't take long to locate my keys, get into my room, find the sink, wash

---

[45] This is one of my milder secret fears: that everyone else takes drastically more time on their appearance than I do, and that they all know secret methods to optimise it. I should probably do something about this, but I have no clue what.

the soap out of my eyes, replace the contacts and then - finally - *victory!*

No need to cancel the celebratory parade for how awesome today will be. Yet.

I scrabble on the floor for a moment, then another moment, and then another slightly longer moment.

I seriously can't find my keys. In making the 'new new plan' I significantly underestimated how much I rely on the ability to see.

The discomfort of squatting and bungling around is adding to the stinging in my eyes, and I realise my new highest priority needs to be getting rid of this infernal soap.

With hindsight, this should probably have been the priority from the beginning.

Taking stock *again*, I come up with a new 'new new plan'. I'll go back to the original bathroom, and wash my eyes out there. Then, using my regained power of vision, it will be trivial to find my keys. After that, I can let myself into my room, replace my lenses, and finally I can leave for breakfast. Still victorious. Definitely.

I stand up, face towards the bathroom and charge ahead at maximum eagerness.

SMACK

I run face first into the wall, having apparently completely lost track of which way I was facing.

I crumple to the floor, like a sack of idiotic potatoes.

At this point, I finally admit that I am defeated.

I have no new plans. No new new plans. No plans of any kind whatsoever. My face hurts, from hitting the wall with it. My eyes hurt, from the chemicals I foolishly rubbed into them. I cannot solve either problem.

As I lie there, blankly failing to handle the situation, I hear the voice of the pretty girl from down the corridor:

"Do you... do you need any help?"

Yes. Yes I need help.

CHAPTER SIXTEEN
An Introduction to Other People

*"In many ways the saying 'Know thyself' is not well said.
It were more practical to say: 'Know other folks'."*

Menander of Athens, 4th Century BC

So far, we've mostly ignored the above advice to 'know others' from long-dead Greek dramatist Menander of Athens, instead narcissistically choosing to keep the focus solely on ourselves.

But, after some investigation, it turns out that other people, arguably, perhaps have some importance in our lives.

You may recall that our initial foray into the world of self-growth was prompted by Socrates the Chicken-Borrower saying "the unexamined life is not worth living."

I like to imagine that it was Menander of Athens' chicken that he borrowed, and that Socrates never gave it back after a disagreement over whether we should 'examine ourselves' or 'know others'. I imagine the argument got so heated that Socrates only relented on his death bed.

I refuse to spoil this by finding out whether they even knew each other.[46]

Returning - momentarily - to reality, it's clear that relationships are a major factor in our goals and happiness. They are central to much of our lives, including friendships, family, business, and even sexual pursuits.[47]

---

[46] Okay, my curiosity immediately took over and I looked it up. Socrates died fifty years before Menander was born, so the only possible explanation is that Socrates invented time travel to borrow Menander's chicken, have this argument, and finally return the controversial poultry from his deathbed. Nothing else makes sense!

[47] An unpopular 1970s board game involving the collection of six types of cheese in somewhat disturbing ways.

Everybody for Themselves

As Menander points out, it's crucial to know others. We long for connection, to be understood and to be loved. The feeling of contentment and safety that comes from being loved is one of the deepest sorts of happiness, like licking the top layer of crème brûlée from a spoon made of serotonin.

However, it's a sad fact that too much of anything, however positive, becomes negative. Too much food, too much chocolate, too much sex, too much sunshine... even drinking too much water can be dangerous.[48]

Healthy dosage applies to relationships, too; it's possible to overindulge our natural desire for connection, transforming a positive source of happiness into an addictive need for validation.

Striving too hard to meet this need is a custard trap. We keep running, with no end goal in sight; always needing to meet more new people, to find a better partner, to have more friends, to gain more followers online, more likes on social media...

Counter-intuitively, prioritising relationships too highly leads to lower quality connection; we can never be truly honest with people if we need them. It can be easy to find yourself dependent on those around you, even while hiding your sadness, fears and troubles from them.

We all must learn to meet this need for connection in the right way: from within, rather than through friends, sex, the number of messages we receive, or finding the 'perfect' partner.

This is an idea that we easily deflect. If we're dead set on finding that perfect partner, being told it won't guarantee happiness just sounds wrong. But even the ideal partner could never bring lasting contentment.

You might think our need for connection would be solved forever by someone who *wants* to constantly provide for all our emotional needs. But even if, by some miracle, we encounter the mythical 'perfect person' we are not going to be happy forever. In this utopia, we fear change: anything that unsettles our perfect

---

[48] I found it oddly reassuring to learn that even faithful old water can be lethal. At some point, you have to just give up worrying.

situation produces anxiety. Our partner wants to take up a new hobby? Could this be the beginning of the end?!

We haven't filled the original hole, but merely covered it. The trap is no longer attempting to find the perfect partner; instead we exhaust ourselves fruitlessly fighting to keep a fragile situation from changing. Because we're incapable of meeting our own needs, we must battle anything and everything to hold onto the relationship. Contrast this with a healthy relationship, where both partners are capable of fulfilling their own needs, and so neither has to fear change.[49]

So, problems arise when we try to use others to fulfil all of our needs. But we can hit similar problems by ignoring our own needs in favour of others.

If you've ever travelled by plane you'll have heard the advice to make sure your own oxygen mask is fitted properly before helping others. A dark part of me is always amused by how calmly this is illustrated. They show a relaxed adult carefully fitting their mask, before helping the contented child next to them.[50]

This advice exists to counter our instinct. We are programmed to help those who depend on us. Usually this instinct is helpful, but in this case it's the wrong thing to do. We must look after ourselves first.

Similarly, we instinctively seek approval from others before we attempt to get that approval from within. But to live a contented life we sometimes must put ourselves first.

Everything I've said so far is pretty obvious. In fact, let's summarise:

Super-Obvious Truth #1
Other people are great, but we cannot rest our hopes for happiness solely in them. We must love ourselves first.

---

[49] Unless the particular change is, say, a dinosaur stampede or meteor strike, when fear is probably an appropriate response.

[50] I always wonder how it would go down in a real emergency. There's probably a good reason that airlines don't show an adult callously ignoring a suffocating child while they fit their own mask. It's probably the same good reason that I don't produce airline safety videos.

Super-Obvious Truth #2
It's okay to make ourselves a priority.
In fact, it's better than okay: it's necessary.

And, yes, before my inner critic starts complaining, I could have just said these obvious truths in the first place.

Inner critic: Or not at all...

Well, there are good reasons to state the obvious. Unless we consciously check, we can be unaware that we're ignoring it. Insight doesn't magically arrive out of nowhere; there's no automatic process that checks our actions are consistent with our beliefs.

If you'd have asked me some years ago if I put relationships in the correct priority in my life, I'd have said yes. But my actions weren't consistent with this: I was relying on the validation of friends, on making people laugh, on meeting girls. My happiness was fragile in that it required these responses from people, or I felt empty, worthless, or non-existent. Yet I would have professed to believe I had my priorities correct.

If you're comfortably self-fulfilled and enjoying your relationships without *needing* others, then that's excellent.

But if you haven't checked, how do you know that's what you're doing?

Interacting with Other Humans

All relationships take place in the external world, but I find it fascinating that a significant amount of any relationship actually takes place internally. Relationships are like icebergs.[51]

Let me explain. I have often been puzzled at how people I find boring have so many friends.

I'm not proud of this judgemental thought. I know we're not obliged to find everybody fascinating, but I prefer to find positives in people when I can. Even so, after spending hours with someone I find dull, I've wondered at their social life. What do they talk about with their friends? What do their friends see in them?

Eventually I realised I was looking at it the wrong way. I believed that being bored in someone's presence meant that they were inherently boring. That if you cut them open in some sort of

---

[51] Slow, cold, and covered in penguins..?

(humane) cutting-open-device that you would find *BORING* written through them like a disappointing stick of rock.

But, clearly, their friends can't find them boring, or they wouldn't be friends with them. So they *can't* be inherently boring. It's as if the human-cutting-open-device would find *BORING* inside them if I was operating it, but somebody else might find *INTERESTING* or even *FASCINATING*. Changing who operates the device completely changes the result.

This is because 'boringness' is a property of the relationship between me and them. They aren't boring. I'm not boring. But the *combination* of the two of us is boring.

Inner critic: "I'm not boring"?! You're certainly fooling me with all this repetitive going-on about being boring.

GK Chesterton said "There is no such thing on earth as an uninteresting subject; the only thing that can exist is an uninterested person."

Saying this about a topic is unremarkable. We know that some people are interested in, say, politics even if we ourselves are not, so we don't slap the *BORING* label on all of politics: it is just boring *to us*. But we fall more easily into this trap when it comes to other people.

We falsely ascribe characteristics to others without recognising our role in bringing them out. Labelling people as *BORING* - or anything else - is a trick of the mind, but we believe it to be true because we can never see another point of view but our own. We are always the ones operating the humane-cutting-open-machines.

When I'm with Excalibob, we have fun, so I think he is fun. But when he's with Sarah, they don't talk much, so she thinks he is uninteresting.

Both labels are wrong: the dynamics of each relationship are brought about by the combination of people, not by fixed qualities of either individual.

None of us are objectively anything. Different people bring out contrasting characteristics in us.

So when we experience people as 'irritating', 'boring' or even 'outrageously sexy' we think that we are describing something objective about them. We aren't.

The labels look like they belong to the other person, but we would be more accurate to label the combination of people involved. If you like, 'boringness' exists *between* two people, not in either one.

This can be a freeing realisation. Sometimes people will tell us we are angry, abrasive, horrible or talkative, and we believe it without question, without thinking "hold on, this is just a label they invented." These labels are only *their* outputs on the cutting-open machine, not some objective description of reality. People can only ever describe their experience of 'the combination of the two of us', never a universal description of ourselves.

We are never defined by labels; not even our own. If we are told we are selfish, we can be unselfish. Labels aren't limits; only somebody's singular opinion.

Recognising that relationships arise out of combinations, and not out of fixed characteristics, increases our options. By default, the combination of Sarah and Excalibob is boring, and that's fine: neither of them need feel bad about that. They will doubtless have better combinations with other people. But if they wanted to, they could change themselves to change that relationship.

Often this is a bad idea. We don't want to become chameleons, constantly changing ourselves in different company to get one hundred percent of others to like us. This is just another exhausting custard trap.

Instead, we can recognise that we combine better with some people than others, and to prioritise spending time with those we fit with easily. If we don't mix well with very many people, we have the additional option to work on changing ourselves to combine more easily.

Sticky Labels

There's a big difference between the way we label ourselves and the way we label others.

When we act angrily we usually don't think "I am an angry person", but instead: "I am in a bad mood." We see our actions as a response to our circumstances, not as an expression of a permanent personality trait.

For example, we may see somebody kicking a ticket machine and think "what an angry person." But, from their point of view, they are responding rationally to their circumstances.

Maybe they had an argument earlier, then a delayed train journey full of screaming children and barking animals, and now they're late for a life-changing interview and the ticket machine has swallowed their card. If this happened to us we would find it quite understandable to furiously boot a ticket machine until our feet hurt. But when we look from outside at the same behaviour, we don't have access to all of their thoughts, feelings and reasons, so we label them *ANGRY*.

This tendency to ascribe fixed personality traits to others, while explaining our own behaviour as a temporary reaction to our circumstances, is known as the *fundamental attribution error.*

Being aware of this common error helps us to be more fluid in our image of other people, making us more tolerant and willing to forgive. It allows everybody room to change and grow.

Sometimes we overcorrect for the fundamental attribution error, and start labelling ourselves with the same abandon with which we label others. We react angrily - maybe only once - and label ourselves as *ANGRY* forever.

This is the exact wrong way to handle the double standard of the fundamental attribution error: the true solution is to *stop labelling entirely.*

Instead of unhelpfully labelling ourselves as *ANGRY* after an outburst, we compassionately aim to change our behaviour. And we offer the same latitude for growth to anybody else. No need for labels at all.

We need to remember that our concepts of other people only exist in our head. We make mental models of others, made up of labels and a rough simulation of how we expect that person thinks and acts. But these models aren't what's real, people are.

This leads to a further problem: the temptation to respond to the labels we have stuck on our mental model, rather than to the person themselves. We don't always recognise when we are reacting to a label, and when we are reacting to reality.

While it's reasonable not to immediately trust somebody who we've previously labelled untrustworthy, we have to allow people to change. Labels are like unquestioned beliefs that need updating. Does the concept in our head match reality? Perhaps not, but updating our labels can only happen if we see the person and not the label, and make the effort to keep our model in line with reality.

Even positive labels can be troublesome. My brain slaps labels on people I like: maybe *FUNNY*, *FRIENDLY* and *SOURCE OF ENTERTAINMENT*. Maybe after a while I label them *TRUSTWORTHY* and start sharing intimate secrets with them.

Then, the inevitable happens, and it turns out that my new friend is only human, and they upset me. Perhaps they betray a secret. Or perhaps they are simply in a bad mood and fail to be a *SOURCE OF ENTERTAINMENT*. My mind feels betrayed that it has to reassess its labels: this person isn't living up to the concept of them I had constructed in my head. *How dare they not exist to entertain me!*

Hopefully, that's an exaggeration. Most of us are aware that nobody else exists purely for our entertainment or support, and that nobody lives up to the labels we assign them (positive or negative) one hundred percent of the time.

But this labelling and judging-by-labels isn't a conscious process, so it is easy to be dismissive of those we have negatively labelled, and to be disappointed when those we positively labelled turn out to be merely human.

Similarly, we can feel great pressure to live up to the labels others have of us. We want to be seen as strong, even if we feel empty or sad, so as not to challenge the positive way others see us. We can fear that others value their image of us more than their actual relationship with us.

Let's summarise the obvious truths again:

Super-Obvious Truth #3:
Labels of others are only our personal, subjective opinion, not some objective, measurable description of them.
The same goes for their labels of us.

Not-Quite-So-Obvious Truth #1:
We assume our behaviour is explained by circumstances, but
that the behaviour of others is due to personality.
E.g. We snapped at somebody after a tough day... but they
snapped at somebody because they must be a horrible
person.

What's the solution to all this labelling stuff?

Being aware is generally enough. We can't abandon labels completely; our brains fundamentally must construct mental images of others, or we'd forget who they were every time they left the room. This requires using labels.

But we shouldn't get these labels confused with reality. We have to remember that we don't have access to anybody else's inner world. And we have to make continual effort to see past labels and relate to the person.

Letting go of labels and seeing everybody as a fellow human in every situation is hard work (and probably impossible to do perfectly), but making the effort can lead to more genuine relationships.

The Centre of the Universe

In quantum physics, there's a concept colloquially known as the 'observer effect', where the act of measuring something changes it.

At first glance, it appeared that our universe has a fascinating property at sub-microscopic scales where measurement affects what actually happens.

There's a particularly famous experiment called the 'double-slit experiment' where (in over-simplified terms) we can prove that a tiny packet of light travels through two slits *simultaneously.* This is cool enough, but it gets crazier. If we measure which slit it passes through - without changing anything else - it only goes through a single slit.

Fortunately for our sanity, what counts as 'observation' in a quantum mechanical sense is nothing like a human consciousness 'observing' something. Sadly, atoms don't care whether humans are watching. Our use of language is misleading: "observation" in physics is not about consciousness becoming aware of something, but simply about atoms interacting.

I find this a shame. I'd love to live in a universe where atoms know when they're being watched. Not only would it provide opportunities for humour (who wouldn't enjoy scaring a cloud of hydrogen by leaping out and shouting "BOO!" from behind a corner?), it would feed that part of us that longs to feel special.

Each of us is the hero of our own story. It's a truth so obvious that we rarely think of it, but the fact that all of our experience happens to *us*, specifically, causes us to subconsciously believe that we are the centre of the universe. We may not see ourselves as a great hero. We may even see ourselves as a villain, at times. But we are unavoidably the central character.

All children believe this. To them they are unarguably the centre of the universe. But while most of us grow out of believing all our needs are a simple scream away, it remains tempting to attempt to control others rather than relating to them. When we forget that the person we are talking to has as rich and complicated an inner world as ourselves, we open ourselves up to frustration.

We cannot control other people. Ever.[52] We can't make them like us, love us, obey us, drop their goals in favour of ours, or do anything at all.

There are further consequences to the fact that everybody is the central character to their own story.

We are only ever aware of anyone else's experience as an abstract idea, but we experience our own lives as a vivid reality. This is probably a good thing; the world is too big to be consciously aware of the lived experienced of everybody all the time. If we somehow achieved this level of awareness, we'd be overwhelmed by pain and tragedy merely by watching the news.

But, for some, discovering that we aren't central to anybody but ourselves can be a painful experience. We can fail to learn the lesson, and regularly clash with reality, as it repeatedly demonstrates that it does not revolve around us. Or we can learn the lesson too well, and lose faith in our own worth.

It's not easy to remain in the middle ground, which says: "I am worthy and important... but so is everybody else."

---

[52] Except, I guess, for parents of small children, although they may well laugh at the idea of 'having control'.

A useful repercussion is that nobody is as focused on us as we are on ourselves. I often replay conversations in my head afterwards. Or - if I've said something especially witty - I'll replay it internally while the other person is actually still talking. I'll be physically nodding and pretending to listen while the excitable cast inside my head is performing a full action replay of 'Me Being Hilarious' for my own private entertainment.

Nobody else is as impressed with me as I occasionally am. But this works both ways: nobody else is as judgemental of me as I generally am. I'll walk away from a perfectly fine conversation thinking "I can't believe I said goodbye like that, that was so awkward. I'm useless at life!"

Meanwhile, the person I was talking to didn't notice anything strange at all. They certainly weren't thinking about how awkward my goodbye was, and definitely not that they now hate me for it, despite how things are playing out in my head.

Replaying goodbyes - or conversations, or entire nights out - is apparently a common phenomenon. This is symptomatic of a social insecurity, believing that everybody is constantly judging us as we do internally. In reality, it's doubtful anybody ever notices the particular way we say goodbye. Unless we fall cartoon-like into a bucket of shellfish and smash a pile of crystal glass on our way out.[53]

Also, the consequences of being judged are rarely as harsh as we believe them to be. With the exception of the first few years of life, our physical survival is not dependent on the constant positive thoughts of those around us.

Sure, it's great for people to think well of us, but that doesn't mean we need to live in fear of their judgement.

Let's throw these truths up into the ongoing summary of obviousness:

Super-Obvious Truth #4:
Nobody judges us as often, or as harshly, as we do ourselves. They are too busy judging themselves...

Super-Obvious Truth #5:
... and even if they were, it's just thoughts in another's mind.

---

[53] Which would only endear somebody to me, if anything.

If our happiness relies on other people thinking a certain way about us, it is fragile. No happiness built purely on others can be secure.

We must analyse where our self-worth comes from, and discover the root beliefs we are holding onto: perhaps "everyone must like me", or "if I am single my life is not worthwhile" and apply our techniques for dislodging painful beliefs such as these.

Don't Talk To Me About People

This whole "know others" thing sounds like hard work.

Ensuring relationships are in their proper priority; abandoning labels in our views of ourselves and others; remembering that we are not the centre of any universe but our own... and that so is everybody else...

It feels like it'd be easier to just give up, and be a squirrel instead.

But I looked it up, and apparently squirrels also have a complicated social system. Not to mention they have to spend months foraging for food, then digging up and eating soil-covered nuts during harsh winter months.

On balance, I prefer having clean, edible nuts that remain unburied all year.

Even considering all the additional difficulties of being human... we can work on being better. Squirrels can't.

So our final truths:

Super-Obvious Truth #6:
All we can really do is accept others as they are,
and hope they do the same for us.

Super-Obvious Truth #7:
It's probably not worth giving it all up to be a squirrel.
Stupid squirrels.

REQUIREMENT:
Approval For Everything

"Is it alright if I ask you a question?"

"Sure, go ahead."

"Thanks, Excalibob. But first, d'you mind if I ask... you know just now when I asked if I could ask you a question?"

"Yes..?"

"Was that alright?"

"Yes. It was fine."

"Thanks Excalibob... er... Is it okay that I asked a moment ago if it was alright when I asked you about asking that question?"

"Yes. Listen... you don't need my approval for everything, you know."

"Oh. How much approval should I ask for, Excalibob? Is this much okay?"

"If you're asking me, then you can't understand the answer."

"Oh...

...

...

Okay."

CHAPTER SEVENTEEN
Growing Solo

"Whatsoever is delighted in solitude, is either a wild beast or a god."
Francis Bacon

As a teenager I played in a youth orchestra that occasionally went on coach tours to Europe.

In case you're impressed by this, I shall redress the balance by pointing out that I played the tuba. No longer impressive, but at least vaguely amusing. Story of my life.

One day, in some country or other, we were setting up at an outdoor stage. This mainly involved tracking to and from the coach carrying various heavy bits of equipment. As I returned for another trip, I saw a bandmate bending over a box of music stands. Being a teenage boy, with correspondingly limited senses of humour and correct behaviour,[54] I thought it would be funny to slap him on the backside as he picked them up.

I raised my arm and stepped forward, winding up for a significant backside-slapping. My hand positively whooshed, tides of air fleeing before my almighty impending slap.

As impact approached - within inches of connection - I had a sudden horrific realisation. This wasn't my friend at all.

It was the conductor.

Adrenaline blasted through my body as I instantly went into panic mode. With superhuman effort, I halted the momentum of my flying hand, only milliseconds before delivering a distressingly inappropriate smack to the behind of the esteemed musical director.

I sidestepped neatly, and continued without breaking stride. I kept my hand glued to my side in the unnatural manner of a footballer pretending he hasn't illegally handled the ball.

---

[54] No offence intended to teenagers more mature than I was.

I flushed red and looked furtively around. *Had anybody seen?!*

No. Nobody had seen a thing. I was safe! I'd come within millimetres of an exceptionally awkward social mishap, and somehow gotten away with it.

It was years before I told anyone that story. I was so embarrassed by something that *hadn't even happened* that I was unable to bring it up until there was a safe distance between the telling and the incident.

It taught me two crucial lessons. First, don't attempt something so idiotic in the first place. And second, what we do when we're alone is important.

If we can't be happy alone, then we undermine our ability to be happy with others; our time with them is impaired by the constant fear that they might leave.

Feeling happy, safe, or comfortable only when we're with other people is a thin crust on top of the sea of custard, rather than the true solid foundation we are aiming to discover.

To make it to solid ground, it's crucial to investigate our relationship with solitude, which is a necessary, but often neglected, component of our lives. Even the most extroverted person can't live in an environment of constant stimulation.

Inner immature schoolboy: But that sounds fun.

Behave, brain!

Solitude doesn't have to be a soul-searching spiritual quest: it can simply be a pleasant way to spend time.

And we require at least *some* time alone with our thoughts and feelings to truly commit to self-growth. When we're surrounded by others we are bombarded by their wants and desires, which can shut us off from our own wishes. Our brains need time to process our experience.

Vertyness of All Kinds

In a 2014 study, a significant number of people chose to give themselves an electric shock rather than spend a short amount of time alone in a room.[55]

Spending time with ourselves *surely* cannot be that unpleasant! Imagine how much happier life would be if time alone - which is

---

[55] See 'Further Reading' for details.

inevitable - could be enjoyed, rather than considered to be worse than an *actual electric shock.*

Of course, this isn't a universal response. Humans are diverse. And so we have a wide spectrum of reactions to solitude. Part of this spectrum is explained by what I will vaguely term our 'vertyness': whether we're more *introvert* or *extrovert.*

Vertyness is a familiar concept. Typically, it conjures an image of introverts as quiet and reserved, and extroverts as chatty and loud. However, it isn't actually defined by how outgoing we are, but by where we get our energy from.

Introverts gain their energy from time alone, and spend it during their interactions with others, while extroverts gain energy from being around others, and find it draining to be alone for extended periods.

Even if we know ourselves well it's easy to get the balance wrong. An introvert may push themselves to socialise beyond their energy reserves, or an extrovert may work in a solitary environment and wonder why they are feeling so drained.

While we need to know our vertyness to manage our energy, it's important to remember it may change from time to time. We don't need to stick an unchanging, inflexible label on ourselves that says "EXTROVERT FOR ALL TIME".[56]

Like most of our personalities, this is a scale, not a binary classification. Perhaps we are extroverted all the time, perhaps we're mainly introverts, perhaps we change at different times in our lives. I was recently introduced to the word *ambivert:* after some time with people, ambiverts crave solitude, then after time alone, they crave company.

Inner critic: Isn't that just, you know, being human?

Pretty much, yes, inner critic. But it's a nice word, anyway. If these labels help, wear them (lightly, as with all labels); if they don't, then don't.

The only reason this matters is to understand and accept ourselves. It's not about being part of one club or another; it's about owning our desires. Introverts shouldn't feel guilty about requiring

---

[56] Unless you want to, and you don't mind scaring away the occasional introvert.

downtime, and likewise for extroverts managing their own needs and energy levels.

Everybody has social needs, and we all meet them differently. Introverts are as able as extroverts to have large social circles and to be the life of the party (should they want to be) - but they have to do so in a way that respects their nature. Equally, an extrovert may only wish to have a few close friends.

Once we know what we want, socially speaking, we can work to get it. But we must do so in a way consistent with our natures. Striving to be like somebody else is exhausting, while being ourselves is not exhausting.

To live a balanced life, we want to live in accordance with our nature, but we may need to oppose it a little. Our *akrasia* - sorry, inner resistance - is easily tempted into using our vertyness as an excuse to avoid growth or action, whether we instinctively hide alone or in a crowd.

The introvert who values relationships needs to do the hard work of dipping into their energy reserves by socialising. Similarly, an extrovert who values self-growth needs to spend some energy developing their ability to be alone.

For extroverts in particular, the necessary time alone for self-examination entails an extra cost. Of course, anybody could avoid confronting themselves by constantly manufacturing busyness. But extroverts have a handy excuse: "I'm an extrovert so I don't have to do all that self-examination stuff!"

Only you can determine how far you need to oppose your natural instinct in order to grow.

Fearing Solitude

If we're all different, isn't it conceivable that only introverts need solitude? Isn't solitude bad for extroverts? But couldn't introverts get too addicted to being alone?

What if we all went into solitude for a week - would it cure the common cold and other infectious diseases that need to keep moving in order to exist? Is this too many questions? What about now?

Some of us struggle with solitude beyond what is due to our, er, vertyness.[57] Any reason we fear time alone will inevitably be personal; there are as many possible reasons as there are people. From my own experience I can identify a few struggles with solitude.

Sometimes we fear the judgement of strangers. Many years ago, I had a few days alone in Sydney as I waited for my friends to arrive in the city. Bored of sightseeing, I decided to go to the cinema. I was more conscious of public judgement in those days, so I felt a little nervous as I approached the front of the ticket queue, alone.

I muttered as quietly as possible to the girl behind the counter.

"Er... one... for, er, Mean Girls... please..."

It was nearly a whisper. Her response was less so.

"WHAT DID YOU SAY? ONE FOR MEAN GIRLS IS IT? JUST ONE? ONLY YOU, IS IT? TO SEE MEAN GIRLS? ALONE, RIGHT?"

At least, it seemed that way in my mind. Looking back, it was probably my own hyper-awareness that made her appear mortifyingly loud. I doubt anybody else noticed.

I was so focused on myself that I imagined judgemental thoughts on behalf of everybody in earshot. Now, of course, I know that these thoughts probably don't exist, and certainly don't matter.

Fear of solitude might not be about judgement. A common terror of mine is imagining my failing to cope if something goes wrong. I am unsure why; there hasn't yet been a situation where I've been truly flummoxed.

Recently, for example, I accidentally flooded the house. The first hint something was wrong was when all the electrical power shorted, and I suddenly remembered that I'd left a bath running. It had overflowed through the floor and into the electrical box below.

I handled this unfamiliar situation adequately,[58] despite my regular fearful belief that I might not manage if something goes wrong when I'm alone.

Some anti-solitude feeling is likely rooted in a widespread modern fear: the Fear of Missing Out, or 'FOMO'.

---

[57] I'm going to stop with the made-up word now. I don't think it's catching on.

[58] Admittedly, my first reaction was to panic and pointlessly search the shed for nothing in particular. After a few minutes, I realised I should probably just find some towels instead of looking for a Magic Flood Fixing Machine I might have bought and forgotten about.

FOMO is the anxious belief that we are missing something incredible or important that is happening somewhere else. For me, this fear surfaces in two ways.

Firstly, I had picked up a false belief that rejection lasts forever, while acceptance must be continually restated. Missing out on a fun activity only once would lead to disproportionate anxiety, as it subconsciously felt like I'd been permanently expelled from my entire social life. Naturally, this isn't how relationships work in reality. Using the belief-dissolving tools we discussed earlier, I was able to dislodge the power of this particular belief.

Secondly, I struggled against my introverted side requiring time to recharge. I craved time to replace my energy levels, and feared taking it because it meant "missing out." The inner voice of the Pusher never allowed me to be alone; alone time was wasted time.

The key to dissolving this fear was the realisation that my life doesn't have to be observed to have value.

Inexplicably, part of me subconsciously believed that my life only mattered if other people saw it mattering. Any accomplishment I made had to be shared.

Of course, it's wonderful to share success. Who doesn't love the idea of running ecstatically down the street shouting "SHE SAID YES, SHE SAID YES" to everyone you meet?[59]

But there's a subtlety to sharing accomplishments. It's a slim line to cross from "I'm enjoying sharing this success" to "I can *only* enjoy success if I share it."

Crossing that line has terrible consequences for our inner peace.

When we believe we need others to validate us, we implicitly believe that our value is *determined* by others. Quiet moments alone, such as admiring a view or making a delicious sandwich, have no less value than moments that are shared. But it's easy to fool ourselves into thinking otherwise.

In this mode, we need regular affirmation of our worth, our purpose, even our sense of self.

But the truth about our worth is that it does not reside in other people. It is not given to us by other people. It does not have to be affirmed, confirmed, approved or generated by other people.

---

[59] I like to do this no matter what the question was. "What does 'oui' mean in French?" is a good one.

My life would still have value even if - for the rest of my life - I never interacted with, or was witnessed by, another person.

Recognising this fact is a necessary foundation to our self-worth. Self-worth is *self*-worth because it comes from within. Otherwise it's just "worth". Worth from others is pleasant, but fragile.

My mind had latched onto this belief that I needed validation from others. Like many of my hidden issues, I wouldn't have said that at the time. But my behaviour proved me wrong, as I found it impossible to rest while alone.

I kept going on holidays with the intention of recharging. But I couldn't switch off, kept uncomfortable by the voice of the Pusher and the sense that somewhere out there was some fun I was missing. Wherever I was, I was unable to simply enjoy myself. It was as if 'this fun here' was never good enough; I needed 'that fun there' that was, by definition, happening somewhere else.

These attempts to relax were made worse by the nagging belief that this failure to be content must indicate something was wrong with me. An uncompassionate inner voice would pipe up: *You can't even enjoy a relaxing weekend in a country cottage, what's wrong with you?* I would beat myself up for my inability to rest, which made resting harder still.

I had to untangle each in turn.

I had to quieten down the voice of the Pusher. I had to self-compassionately stop berating myself.

And I had to dissolve the fear of missing out by embracing the belief that *my life has value even if no-one else validates it.*

Without this final step of discovering self-validation, I would hate even otherwise happy times, due to subconsciously believing that a witness was necessary for my happiness.

In reality, we can enjoy ourselves without needing permission or validation.

Tell My Friends They Are No Longer Required

Historically, some people *really* liked the idea of solitude.

You may have heard of 'anchorites', the hardcore medieval religious who devoted themselves to silent prayer by walling themselves into cells, their only contact with the outside world being the reception of food through tiny windows.[60]

We don't have to wall ourselves into a cell to explore solitude. Neither should we get rid of everybody we know.

For those of us who aren't feeling anchorite urges, we only wish to free ourselves from *needing* people.

Wanting people instead of needing them allows us to choose how much time and energy to spend on others. This has a double effect: not only do we become more able to enjoy time alone, but time with others is more pleasurable when we choose it rather than require it. Our time becomes a gift, which can be reciprocated.

It is a pleasing paradox that validating ourselves makes us more attractive to others. We become easier to be around, no longer demanding anything from anybody. Needing people has the opposite effect, of driving others away and making relationships weaker. Self-validators are sources of energy, rather than drains.

We cannot rely on having company whenever and however we want. It's impossible, and requires us to resist reality every time circumstances dictate we will be alone for a time.

Solid ground means not being buffeted by circumstance, especially inevitabilities like being temporarily alone.

If we end up in a follow-up experiment to that study, we don't want to have to choose an electric shock. Let's develop our ability to enjoy time alone with our thoughts.

SORT-OF-EXERCISE: Questions of Solitude

There's nothing worse than exercises that are just lists of questions.

Inner critic: "Nothing worse"..?! How about your worst enemy substituting your toothpaste for solid urine?

Cow's urine. From a cow that also hates you.

... erm, well, er, okay, yes. That's MUCH worse. And frighteningly specific.

But, obviously, I didn't mean it literally. I just meant that I personally hate lists of questions in exercises. I think guiltily "I should probably answer these", and then I don't. Then I imagine all

---

[60] I have no idea what they did about bathrooms, and nowhere near enough curiosity to find out.

the people who are probably much better at doing these exercises than me because they have iron discipline and I don't, so I skim over the questions and don't bother actually answering them or learning anything at all. It's a terrible experience.

Inner critic: I can see that I'm not needed for this section. You're doing a fine job, carry right on.

Yeah, I guess that was needlessly self-pitying. But I suspect I'm not alone in feeling guilt at failing to *do* these sorts of exercises.

Having said all of that, I haven't come up with anything better. So this is about to be nothing more than a list of questions. Sorry.

If you insist, you could imagine you're in... errrr... a mansion in your mind, and each room represents... eeehhh... a question. And in each room you have to... mmm.... answer that question.

You can imagine a guide asking you these questions as you tour the Mansion of Your Mind. What a super idea for an exercise, right?

EXERCISE: A Mind Mansion.[61]

Visualise yourself in a Mind Mansion talking to the resident butler. Or, if you prefer, just pause to consider your answers. Whatever works. Each question - sorry, room - builds on the ones before.

Am I an introvert, an extrovert, an ambivert, or in between?

If the answer is not obvious, visualise yourself alone, or with people, or both. Which brings you the most energy?

Inner critic: Hold on. How do I visualise myself "BOTH" alone and with people? Honestly, I had extremely low expectations for this "Mind Mansion", and you still managed to disappoint me.

Hey, please don't interrupt the exercises. The awesome power of the Mind Mansion is not to be trifled with.

How much do I value relationships? Does my time spent on them reflect this? Do I leave time for everything else?

How much do I value time spent on myself, and on self-growth? Does the amount of time I spend reflect this?

---

[61] Definitely Not Just a List of Questions.

How much of my self-worth is drawn from others? Who decides whether my accomplishments are successes, or failures?

How much time would my ideal self spend alone per day, per week, per month? Is this more or less than my 'real' self?

Is there any resistance or fear around spending more time alone? What about more time with people?

What thoughts or feelings prevent me from being comfortable alone (if any)?

What thoughts or feelings prevent me from being comfortable with others (if any)? In what situation(s) do these arise?

Can you identify the beliefs that cause these feelings?
E.g. "My life has value only if others say it does", "Life is always happening elsewhere", "Nobody wants to be around me", "I have nothing to offer", "Being alone is frightening."

Go as deep as you can to find the *root* belief by repeatedly asking why. For example, if you think being alone is frightening, ask why. Then ask "why" to the answer to that question, and so on:

Being alone is frightening... because I am missing out.
Why am I missing out?
Because I always miss out.
Why do I believe I always miss out?
Remember missing that party invite when I was six?
Why do I believe not being invited to a party when I was six affects me now?
Er. That's a good point.

Obviously, that's a contrived example. But I have found that at the root of an anxiety there's often some specific incident. Challenging my mind to not generalise from such incidents helps dislodge the anxiety.

Ask "why" until you've reached the deepest level possible, where you can work on the belief with your tools: is it helpful, is it true, can I challenge it, can I change it, can I replace it, etc?

The immense healing power of the Mind Mansion has hopefully encouraged you to consider how you relate to being alone. It may not seem it, but this is a powerful step towards contentment.

VOLTAGE / CURRENT
Another Critical Interlude

Hold on a moment. I have some objections.

Of course you do. Go right ahead.

Well, actually, there's only one objection. But I'm sure I'll think of some more as we go.

Fine.

Wait, why are you being so accommodating?! It's making it hard to object in a discomfiting manner.

Is it?

Damn it. Stop! Anyway, here's what I planned to ask, before you were so annoyingly polite and welcoming to me. Who's got time for any of this stuff?

Time? For what stuff?

For, well, all of it. All this 'learning self-compassion and getting to the bottom of my limiting beliefs' stuff.

And now you're talking about 'practising solitude' and figuring out what our reaction to being alone means for us. How is anyone supposed to actually DO any of this?!

We all have lives to live, and laundry to do, and meals to cook, and responsibilities and plans and... isn't it a bit much to expect us to somehow find time to 'analyse our reaction to being alone'?!

You think the temptation to ignore everything and just get on with life had never occurred to me?

I don't know if you remember, but it was precisely repressing all of this stuff for years that led to some extremely unpleasant and anxious times.

Anyway, none of this is obligatory. There's no Self-Growth Police coming to check you have correctly calibrated your feelings towards solitude. It's not like I'm advocating for every single person to immediately go on a silent retreat in the countryside right this minute.

If nothing else, that would massively drive up the price of relaxing holidays, which is the exact opposite of what I'd like to happen.

It's just... it all feels like so much to do.

Yeah, I get that. But taking time out for quiet is doing less, not more. It *sounds* like an additional thing, but it aids our ability to handle everything else, right? Like meditating for a few minutes in the mornings; it's extra time spent, but it helps with the whole day.

It could be as simple as taking a few seconds to examine why you overreacted to the workplace microwave already being in use at lunchtime: is it because you're hungry, or tired, or because you've been compromising all morning and this is the final straw, or what? Learning to recognise what affects our mood is powerful: a lesson we learn once can be useful time and time again.

And it doesn't have to take up all our time. That's just resistance talking again.

Maybe. But now I feel ridiculous for complaining about it. It's not even a real problem. People are starving and dying and I'm feeling stressed at the thought of finding time to look after myself.

That sounds like a familiar guilt. Look, feeling overwhelmed is perfectly normal from time to time. It doesn't mean you don't care about other people and their problems. It just means that you felt overwhelmed for a bit.

Ironically, it'd probably help if you took a bit of time out for yourself.

This is weird. You have actually helped. A bit. I wasn't expecting that.

Me neither. Maybe I'm getting better at this.

THE LITTLE FLOWER
That Grew In The Mud

There was once a little flower who looked at all the other flowers growing nearby, and thought "Oh how pretty they all are! I hope I'm as pretty as they."

A bee came along, and the flower tried her hardest to look pretty. But the bee went to the other flowers, and never returned. The little flower thought "I must be an ugly little flower", and felt sad.

Soon, the little flower watched some caterpillars feeding on leaves, and then turning into butterflies.

"Why do they not want to eat my leaves to turn into butterflies? Truly I must be the worst little flower in this whole flowerbed!" thought the little flower, even more sadly.

Later, a child came along and exclaimed at the beauty of the flowerbed. The little flower felt a surge of hope.

But this too turned to disappointment as the child knelt to smell the other flowers, ignoring the little flower entirely.

"I must be a repulsive little flower indeed", thought the little flower, wishing she'd never stuck her head up to see the sun at all.

When a dog came sniffing around the flowerbed, the little flower hardly bothered to look up. She barely watched as the dog curiously poked around. She didn't want to be rejected once more.

The dog cocked its leg and urinated, soaking everybody she'd ever met in piss. Except her.

The little flower felt a surge of joy. "Hahaha! They got covered in wee! I hate those guys, this is the best day ever", she thought, victoriously.

She might have been a flower, but she wasn't always very nice.[62]

---

[62] Then again, occasionally we all enjoy the Dog of Life urinating on those who've been more successful than we have. But it's an empty triumph. Even if it is funny when it happens.

CHAPTER EIGHTEEN
Apples & Pomegranates

*"Her lips were red, and one was thin,
Compared with that was next her chin,
Some bee had stung it newly."*

*Regarding a misfortune on a wedding day,
from 'A Ballad upon a Wedding' by Sir John Suckling, 17th Century*

Sometimes I hate when other people are happy.

I mean, obviously, I'm very much pro-happiness for all. I'd love to see a world in which we're *all* happy. But actually SEEING someone else physically being happy? Disgusting.

Misery loves company. But what it loves even more is leaving everyone else behind in their misery while we disappear to a hammock on a beach with a cocktail in hand.

Hopefully I'm not alone in having a cartoon devil on my shoulder whispering such jealousy. Someone I know - definitely not me, honest, I'm talking about a friend, and certainly not using a thinly transparent cover for myself - recently travelled to Australia. It was winter back at home and I - I mean, my friend - regularly checked the weather forecast for the UK, hoping to see freezing cold snowstorms so I - okay, yes, it was me all along - could *really* enjoy the sunshine of the Australian summer, in the secure knowledge that my friends and family were suffering in the cold.

I am not proud of giving into the impulse to taunt my friends by sending them pictures of myself on a beach while they were stuck with winter. This kind of comparison is poisonous. Though I am pleased it doesn't take long on social media to see I'm far from alone in this impulse to show off.[63]

Constant comparison is a powerfully self-destructive habit to acquire.

---

[63] Although even being pleased about this is itself a comparison. Damn.

I have compared myself to other people so often that the neurons in my brain connecting my conscious mind to the 'comparison centre' are as thick as ropes through overuse.[64]

I constantly compare myself to everybody. In every possible way. Whenever I meet - or even see - someone, I wonder if I could do what they do. Could I be a painter? Are they better than I am? Cooler? More attractive? More intelligent? More successful? Should I feel superior to them? Or inferior? I instinctively put myself in everybody else's position. All the time.

Even when listening to the radio in the car my attention inevitably wanders. Would I be better at being a radio host than this guy? I probably couldn't cope with the hours, or the public pressure. Though I would surely have asked a better question than that. This interviewer is *useless!*

I can find myself lost in an elaborate fantasy career before jogging back to reality. It's an autopilot experience. One moment I can be consciously driving, the next I'm imagining exactly how I wittily greet the receptionist on the way into the broadcasting studio in the morning.

Of course, a mere fantasy about being a radio host - or whatever daydream I get lost in - isn't necessarily bad. It becomes a problem because of the incessantly negative nature of these comparisons. I look at all the ways I fail compared to whoever I'm imagining myself as. *They obviously work out. I'm lazy and weak. They seem so happy, why can't I be content with my life?*

While watching the television: why aren't I an expert in 17th century paintings? Why can I not rewire the electrical connections of a house? Why am I not called upon to provide expertise to the news? Not even the local news wants me! I unfairly compare myself to the best in every field, and inevitably come up short.

You might think that I could balance this out by comparing myself favourably to the worst in every field. You would be wrong.

When I compare myself favourably I merely beat myself up in different ways. Perhaps I feel like a bad person for making the comparison at all:

---

[64] Metaphorically speaking. I'm pretty sure if my neurons actually were that thick, I'd have bigger problems.

"How dare I look down on this person? Who am I to proclaim myself better? I am a terrible person."

Or, if they are experiencing some misfortune, then I feel terrible guilt for being unhappy in my own life:

"Look at them, suffering in that awful situation, and yet they seem happy. How dare I ever complain about anything!"

Comparing myself to somebody else makes me feel awful, no matter what the outcome. I have, at times, beaten myself up for not handling the pressure of an imaginary murder trial as well as accused murderers in television shows seem to manage it. That can't be right.

Thanks for Sharing

I don't believe I'm alone in this constant comparison habit. It looks as if many of us are hopelessly addicted in much the same way.

We are constantly encouraged to compare our achievements, looks, possessions... virtually all aspects of our lives to one another.

You might think "well, as long as *everyone* is addicted to comparison then I don't mind doing it". Uh-oh, SUBTLE COMPARISON ALARM. Unfortunately, that is itself a comparison. We can't use comparisons to justify our comparison addiction. If it's self-destructive, it's self-destructive whoever does it.

It seems to be basic human nature to compare. And if that's true, then it must have a positive aspect.

I can see how a little friendly competition could motivate us. I expect most parents have, at some point, encouraged their children to finish their meal with a guilt-inducing "There are children starving who'd be grateful for that, so finish it all!" But, if we're honest, most comparison isn't of a positive, motivating kind. Mostly, we don't use comparison as a healthy motivator and then move on. Nor are we kind to ourselves in our observations.

Comparing is generally weighted against us. Remember, only we are privy to all the troubles we suffer with, and the dark thoughts we bury behind a mask. We only see the surface when we look at others. We may think they have it easy, but perhaps they're just adept at hiding their struggles.

When you watch a duck swimming, it appears to gracefully slide over the surface. What we don't see is that underneath the water it is actually ~~riding a tiny motorboat~~ kicking frantically. All the effort goes unseen.

We cannot ever see the tremendous effort others may be putting in beneath the surface. A comparison from inside our heads to the outer surface of another person can never be fair, which is why we nearly always lose.

This is not simply the old cliché of comparing apples and oranges. Comparing our inner lives against others' surface presentations is comparing apples against *sentient apples that worry about whether or not they're good at being an apple.*

Even if these comparisons were a good idea - and they're not - they are inherently unfair, and are therefore not worth our time.

Comparison Projection

Comparison doesn't even have to be against other people. Some of the worst comparison can be against our ideal selves. Recently I was playing the piano. As I played the high notes, I noticed they were a little out-of-tune. My thought process went something like this:

- Those high notes are a bit out-of-tune.
- I haven't tuned this piano for ten years.
- I bet proper piano players tune their pianos *all the time.*
- I'm a terrible person.
- I don't deserve a piano.
- This is why everything around me is in a constant state of decay.
- I am in a constant state of decay.
- I am dying.
- Everything is hopeless.

These astonishing leaps of thought took place in less than a second. My lack of perspective is almost impressive in its ridiculous scope. It came about because I compared myself to an imaginary perfect version of me. This fictional ideal me never gets behind on chores, or makes any mistakes at all. His piano is always perfectly tuned.

But he doesn't exist. It is unreasonable to try to live up to such an impossible standard. We all make mistakes.

We can take this a step further by projecting our ideal selves onto other people. We imagine they have access to the same imaginary ideal version of us that we do, and that they also find us wanting in comparison to the fictional model.

For example, sometimes I have to visit a world in which my comparison-addicted brain immediately makes me feel inferior. Perhaps I have to drop my car into the garage, where I will compare myself to a version of me who can repair engines. *You're not a proper man; if you were, you could fix your own car.*

As I talk to the mechanic, I imagine that he - or she - looks at me with the same judgemental attitude I do. Of course they don't: if nothing else, if everybody was an expert mechanic they wouldn't have a job. This comparison takes place purely in my own mind.

Or perhaps I have to go for a haircut, where I am forced to confront my terror that I never understood how you're supposed to know how your hair could or should look, or how to ask for it... if you even knew what it was. I'm usually reduced to asking for "less hair, please". My mind pops up with a comparison: *You're too much of a typical man to know how to look after your appearance.*

And again, I imagine that people around me make the same judgemental comparison against this ideal version of me that can handle every situation perfectly.

You may note that none of this is particularly rooted in reality. These two examples even contradict one another: I'm not a proper man; I'm too typical a man.

Not to mention that I have no idea if people think these things of me or not. I'm not psychic.

But the truth doesn't matter. I am hurt simply by making the comparison.

Leaving The Comparison Game

It's a freeing truth that other people generally don't care whether or not we're in a relationship, what we're doing with our lives, how fat we are, what size our new television is or what we're wearing. These imaginary judgements are invented by our minds. The only person keeping any kind of score is ourselves. And we're scoring a race which only exists in our minds.

How insane is it to feel terrible over a game that we invented for ourselves and can step out of at any time?[65]

Sometimes we externalise our personal comparison game, turning life into something we "win". It might be about income, the size of our house, our job title, our family, our holidays, or anything.

But nobody else is playing our game, so we brag, finding excuses to drop into conversation how well we're doing at our personal game. This bragging serves a dual purpose: it makes us feel (temporarily) good, and it validates to us that our personal comparison game is real. When we're invested in the game, we need other people to validate that it exists.

Worse, we can be dragged into other people's comparison games. We see them bragging about this, or that, and we mistakenly think we need to do well in *their* race to be happy in *our* lives. We don't.

This race cannot be won. Not only because it doesn't exist (though that is, admittedly, a major drawback), but because it's impossible. It's yet another custard trap - a foundation that is only solid for as long as we're wasting energy on it.

So what if that person has a bigger house? Someday they will meet someone with a bigger house still, and they will feel sad. Meanwhile, you can opt out of the game entirely and judge yourself only on your own merits and by your own criteria. We don't need to buy into other people's comparisons, just as we don't need to make them ourselves.

A need to feel superior is a mask over a lack of belief in ourselves. If we truly believed we were good enough, then we wouldn't need to compare ourselves, even favourably, with other

---

[65] As always, don't beat yourself up for playing!

people. We'd be content that we are worthwhile as we are, in all our imperfections, perfections, and struggles to improve.

Constant comparison is exhausting, whether it's based in feeling superior or inferior.

Can't Comparison Be Good?

Can't comparisons be helpful, motivational, or inspirational? Well, I suppose I could decide to learn to fix my car myself. That would be great.

Inner critic: As long as I don't have to get into any vehicle after you've messed with the engine. I don't want to "practice acceptance" on a high-octane fuel explosion, thanks.

For any change to be genuine it has to be for myself, and not to appease the judge inside that finds me wanting. That judge can never be appeased, only silenced. To fully appease him, I'd have to learn plumbing, plastering, rewiring a house, animal husbandry, cooking, sewing, the native plant species of Australia, and who knows what else.

Nobody can be the best at every possible area of life. While managing to keep their piano fully tuned at all times.

Inner critic: Maybe you could simply learn how to ask for a haircut? Is there an evening class for that?

Very funny. Let's take the original question more seriously, though: couldn't envy inspire us to achieve great things?

I feel safe to say that the most common outcome of envious feelings is simply bitter moaning and complaints at the success of others.[66] Usually we recognise this moaning is unattractive so we keep it inside our heads, though perhaps with close friends we may share some mutual envy out loud.

Maybe I'm being unfair. Let's imagine envy actually inspires us to take action. Are we all now contented, in this (fictional) world of inspirational envy? Sadly not. If envy was our primary motivation, then in reality we don't want what we think we want. We only want to win the comparison game!

In a world of positive envy, reaching goals doesn't bring any happiness. Instead, our goal shifts further away, to envying the next

---

[66] Speaking for myself, I guess. Though I'll drag as many of you down with me as I can! Misery loves... ah, damn it, I'm doing it again.

person and coveting something else. Our motivation was never the goal in the first place. It was to win a comparison game. We are always unhappy at our perceived lack compared to the next person.

This endless running on a conveyor belt towards a destination that never comes into sight... does it sound familiar? Running constantly without being able to stop and enjoy what we have? Custard traps show up all over the place.

We escape this trap by choosing our wants ourselves, without rooting them in comparison. I'm not saying our goals must be selfish, only that we must *choose* them ourselves.

For example, I might desire to make my partner happy, or for my children to have a life filled with opportunities. But I am choosing those goals for myself, not out of a desire to beat other partners or parents in a game of my own invention.

Comparison can be so toxic that it poisons even such positive goals. Perhaps I want to make my partner happy, but not because I am a mature person who values their happiness, but because I am comparing myself to her ex and I want to SMASH HIM INTO THE METAPHORICAL GROUND BY BEING BETTER THAN HIM.

You can see how my goal of making her happy is undermined by my competing with a ghost from the past. This is a war I can never win, and ultimately it takes a toll on the relationship.

"Ha, remember how you said your ex couldn't twirl spaghetti properly? Look at this! I'm a CHAMPION!"

Competing for positive reasons is just as destructive as normal envy. The only way to contentment is to quit the comparison habit altogether.

Breaking Our Comparison Addiction

If we're accustomed to using comparison to provide motivation, it can feel like we will never aim for anything if we stop comparing.

But it's not a contradiction to be content with ourselves, and yet to have goals and wants. It only seems like a contradiction if we're addicted to comparison and the thrill of feeling superior.[67] It's a lie from our minds that without comparison we would have no motivation.

---

[67] Or the reverse self-pity hit of feeling worse off, which can be equally addictive.

The antidote to this compelling lie is simple. Motivation does not require comparison. We can break the link between attaining our desires and winning an imaginary race against other people.

There are some familiar ingredients in this comparison habit: lack of self-compassion, limiting false beliefs, and emotional reactions to thoughts.

As acquisitive animals, it's natural to fear that what we have is not enough. Or even that what we *are* is not enough. This 'not enough' mentality is at the heart of many problems. To live on a solid ground, we need the capacity for satisfaction in what we have and who we are.

This doesn't mean giving up on growing, on improving, or even on acquiring more. Just as we shouldn't be motivated by fear, our desires shouldn't be based on comparison, but on genuine wishes.

Inner Questioner: (showing up for plot purposes) I have a convenient question for you! Are there any awe-inspiring ancient quotes that make comparison sound poetically terrible?

Yes. Check this out, from the Bible:

"The life of the body is a heart at peace; but envy rots the bones." Proverbs 14:30

Rots the bones! Could the writer of this proverb have hinted at the metaphor of custard any more perfectly? The solidness of bones becoming soft and rotting away, just like the solid ground beneath us turning to custard.

Inner critic: That's a stretch. Are you claiming the writer of the Book of Proverbs was setting you up for a metaphor about custard some thousands of years later?

Maybe. We can't rule it out.

Either way, this is a gloriously tangible image for how envy eats us away from within, transforming our solid foundations into liquid under our feet.

Ending the comparison habit prevents us from hurting ourselves pointlessly at others' success. Or from rubbing our victories in other's faces, in a misplaced desire to validate ourselves.

So, what's our plan for unlearning this particular habit? Just before I tell you, I have to send a quick message, sorry. Won't be long.

"Just written my chapter on 'Comparisons' and am taking in the sunset from my new holiday home on the moon with a nice glass of port #bliss #bestdayever"

Okay, I'm back.

We must realise how pointless the addiction to comparison is. Perhaps that couple do have the perfect life. Everything is exactly ideal. Their relationship, their jobs, their family and their lifestyle are all exactly how they want it. Does that mean we ought to be less happy with our own lives? Of course not.

Our ability to be happy can't be contingent on others having less than we have, or we will never be happy.

As always, our first practical step is to become aware of the habit. Aim to catch ourselves in the moment of comparison, and to remember that it isn't necessary; there is no objective standard we must meet, the race is imaginary.

We also want to notice when we are externalising our comparison game. We especially shouldn't validate ourselves by attempting to make others feel inferior.

Sorry, I've just remembered another message I need to send. I'll just be a second, again.

"Anyone else ever get tired of having too many awesome friends? Just give me an evening alone, amirite. #seriously #havingittoogood"

When we notice we are comparing ourselves to others, however subtly, we don't have to engage further. Awareness is the first step towards change.

Oh dear, sorry, can you wait just one final moment? I really ought to employ a social media manager.

"Just heard the agent messed up my bid on the new mansion #cantgetthestaff #seriouslyhesfirednow"

It's critical to be self-aware. It's so easy to engage the comparison habit without realis...

... oh. Sorry. I'm going to go scrub my social media a bit, and change my thinking patterns a little for the future.

Once we develop this self-awareness, we have a number of options for breaking the habit.

We can say to ourselves as we catch a comparison (whether in our favour, or not): "This thought is unhelpful so I'm not going to fuse with it."

We want to engage with each comparison individually, and remind ourselves that we are enough as we are. Note that yes, perhaps this person has something we want, but that doesn't mean we are worthless.

Even if we never have *everything* we want, our life remains worthwhile.

We can also - if appropriate - remind ourselves that we are working towards whatever our ambitions happen to be.

After thinking "Someday I want to have a family like that", resolve to take a small action towards the goal. Comparisons sometimes hurt because we leave them as empty unfulfilled wishes.

Lastly, we can remind ourselves of something positive. When we compare we automatically feel as if we are lacking, and forget all we have that's already good. Taking a moment to be grateful is a powerful antidote to the negative emotions of comparison.

So:

Notice it. Gratefully recognise something good in our lives. Then, either take action, or let go of attachment to the goal.

Deeply ingrained comparison takes time to erase, but it is possible. Be aware of your inner monologue, and catch comparisons as they happen.

I know someone who freed themselves of this comparison habit, so it must be possible, but then, they're so much better at that sort of thing than me, and I'm useless at it, and terrible in general, and...

... damn it.

THE SURPRISINGLY ONGOING ADVENTURES OF McBIGGS
Hero-Still-At-Large

McBiggs slammed the door to the lab shut and collapsed back against it, expelling a powerful blast of air from his lungs.

A lesser man might have merely sighed, but not McBiggs.

So he sighed, just to prove a point. He didn't like being limited, even by his own awesomeness.

He couldn't believe he was still alive. He thought back to what had happened after The Thing had caught him unawares. It had reached out to devour him - or hug him. Or something.

I should really figure out what it is they do, one of these times.

It had been upon him before he could react.

There was no chance of escape. This was it. It was over. The moment had seemed to stretch out forever, as the few instants that remained to him expanded to infinity and disappeared in a flash.

Instinctively, he had tensed and loosened all his muscles at once. (And THAT had taken some cleaning up, afterwards.)

In his panic, he had screeched the air out of his lungs: "EEEEEEEEeeee!!!"

Amazingly - and he still couldn't believe this had happened - The Thing stopped, just brushing his face with its arm (or tentacle, or something - McBiggs didn't want to consider the other possibilities in too much detail).

It made a slithering sound, almost in puzzlement.

And McBiggs looked it right in (what he hoped was) its eye, and in that instant he truly saw The Thing - any Thing - for the first time.

The Thing was lost, alone, frightened. Like him, it was a living being just trying to make its way in a harsh and unforgiving universe. Like him, it didn't understand what was happening. Like him, it was scared.

It probably didn't know what McBiggs even was. Maybe it had never seen a human before. Maybe it didn't understand The Incident any more than he did.

Somehow, across the vastness of their difference, they perceived their shared connection.

Neither could reach across the void that separated them, not only from each other, but even from beings of their own species. Somehow that shared loneliness and mutual pain united them on a deeper level still. A level McBiggs had never perceived existed. Until now.

He felt warmth stirring inside him, and somehow he *knew* that The Thing felt it too. Depth of understanding flooded McBiggs.

To his astonishment, McBiggs felt great love welling inside for The Thing, for this fellow life. The love rushed and expanded in an instant, taking in all the lives that existed across this whole flaming universe.

His family, his friends, his enemies, strangers... even those who tried unsuccessfully to bully him at school flashed through his mind. And he loved each of them.

Something about the way The Thing's eye - hopefully an eye - oozed towards him told him that this love was reciprocated.

They *understood* one another.

They *loved* one another, as McBiggs had never felt before.

This had made it a little more difficult than he'd anticipated to headbutt The Thing to death and carefully blast its still-warm corpse with one shot from his Super Serious Laser to confirm the kill.

McBiggs was having to take a quiet moment to recover before he resumed crossing the ship.

He made a mental note to be more loving to everyone and everything in future, and opened the lab door.

Not far to go now.

CHAPTER NINETEEN
The Unbridgeable Divide

"We're all islands shouting lies to each other across seas of misunderstanding" - Rudyard Kipling

A fictional statistic I just thought up indicates that books are exactly twice as enjoyable if they contain a story set in Paris. So let's have one of those.

The second time I visited Paris was mostly a solo adventure. I spent a couple of days staying with a friend, and then a few more exploring the city alone. On my last night, I decided it was time to head out in search of some social interaction.[68]

I'd spotted a fun-looking bar near my borrowed flat, so that was my first destination. After a lonely half hour at the bar, it was apparent that this wasn't the most sociable place, and I decided to cut my losses and head home.

As I left, I remembered seeing an Irish bar the previous day. It was on the other side of town, but fantasies of happy adventurers, interesting conversation and plenty of beer filled me with renewed determination.

Forty-five minutes later, I arrived at the Irish bar. It was dark, dingy, sticky and banging with electronic music. There was no conversation. Or happy adventurers. Or even any other customers. But I'd come a long way, and maybe there'd still be beer.

I leaned on the bar and waited for the single bartender to notice her only customer. After a couple of minutes, she shot me an angry look, which I took to mean "What the hell do you think you're doing here? GET OUT!"

I valiantly pretended to take a phone call, and left.

This was an even worse setback than the first bar, especially since I'd travelled so far to experience it. I admitted defeat, again.

---

[68] Not a euphemism; I just thought some conversation would be enjoyable.

But, as I trudged back towards the metro, I happened upon a second Irish bar. My optimism won the ensuing internal battle against my experience, and I headed in.

This bar also lacked the camaraderie I had dreamed of, but at least they had some functioning light bulbs and my feet didn't stick to the floor.

I soon got served, and settled in to watch some football. As a traveller alone in a strange city I wasn't in a position to be picky. Sometimes watching French football with nobody in particular is the best we can hope for.

A short while later, I was drawn in by a discussion between the waiter and a girl sitting alone at the adjacent table. She was staying briefly in Paris. A fellow lone traveller! Finally, a chance for some conversation. Maybe I could salvage the evening's imagined adventure.

Unfortunately, I'm not very good at talking to strangers in bars, especially when the stranger is a pretty girl. I tried desperately to think of what I could say that wouldn't sound like I was trying to chat her up, but inspiration failed to strike.

After what felt like an anxious eternity - but was probably only a few minutes - I decided that I had nothing to lose. As I hadn't thought of anything original to say, I went with the least intimidating thing I could think of.

Heart pounding, I spoke up.

"Excuse me, sorry to interrupt, I couldn't help overhearing... you've just come back from the Far East?"

Not bad on the whole, perhaps a little pathetic, but it wasn't overly intrusive, and it hopefully communicated that I wouldn't be offended if she didn't want to talk. Five out of ten, I think.

She smiled. "Yeah, that's right, why did you want to know?"

Suddenly, the bottom fell out of my world. My mind was blank. I'd used up all of my limited supply of conversation just on saying, essentially, "Excuse me."

I HADN'T PLANNED FOR A SECOND LINE!

I couldn't say *nothing*. Some unknown part of me took over and leapt in heroically with the delightful line:

"If you want I can just fuck off if you like?"[69]

This pathetic display was apparently somehow endearing. She laughed, and we went on to talk for a few hours, ordering more drinks and swapping travel stories. I rarely get talking to absolute strangers, and, in the end, had to count this as a victory, of sorts.

I am unsure what moral to draw from this story. Possibly "human interactions are confusing" or maybe "you should trust me even less on this subject than the low bar I've set on any other."

Still, only a true master of human interaction would ever make such a basic mistake as immediately encouraging the other person to tell them to fuck off for no reason. Therefore, it would be rude of me not to dispense my wisdom regarding interpersonal relationships.

Inner critic: ...

Did you say something?

Inner critic: No. Your audacity at even making that joke has rendered me speechless. Honestly, I think you've somehow blundered into a better technique for mental peace than anything else you've put in this 'book' so far.

Forget transforming inner voices into a "positive force for encouragement" or whatever other garblings you've spouted. Just make an outrageous claim like "I am a master of interpersonal relationships" and I'll silently brood on it for days.

I think it's obvious by now that I am generally joking, Mr Humourless.

Still, having demonstrated my lack of expertise on actually talking to people, it's probably for the best that we've had three-and-a-bit chapters on 'Others' without touching explicitly on relationships, be they friendships, romantic, colleagues, strangers, spouses or an unholy union of all of the above.

And there's just *one* more thing to talk about...

---

[69] Yup, in those exact words.

A Possibly Depressing Thought That's Actually Quite Cheering If You Really Stick With It To The End

I'd like to discuss something that we would probably prefer not to think about. I'd like to talk about the frightening truth that we are all fundamentally alone.

Inner critic: Bloody hell.

Nobody can bridge the gap between themselves and the rest of the world. No matter how much of our lives we share, there will always be aspects of ourselves that others can never know. In fact, there are always aspects of ourselves that even *we* don't know! Just as we can't expect anyone to fully know us, we cannot experience anyone else's life, mind, or feelings. We can never fully know anybody.

Worse - yes, sorry, it gets worse, though we're nearly done with the depressing bit - we are all born alone, and we all die alone.

Inner critic: Flipping heck.

Admittedly, other people are usually physically present at both of those times, but they are unable to share the experience of 'being born' or 'dying' with us. These important transitions are a completely solitary experience.

Put into such stark terms, this sounds frightening. "Dying alone" must be two of the most terrifying words to combine in the English language. Right up there with "zombie shark", "spider torture", "clown disease" or "vegetarian restaurant."[70]

This gap between individuals is totally different from solitude, which, by definition, ends when others are around. No connection can ever cross this fundamental gap.

I want to attempt to take any lurking terror out of this idea, but to do so we must talk a little about normal loneliness.

---

[70] Sorry, vegetarians. If it makes you feel better, it's because I secretly suspect you're a better person than I am.

Alone in Isolation

Feeling lonely is commonplace. Most of the time it's a harmless signal that we'd like to spend some more time with other people. We are social animals. Even after cultivating our ability to enjoy solitude, it's natural to require company.

This normal loneliness is caused by *interpersonal isolation* and is solved by connecting with others. Merely spending time around people is not enough; a genuine connection is important. It is positively easier to be lonely in a crowd, if we're surrounded by people we cannot connect with.

However, occasionally we experience a purer form of loneliness: *existential isolation.* This is the aforementioned realisation that there is an impossible-to-cross gap between ourselves and everybody else. That there is a deep level on which we cannot ever communicate or be understood.

Inner critic: I can sense he wants to drive this point home. Any second now, he's going to crack out some spurious scientific comparison...

You may recall hearing that atoms are made of protons, neutrons and electrons.

Inner critic: And a shoddy diagram...

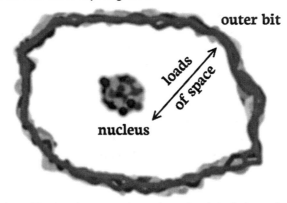

Figure Some-Number. An extremely precise and artistically brave drawing of an atom.

Almost all of an atom is empty. There's a tiny blob of protons/neutrons in the middle, which is where we find virtually all of the mass. This central nucleus is surrounded by a vast emptiness, and then by a cloud of electrons.

It's mind-blowing to realise that every object we have ever touched is 99% empty space. Even our bodies are 99% empty space.

Inner critic: It's not that surprising. For example, I am unsurprised that 99% of your brain is empty space.

Even more incredibly, in most interactions these central parts of the atom (the bits that contain all the mass) never touch each other. This means that when you physically touch something, the mass in your hand doesn't even get close to touching the mass in the object. As your hand and the object approach one another, the clouds of electrons on both sides repel.

Since almost all of the matter is contained in the nucleus, and since nuclei never touch one another, there is a very real physical sense in which we have never touched anything in our lives; what we experience is only the electrical interaction between fuzzy clouds of electrons. The heavy bits of the matter remain separate.[71]

This is like our social connections. We connect with one another, we learn about one another, we form friendships and relationships and love one another. But just as the nuclei of atoms never actually touch one another, we remain inescapably separated from other people. We cannot fuse with somebody else, we cannot read their mind, we cannot truly know everything about them. And nobody can truly know us either.

Existential isolation surfaces as an emotional experience of this lonely truth. If we aren't adept at understanding our emotional currents we might get the feeling confused with interpersonal isolation.

After all, it *feels* like loneliness. And we know - or think we know - the cure for loneliness. We need more friends, or a new romantic relationship, or to fix a problem in our current romantic relationship. But this type of isolation isn't one that can be solved by throwing people at it. Either literally or figuratively.

In fact, if we try to plug the hole of existential loneliness with people, we might make big mistakes.

For example, perhaps one day I stumble across the feeling of existential isolation.

---

[71] My Inner Pedant wants to point out that I'm over-simplifying the physics for the sake of a simple analogy. Although the point is basically true: nuclei don't get close to touching in everyday circumstances.

Inner critic: Is that a thing that happens? To normal people? Is it even possible to "stumble" across the feeling of existential isolation?!

It's normal for our subconscious to be aware of this loneliness, yes.[72]

Isolation is arguably a major drive behind our desire to socialise: to lose ourselves in a crowd and forget for a moment that we are separate beings. Many ecstatic experiences have that exact feeling of melding with others; from chanting at football matches (or churches), to dancing in clubs, to sex.

This lonely awareness lurks beneath the surface for all of us. Maybe it has never directly emerged for you, and maybe it never will. But it can lie beneath seemingly unrelated issues and undermine our contentment without our realising, so it's worth exploring the idea.

Mistaking existential isolation for basic, common loneliness causes problems. Perhaps it makes me break up a perfectly good relationship because I wrongly think "I've must have picked the wrong partner, they're obviously not meeting my needs."

Inherent isolation is a need they could never have met, so this is a terrible reason to split up. Similarly, it's an equally bad coping strategy to start a relationship just because one happens to be available.

We need healthy ways to handle this feeling, or we will become despondent that we can't shake it no matter how many people we surround ourselves with. No partner, nobody at all, can settle the issue of existential isolation. Only we can do this for ourselves. Stuffing people into the existential black hole is unhealthy for us, and for our relationships.

This is why we must face this fear rather than taking the easier path of ignoring it; unfaced, it can have terrible consequences.[73]

Repressing existential issues such as isolation (or other cheerful notions such as death and the search for meaning) can cause them to surface in seemingly unrelated anxieties.

---

[72] Well, of course, by definition I can't know what my subconscious is aware of. But it sounds plausible, so let's proceed as if it's proven. And not just, er, made up.

[73] If you like, you can imagine a spooky ghost making that warning: "Face your existential fears, or there will be TEEERRRRIBBLE CONSEQUENCES!! Terrible consequences, I tell you!!" There's no good reason to do this, but it might be fun.

Some argue that *all* human anxiety is simply existential fear, claiming that this fundamental angst gets translated into other contexts because we're unwilling, or unable, to meet the fear at the source.

Apparently, to some deep part of our subconscious, it seems preferable to develop a phobia of carrots (or however the fear surfaces in our individual case) than to work through tangible existential angst.

I have no idea if this is true or not, but plenty of clever people argue it is,[74] so I might as well plunge into the world of existential terror. And if it helps handle other - seemingly unrelated - issues then that's a bonus.

Let's see what can be done about the fundamental separation of all humans.

We're All Isolated, Together

Naturally, many wise people have thought about our isolated state over the centuries.

Disappointingly, they haven't come up with one, single, obviously correct solution to the problem. But this is actually good news.

It means we don't need to pressure ourselves to solve the unsolvable.

Short of redeveloping the entire universe, and giving all humans mind-sharing telepathic powers, this is simply how life is. When our wishes are in conflict with reality, we have no option but acceptance.

But can we go further than mere acceptance, and take the sting out of isolation entirely? Yes, actually. Inspecting it more closely, suddenly the idea doesn't seem so frightening.

Inner critic: Wait, what? You've spent pages talking about how terrifying this whole isolation thing is, and now suddenly it's not scary at all?! Explain!

Yes, exactly. The *idea* of isolation turns out to be more frightening than the reality. Now I've spent so much time immersed in the idea, I realise that everything is alright.

---

[74] Including Dr Irvin Yalom, whose books introduced me to this concept. See 'Further Reading' for details.

We clearly can tolerate the reality of isolation; we've been tolerating it ever since we were born.

At first, I was afraid to confront the very idea, as if *thinking* about isolation could magically make it worse. But my thoughts don't affect the universe like that (or I'd have won the lottery several times by now). Realising the truth of the human condition doesn't make it harder to endure. And as soon as I accept it's okay to think about scary 'existence' stuff, the fear disappears.

Clearly, the existence of existential isolation can't condemn us to loneliness. In fact, every moment of genuine connection we've ever experienced occurred in *this universe*, where we are all separate beings. So perhaps this separateness isn't as powerful it seems.

I appreciate that, to some people, this whole chapter may seem like pointless overthinking. But there are those - myself included - who worry explicitly about things like this, and so finding a new way to view isolation can be freeing.

It is possible to go further still, and to turn the concept of existential isolation into an actual positive.

The knowledge that we are all essentially alone paradoxically unites us. We are all in the same boat. From the lowliest to the highliest (yes, inner critic, I am aware that is not a word) we are all undertaking this scary-when-you-really-think-about-it journey from birth to death *together*.

This fact can act as fuel for our relationships. When we see others as being like us - frightened, looking for reassurance and companionship in a lonely universe - we view them more charitably. We can't help it. As humans, we are (most of us) naturally empathic. When we recognise the suffering of another, we feel naturally more predisposed to them.

Hence, a reminder of shared universal suffering can make us feel a greater charity towards *all* our fellow humans.

I'm using the word 'charity' deliberately. Charity is a word that is disappointingly weakened in its modern form. It evokes images of milky well-wishing. It has undeniably positive associations, but not powerful ones. Which is a shame, as charity is derived from a powerful word: the old Latin word *caritas.*[75]

---

[75] WARNING: Inexpert diversion into linguistics ahead. See 'Further Reading'.

Caritas was used in Latin to translate the word "love" from ancient Greek. Well, one of the words they had for love. Ancient Greek had four words to precisely convey the many concepts we mush into the single word "love". For ancient Greeks, "love" could be any of *eros, agape, philia* and - unfortunately for poets everywhere - *storge.*

Incidentally, I have some unrelated thoughts on the excellence of Ancient Greece.

Inner critic: A diversion within a diversion? Oh, I expect this to be informative, enlightening and well-researched, and not at all a waste of time.

I once spent some time in South America trekking over old Incan pathways. Incan roads are scenic, but they are not particularly efficient, mostly being lengthy zigzagging dirt tracks up and down mountains.[76]

As I walked, I couldn't help but wish that some other civilisation - say, the Romans - had popped over to South America with a good old-fashioned road-building regiment to flatten out some mountains and lay a proper straight trail.

As my feet ached, and my back complained at carrying half my body weight up yet another mountain, I had a further realisation. While the Romans may have beaten the Incas when it came to roads, the Greeks had a better idea still: don't bother with roads at all. Instead, chill out in comfortable togas, drinking wine while discussing philosophy.

And so, my grand realisation was that I would rather sit around and drink wine than trek up mountains in the rain for days on end.

Inner critic: So, your point is that Greeks were great because they aren't famous for building roads? Real genius-level stuff, there, Neil. Well done. What has this got to do with anything, again?

Not much, admittedly. I did warn you it was unrelated.

Anyway, as I was saying, of the four words for love in Ancient Greek we are most familiar with *eros* (erotic love) and *philia* (stuff we like). We're less familiar with *storge*, which denotes general affection.

---

[76] Though mainly up, it seemed, in contravention of all physics.

But the final word for love - *agape* - is the best. *Agape* is the purest form of love. It dispenses with complications, with physical attraction, with reciprocation and with thought. *Agape* is simply pure love.

This is the form of love that was translated as *caritas*, from which we get the modern word "charity". And so, when we feel charitably towards people, we are using a word that can trace a relation back to an ancient concept of pure love.

Daily life does not generally promote an attitude of pure love to our fellow people. Maybe I'm unusual, but I find it remarkably easy to go through the day forgetting that everybody I meet is on the same terrifying journey as I am from lonely birth to lonely death. It's rare that I am inspired to love my fellow passengers on public transport by remembering this truth.

Consciously remembering this shared existential isolation can be fuel for uniting us, allowing us to tap into that pure love for our fellow humans.

This contrasts with my usual approach: finding people annoying if they're in my way, and otherwise not thinking about them much (no need for any interruption from my inner critic here, I'm already aware this isn't very nice, thanks!)

Inner critic: Wait. You somehow arrived at the conclusion "love one another" from the fact that we are all fundamentally isolated? Via a linguistically-suspicious diversion through ancient civilisations... which, now that I think about it, was probably just a poorly-disguised excuse to include a weak observation about roads and wine-drinking?

Yes, basically.

Inner critic: Oh. I thought you'd deny it. Still, if you're going to be spouting cheesy and obvious concepts like "being loving to each other is good" at least you're doing it for counter-intuitive reasons like "we're all isolated and lonely in a way that can never be fulfilled." I might let you off the hook, this time.

I guess you could argue that isolation may not be the *best* reason to base our relationships with each other on love.

But given that love is A Good Thing,[77] anything that can remind us to adopt a more loving attitude is positive, for ourselves as well

---

[77] Even if this is strangely unfashionable to admit aloud.

as for society. Even if it's an initially frightening concept, like existential isolation.

EXERCISE: Existential Empathy

Picture somebody you know. Or someone you don't. Or an imaginary person. Picture another human, basically.

Picture them, and remind yourself that they are trapped in their own experience, and that nobody can ever truly know them, just as they can never truly know or understand anybody else. Attempt to feel that void of existential isolation on their behalf.

How do you feel about them? Empathy? Pity? Sorrow? These are only a short emotional leap away from wishing good things for them, and then from feeling pure, *agape*, charitable love for them.

If we can remember that everybody is in that same boat, and form a mental association between isolation and love, then whenever we experience loneliness it reminds us to go out and be loving.

And being loving to others is the easiest and most reliable way to receive love in return, which is the perfect emotional antidote to feelings of isolation and loneliness.

There is something pleasingly neat about using the fundamental bleakness of the universe as a trigger to make us more loving, and therefore more secure and happier. I suspect that pulling this trick off - to the point that it's no longer a trick, but a genuine mode of thinking - would go a long way to quelling our deep existential angst.

PEOPLE ARE MARVELLOUS
But Life is Complicated

We've been talking about other people for a while, with the unstated assumption that both relationships and people are Good Things.

I like this as a default assumption. Despite my occasional cynicism, I like my fellow humans. I think we're pretty good, as a species. And I think the majority of us are worthy of that positivity and trust.

I'd rather live in a world where I believe people are mostly decent - and be occasionally disappointed - than to assume the opposite.

Still, this is only a default assumption; it isn't always true. Not everybody is working to our good. We have to recognise that relationships can hurt, too.

I've talked a lot about acceptance and self-examination, selling them as powerful tools for solving our problems. But, like any tool, they can be harmful if applied in the wrong way. The most important part of any idea is knowing when *not* to apply it.

For example, acceptance doesn't mean meekly going along with whatever bad things come our way, and self-examination doesn't mean blaming ourselves if somebody else hurts us.

Similarly, while it is beneficial to assume people are good, we have to recognise when a particular person isn't living up to that hope. If we're being hurt we ought to speak up about it. Whether or not it's deliberate, being repeatedly hurt - or used, or mistreated - is unacceptable.

The role of acceptance is only to remind ourselves that we cannot always change every situation to match our wishes. It isn't about preventing action.

Relationships are good, but that doesn't mean all individual relationships are worthwhile. And it doesn't reflect badly on us if we can't make them all work out.

People are good, but that doesn't mean that everybody is. Or even that anybody is good all the time.

Acceptance is good, but that doesn't mean we shouldn't act to change harmful situations.

Responsibility is good, but not everything that conceivably *could* have been in our control *should* be. Managing our monkeys is hard.

Self-examination is good, but that doesn't mean everything reflects on us.

Life is complicated, and we can't always live by simple rules. That's okay, as long as we watch out for when our assumptions are failing us.

Love people, accept your emotions, examine yourself to see if it's you that needs to change (this time)... but above all, look out for yourself.

You deserve it.

A RELATIONSHIP
In Fantasy Form

It had been another tough day at the office. Now, only the long, uncomfortable commute back to his empty house beckoned before he would sleep and repeat it all again the next day.

Time for some mental distraction.

He leaned back against the frayed seat cushion, trying to ignore his fellow commuter jiggling in the next seat. He closed his eyes, and indulged himself in his absolute favourite daydream...

His acceptably attractive girlfriend's affordable car was parked outside their average-sized home.

He turned the key and pushed at the door. He hadn't got around to fixing the damp yet, so it wasn't until the second try that it heaved open. He kicked off his shoes, not expecting to be overwhelmed by an affectionate hug as she ran squealing in excitement towards him... which was good, as that didn't happen. Instead, he thought he heard a vague noise of greeting from the back room, which he returned.

"Hey honey!"

He couldn't hear any response over the noise of the television, so he went upstairs to change into comfortable slippers and a t-shirt with a hole in it.

He felt the train slow and opened one eye. Not his station yet. Back to the fantasy.

He entered the lounge. His girlfriend looked up for a second and smiled, before her eyes flicked back to the television.

"Good day?"

"It was alright."

He watched her for a second, contentedly. She was tired and not in the mood to talk. She needed her own downtime after work. He glanced over at the kitchen, where his dinner had not already been prepared by a fictional superwoman conjured up by his imagination. He wanted to have a responsible adult conversation about who was going to cook this evening.

"Do you want a takeaway?"

Her eyes lit up.

"Hell yes!"

He jolted as a trapped businessman prodded him to get past. It had just been getting good, too.

Eagerly, he sat back down and reignited his imagination.

He grabbed the stack of piled-up delivery leaflets and shuffled up next to her on the sofa. Their legs brushed together as they searched for a new place to order from. She passed him the remote control.

"Your choice tonight. But I'm picking the food!"

He slipped an arm around her as she resumed searching, and began to flick through the channels looking for something to watch. Cookery show... no. Police drama... no. The news... no. He kept prodding the remote.

Finally, they settled on both entertainment and a takeaway and sat in companionable silence for a while. Life was decent.

And they'd booked that all-expenses-paid gourmet Caribbean sex cruise for next month.

But, right now, he was enjoying his favourite spot on the sofa, and...

The train stopped again. A flick of the eyes. Not there yet. A girl further down the carriage caught his eye for a second, smiling.

Two more stops to go...

PART FOUR
THINGS

"Things were said, I know not how advised."
Sophocles

CHAPTER TWENTY
A Superficial Baptism

"It is the property of fools, to be always judging"
Thomas Fuller

"Why does Thomas Fuller use commas like that?"
A Judge, or Fool

One day I was musing about external influences.

The modern world is a constant assault of advertising, billboards, signage, the internet, mobile phones and noise. Surely this was unhealthy for our inner peace. Or so my thoughts went.

I made the well-intentioned decision that, for the rest of the day, I would avoid *all* external influences and information. It would be an experiment. Maybe I would discover a new way to relate to the world, and a corresponding increased serenity.

Only moments after this decision, I parked my car in a multi-storey car park and headed towards the exit, smiling to myself triumphantly as I successfully ignored the sign on the door to the stairs.

I made it about halfway down the first stairway before I wondered at how strangely empty this staircase was. I was sure there had been plenty of people in the car park, yet nobody seemed to be taking the stairs. Also, it was dark and dingy and I didn't seem to be heading in the right direction. Perhaps I'd gone the wrong way.

I returned to the top of the stairs and back through the door, only to find sirens wailing and overhead lights flashing throughout the whole car park.

People stood by their cars looking at the blinking bulbs, and then at me with confused, pitying expressions.

With a dropping sensation in my stomach I turned to read the sign I had proudly ignored: THIS DOOR IS ALARMED.

Literally the *first* bit of external information I had purposely filtered out was crucial!

Unsure of what to do next, I looked up to the CCTV security camera, mouthed the word "Sorry!" and ran away.

Our relationship with the external world is complex.

It's not so simple as retreating to our inner world; as my tale of idiocy shows, it is important to interact outside of ourselves in the *right* way.

We can't ignore everything. Nor can we unthinkingly absorb everything thrown at us by modern society; if we sponge up the message of every advert telling us how lacking our life is without this or that product, we'll be miserable for all of our days.

So we must think carefully about where we find our happiness, and in the process discover our purpose, goals and values, as well as dealing with the remaining existential issues that confront all of us. No big deal.

Through this, of course, we will discover the Meaning of Life.

CHAPTER TWENTY-ONE
Where NOT to Find Happiness: Part One

"It is not the man who has too little,
but the man who craves more, that is poor."
Seneca

Happiness is in the next thing that you want.
Not the thing you got yesterday. That's old news.
It's the next thing.
Yeah. That thing you want right now. That's the answer.
You need that.
Then you'll be happy.

CHAPTER TWENTY-TWO
Advanced Material Science

"For the world says:

'You have desires and so satisfy them, for you have the same rights as the most rich and powerful. Don't be afraid of satisfying them and even multiply your desires.'

That is the modern doctrine of the world. In that they see freedom. And what follows from this right of multiplication of desires? In the rich, isolation and spiritual suicide; in the poor, envy and murder."
Dostoyevsky

Fantastic news! It's time again to discuss advanced physics. I bet you've been hoping for this for ages. Perhaps you'd enjoy a discussion of quantum effects, relativistic paradoxes and dark energy... and how it all affects YOU.

If so, I'm afraid I'm about to disappoint you.

Inner critic: Pretty sure they're already disappointed. They'll have figured out by now it's not going to get any better.

Oh, hello again, you. I'm afraid that wasn't a great attempt to derail me. You may not be a positive force for encouragement (yet), but this is below your usual standard of hitting psychological weak spots. You have apparently morphed into an easily-ignorable abuse factory.

Inner critic: Ouch.

Ha. I win this round!

Inner critic: Not so fast! By cheering your victory you're validating the idea of battling against yourself. Didn't somebody say not to do that...?

Curses. I still have much to learn, it seems.

The Physics of Embarrassment & Desire

There's a tension between two common desires: to be individual, and to blend in with the crowd.

On the one hand, we dream of individualising through a unique, authentic, adventurous life; on the other, we seek to fade into the herd and replicate what everybody else is doing.

Mostly, any individual wants a bit of both. We want to visit the Eiffel Tower, but also to set ourselves apart with a cool story about hiding from a gang of clowns in a Venezuelan brothel, or having an unusual experience in an alleyway in Prague. We create our own balance between common experience and individual adventure.

One familiar shared experience is having a bloodcurdlingly scary teacher. This may not be something we all actually *want*, but for a long time I missed out on this particular ordeal and so never got to bond over the mutual trial.

Until I reached the tail end of my degree, when Professor Terry Fying showed up to teach *Painfully Grim & Strenuous Equations* for a semester.

The Professor opened the course with a fierce stare and the pronouncement "This course is IMPOSSIBLE. You will all fail." Then he threw out a sinner who had dared to arrive only moments before the class began.

He proceeded to lecture on Painfully Grim Equations with a raging intensity, daring us to understand the incomprehensible, before (I think, I'm hazy on the details) casually murdering several of the front row for failing to have passed the course already.

We spent the semester in terrible dread of this weekly torment. Each class my main aim was to avoid drawing unnecessary attention as I wildly scribbled notes. But Fate had other plans...

Okay, that's obviously overstating it a little. Fate, the person, doesn't exist. And if they did I'm sure they'd be too busy dealing with world leaders and the like to care about mundane issues like me getting into trouble once in a lecture. Still, it makes it more fun if we pretend that Fate was watching and the destiny of the world hung in the balance. So let's do that.

Fate was about to intervene...

It was a quirk of my afternoon routine to enjoy a bottle of cherry-flavoured fizzy drink. So, during one lecture, I opened a drink. *Pssssssssssshhhhsshh.* I had only half-loosened the bottle cap when the professor ferociously spun away from the blackboard, glaring at me in sheer disgust that I had dared to interrupt him. The message was clear: *NO NOISY DRINK FOR YOU.*

I meekly slid the bottle back into my bag. No drink for me.

Two thirsty hours passed. I tried not to obsess over the refreshing taste of my cherry-flavoured fizzy drink as we scrawled down grim equation after grim equation. This was hell.

Albeit a mild, educational hell.

The next week I was determined not to repeat my mistake. I arrived early to open my drink in advance.

Pssssssssssshhhhsshh. The gas escaped harmlessly before the professor had even arrived. Victory. I screwed the cap halfway back on, ensuring not to *fully* tighten it, in case the gas built up again during the early part of the lecture. I wanted to be sure I could enjoy my drink in comfortable silence.

Later, as the lecture was in full grim flow, I decided to sip my cleverly-prepared drink. I reached carefully downwards. Gently gripping the neck of the bottle, I lifted it oh-so-slowly, hoping gradual movements would be less detectable to the all-seeing eyes of rage.

Unfortunately, I was a little *too* careful in my picking-up motion. With horror, I felt the bottle slip and drop a couple of feet to the hard floor.

Events developed rapidly.

The bottle made impact, and the fizzy liquid exploded powerfully. Since I'd so *cleverly* left the bottle-cap half-on-half-off, there was no outlet for the blast. But nor was it suitably contained inside the bottle. Instead, it became a cherry-flavoured rocket, spinning around and around on the floor like a tragic firework. I dived to stop it, picking it up and showering fizzy brown sugar over myself and everyone near me as if it were champagne.

Eventually (although it must have been only seconds later), I screwed the cap shut, and sat down in a sticky, brown and despondent mess.

The professor was - along with the rest of the class[78] - glaring at me with a level of concentrated quantum violence that was impossible to comprehend. No equation could represent his level of shock and anger. People had been thrown out for comparatively minor interruptions, so I expected to be ritually disembowelled with a sharpened piece of chalk.

Mercifully, he was so appalled by the level of stupidity required to accidentally create a spinning fountain of fizzy sugar that he allowed me to remain and make syrup-covered notes for the rest of the lecture.

We could draw countless lessons from this affair, though we shall avoid the (many) morals that focus on my idiocy and instead take the opportunity to wonder about the role of *desire* in what happened.

Concluding that "desire was at the root of the problem" feels cheap. Admittedly, without my wanting the drink, the incident would never have happened. But it seems reasonable to want something so simple, and making desire itself into the enemy sounds like a slippery-slope argument to giving away all our possessions and living in a cave. Can't we draw the lesson "don't be so useless at drinking liquid, you fool", and move on?

Sadly not. A central message of this book is to resist rigid thinking and to take off the habitual glasses through which we view the world.

In this case, grasping the reasonableness of the desire prevents us from considering alternative viewpoints, such as "better control of my desires may have avoided this accident, and perhaps even other accidents in future."

Removing desire is a valid way of viewing the debacle. Maybe I could have stuck to nice, safe, unfizzy water. Or just had a drink after the lecture.

So, in an open-minded spirit, let us look at our relationship to desire, beginning with materialism in particular.

---

[78] Apart from my friend who was laughing himself to death, of course.

Amassing Items For Pleasure & Profit

We have a dual attitude towards the idea that "more stuff will make us happier".

Despite the common belief that money can't buy happiness, we tend to behave as if it can. Surely, though, this needs no discussion. Money *can't* bring us happiness, right? Ask anybody.

We all know how this section goes: I jot down some standard wisdom about not needing money to be happy, we all feel appropriately guilty for our ongoing attraction to higher numbers in our bank accounts, and then we'll vainly vow to be less materialistic in future, without changing anything at all. Easy.

Weirdly, however, there is some scientific dissent to this idea that 'everyone knows' is true. I came across a surprising 2013 study by Stevenson & Wolfers which appears to show that perceived happiness does increase, albeit slowly, with higher income.[79]

This is both predictable (people with more money are happy, shocking!) and surprising... money *can* buy happiness?!

Worse, it's also disappointing, as it requires me to actually *think* in order to write this chapter. I had hoped to trot out the standard clichés and then take the afternoon off.

Thanks for nothing, academia.

So. Let's start with the obvious facts.

We all need food, shelter and security. But, beyond this, it's hard to see where deep happiness can be linked to having more stuff.

I expect we have all experienced the emptiness that follows purchases, promotions or other attainments. We know the hangover after the high of novelty wears off, be it a new house, car, job, gadget, or even relationship.

Usually we pretend not to notice the emptiness and aim for the next thing. Another car. An extension to the house. More clothes. A higher salary. Whatever it is, there's a temptation to move the goal higher and higher.

We fool ourselves into believing the next high will be the one that lasts, but when we reach it, it is precisely as temporary as the one before. Then we convince ourselves we never *actually* thought this would be the *final* goal, and aim higher still.

---

[79] See 'Further Reading' for details.

Sometimes we get tired of asking 'what do I want next?' and realise that material possessions are not the answer. With this mindset, they can never be the answer, because there is no possession, set of possessions, or amount of money that will ever be enough.

This is the same pattern we've learned to recognise: endlessly running towards any goal is just another custard trap.

But if materialism is a custard trap, why would perceived happiness apparently rise with higher income? Time for me to wildly speculate...

It seems that the answer must lie in our attitude. Happiness requires the right attitude; one that allows us to be happy with or without money.

It seems plausible that some people will have this attitude and more money. In which case, it makes sense that they might report higher happiness.

I was tempted to do some numerical analysis to model what percentage of people would need to have this happy attitude (assuming it's independent of wealth) to predict the effect measured in the study, but as I was about to begin I realised it didn't matter.[80]

We don't need to treat this as some huge mystery. Is it really confusing that some rich people are sad, and some poor people are happy, while other rich people are happy and other poor people are sad?

It's only confusing if we believe that happiness fundamentally depends on wealth. When we realise that it's mostly our *attitude* that matters then the confusion goes away. While *endlessly* wanting more is a custard trap, merely wanting something isn't.

Recall that to be happy in a relationship, we must be able to feel happy alone. Materialism is similar: unless we can be happy without any given thing, we'll struggle to be happy with it. But that doesn't mean we must denounce materialism in general.

As I've said already: as much as I'd love to produce a definitive list, it's impossible to divide the universe into Things That Are Always Good Or Always Bad For Us.

---

[80] This convenient realisation has nothing to do with my very real desire to take the afternoon off, honest.

We have to figure out if - *for us* - a goal is the fragile custard of a materialistic treadmill, or a genuine desire that may bring some fulfilment.

Any goal can be a custard trap, from wanting a dishwasher, to having to climb a mountain on every continent, to getting a world record, to getting married. But none of these are certain to be a trap: they can all be healthy, life-giving desires too.

It solely depends on our attitude: whether we want it, or "need" it (that is, *think* we need it). Or there's a third option: we may genuinely, actually need it.

Only you can tell if something you want may be a trap for you.

Questions like "do we need wealth to be happy?" seem confusing when we believe traps are universal. But there's no need to be puzzled when we see depressed wealthy people, or happy poor people. Materialism could be a trap for one, and not for another. And the same goes for virtually *everything*.

The confusion arises when we universalise our own experience and assume we're all the same. Since we're all different, we need to put effort into assessing the health of our personal goals.

I'm sorry that this is yet more "you have to do this yourself" work. Believe me, I'm as furious about the lack of easy answers as you are. If it were as simple as "more things and more money can't make us happy, so let's all stop believing that" then I'd have finished this chapter and be relaxing with a glass of wine by now.[81]

Luckily, this is the same type of work we've already seen, applied to a new domain. We identify when we're stuck on these custard traps, and change our thinking to free ourselves from them.

Distinguishing Healthy & Harmful Desires

There exist two extreme positions. Let's exaggerate them both:

To one, all desire is healthy. Popular culture is filled with this narrative; adverts everywhere speak the language of fulfilling our desires and living our dreams. In this world, when we get what we want we will (finally) be happy.

On the other extreme, there is a counter-cultural movement which says that we are happiest when we release desires instead of

---

[81] Yes, the irony that I am wishing for a material thing like a glass of wine is not lost on me. Let's pretend I am making a clever ironic point and move on.

fulfilling them. It says that we are enough as we are. All desires (beyond our basic needs) are unhealthy, or at least unnecessary.

Both of these caricatures contain some truth. Both arise from the same mistake we've already discussed: generalising from our own experience. Because such-and-such a desire was harmful to me, it must be harmful to everybody. Or, taken to its extreme, all desire must be harmful.

As we've seen, we come closer to reality when we recognise that a healthy desire in one context can be harmful in another.

For one person, gaining a promotion could bring genuine lasting happiness. For another, the pressure to climb the career ladder could be a custard trap; each rush of joy at a promotion only a fleeting pleasure that must be replaced by the next. To the first person, the desire for promotion is healthy; to the second, unhealthy.

The same sexual desire could inspire one person to find a partner, or somebody else to cheat and ruin a healthy relationship. The desire to travel could be a healthy ambition, or a harmful wish to avoid reality. It could even be both for the same person at different times.

We must judge each desire in our own personal context, and at this current time. What happens when we fulfil this desire? Will we keep raising the bar ever higher, or is this a fulfilling end-goal?

It's okay if we don't know immediately if a desire is healthy. Understanding ourselves is not easy. By observing the patterns that arise in our lives, we can see if we are repeatedly fooling ourselves that happiness is just one or two desires away. If so, it might be time to change attitude.

If in doubt, we want to keep aiming for our current goals, but to keep checking that we're not secretly stuck on an endless custard trap.

Freedom Through Gratitude

Once we can distinguish healthy from harmful desires, we take a dual approach.

We want to fulfil healthy desires and release harmful ones.

I'm not going to suggest how you might attain your healthy desires once you've identified them. Advice on fulfilling goals and living dreams is commonplace.

Instead, we're going to develop the underrated skill of releasing desires.

This may also aid in discernment of our healthy desires; any that continually return after being released are more likely to bring us genuine contentment. If we release a desire and it doesn't recur, then it was probably something we didn't really need.

Sometimes freeing ourselves from a desire is as straightforward as recognising reality: "I keep thinking I need a raise to be happy. This hasn't worked out for me yet, so maybe I'm fooling myself here."

But for those (more numerous) times when this realisation alone isn't sufficient, there are alternative strategies.

Let's look at an important component of a healthy attitude: gratitude.

Inner critic: Damn that obnoxious rhyme.

Sorry! I didn't think that would bother you. That sort of rhyming kind of annoys me, too, but what's done is done. Nice to find common ground, eh, inner critic?

Inner critic: ... we don't have much in common! We don't! Leave me alone.

Hmm. If you insist. Anyway...

Being grateful is extremely good for our emotional health.

Sometimes our desires distort our sense of perspective. We obsess over what we lack, or believe we lack, and this denies us enjoyment of everything else.

The tunnel vision of wanting something makes us blind to our good fortune. We pass off whatever we already have as somehow "not counting". Rationally, we *know* that owning something already doesn't make it less valuable... but it can feel as if it does.

Like a child who wants a toy until they have it, it's easy to fall into the trap of valuing things for their unattainability.

This is how the eternal cycle of desire perpetuates itself. We discount whatever we have, precisely because we already have it. Somehow it doesn't "count" that we have a place to sleep, loving friends, enough to eat, or whatever we legitimately have reason to be grateful for. It seems as if without 'that thing we want', everything else is worthless.

Reflecting gratefully on the good things we have liberates us from the tunnel vision of desire.

We don't have to float on a cloud of everlasting gratitude - "oh, how wonderful that I'm taking a breath, oh how delightful that I have clothes, oh look at the rain, isn't it wonderful?"

This would rapidly become irritating.

Instead, we would like to become aware of when we're fixating on a desire, and to deflate the fixation with a little perspective-restoring thankfulness.

Gratitude doesn't mean abandoning our goals, or closing our eyes to real deficiencies. Goals are critical to our happiness, and ignoring our desires is as bad as focusing obsessively on them.

But we generally don't need reminding of what we lack. We naturally ruminate on it, at the cost of enjoying what we have. Meanwhile, it's easy to forget to be grateful.

The moment when we finally have *everything* we want is never going to arrive. It can never arrive. It's impossible. If we defer happiness until we have everything, we will never be happy.

The only way to contentment is to be grateful while we head towards our goals. To enjoy what we have and replace "I am lacking" with "I have enough. I am enough."

EXERCISE: Momentary Gratitude. Right Now.

Find something you are grateful for, right now.

Even if you are reading this book in the midst of a fire, with all your possessions flaming around you,[82] you can still be grateful that you are, at least, alive.

And, hopefully, nobody is in such a dire situation right now. Maybe you can be grateful that you're not.

Pick something positive, and don't just think nice thoughts about it; connect with the actual feeling of gratitude for it.

It doesn't have to be a major, life-changing, bubbling wellspring of gratefulness, but you do have to feel the happy, warm feeling of gratitude. At least a tiny bit.

---

[82] Please put the book down immediately and leave the building before resuming this exercise.

Note how long that took. I'm willing to bet you could connect with that emotion in less than a minute once you actively sought it out, and probably even quicker than that.

Feeling grateful for one moment won't do much by itself. But, as usual, if we make it a habit, it can have large effects. We can reduce the constant feeling of lack that underlies so many custard traps.

Detachment from Outcome

It's useful to have more than one way to handle a desire. If we can only be satisfied by meeting all our desires then we are doomed to unhappiness, a slave to our emotions and our whims.

It would be convenient to sometimes recognise that we will be just as happy if we simply let go of the desire.

The necessary skill is *detachment from outcome*. Being overly attached to a particular outcome subconsciously tells us we depend on it. That we are deficient without it. That we *need* this thing, rather than wanting it.

Inner critic: Like that 'non-attachment' thing you made up earlier?

Are you feeling okay, inner critic? That wasn't very critical. You sound like an interested observer. But I'm glad you've been paying enough attention to remember the non-attachment dialogue from way back when we were discussing the present moment. Thanks!

Inner critic: (shuffles uncomfortably) Err, yeah. I mean. It's not like I care, or anything.

Still, I'm touched that you remembered it at all. I expect if I was a reader I wouldn't recall it. I'd probably be thinking "what non-attachment thing? I don't remember that!" and beating myself up for my poor memory.

Inner critic: Technically, it'd be ME beating you up, you know.

Sure. We make a good team.

*Inner critic: *high-five*... Wait... *sudden awkward realisation*... I... I'm... I'm going to go, now.*

No worries, inner critic. See you later.

As I was saying... We want to aim for our goals but without grasping a particular result. To quote an old English motto: *Que sera sera: what will be, will be.*[83]

---

[83] This may have surprised you. It surprised me too! It's not Spanish or Italian at all, it's English, from around the 15th century. Totally irrelevant, but interesting.

As usual, our minds resist this idea, crowing that we must deeply depend on the outcome, or we won't honestly aim to achieve it, but - say it with me - *that isn't true.*

Getting a raise at work is not dependent on anything (in our control) but our performance.

Our private hope for a particular outcome does not affect the end result, except insofar as it affects our work. So it must be possible to work as hard, but without the inner need. We still *want* the outcome, but we let go of whether or not it happens.

If we're successful: fantastic. If not, we can still be content with what we have.

Once we have done all we can to achieve a goal, we let go of the outcome, and choose to be content whatever happens. Relinquishing the desire to control what we do not control is important for our happiness.

At first glance, it seems impossible to do this. How can I want something without being disappointed if I never get it?

I would like to share a super-impressive technique for this. Unfortunately, my two best strategies are irritatingly simple.

Inner critic: I doubt they were expecting super-impressive wisdom, so don't worry too much. Keep to your usual level of, what was it, "irritatingly simple"?

Ah, but simple-seeming things are often the most wise...

Inner critic: Did you make that up? It doesn't make sense.

Ah, but things that make the least sense, make the most sense...

Inner critic: Stop trying to be wise. It isn't working.

Ah, but things that aren't working are often... oh, okay then.

EXERCISE: Observe Desire Coming and Going

The first irritatingly simple method is to merely acknowledge that "I want that, but I don't need it".

Along with adding a touch of gratitude for the good things I do have, this is often enough.

For tougher-to-shift desires, a way to lessen their power is to observe them rise and fall within us.

Sit and meditate for a few minutes. Observe that just as thoughts and emotions arise without cause, so do desires.

You might have an urge to move, to stop meditating, to scratch an itch, to go and work on a project. Watch what happens if you don't immediately give in to the desire but instead passively observe it.

Concentrate on the sensation of the desire. How does it feel in your body to want to go and do something?

Keep observing without reacting. An itch unscratched will fade away if you allow it. We don't always have to give into our desires.

Inner critic: Wait, wait, wait. What if I really need the toilet? If I'm sitting there with a full bladder, that urge isn't going to go away.

Do you want me to have an accident while we're meditating? Because it'll be you cleaning it up.

True, the source of the feeling (in this case, the full bladder) may still remain. But even desperation for the bathroom is a feeling that ebbs and flows.[84]

If you observe it without acting, you will see that it comes on powerfully for a few seconds, and you think *OH GOD THERE'S NO WAY I CAN COPE WITH THIS,* and then some seconds later it fades to a more tolerable feeling. And you've gone another ten seconds without immediately giving into the desire.

We can't go for long without bodily necessities like food, bathroom visits or sleep, and I'm not suggesting that we do. Of course, we must look after our bodies in a healthy manner.

But practising allowing momentary desires to come and go helps train us to release larger desires. If we automatically jump to obey every desire as soon as it appears, then we are slaves to our whims.

We don't fight our wants; instead, we put them down gently. We still have them within reach, without grasping them tightly in our hands.

Unless - and this is important - we're talking about a bottle of fizzy drink in a tense situation.

You should grasp onto *those* very (very) tightly.

---

[84] "Flow" might not be the best choice of word, there. Hopefully, it'll mostly ebb.

CHAPTER TWENTY-THREE
Where NOT to Find Happiness: Part Two

"The greater part of our happiness or misery depends upon our dispositions, and not upon our circumstances." - Martha Washington

There is no SI unit of measurement for happiness.[85]

There is also nowhere you can find happiness.

Searching for something implies that you don't have it. Nothing could be worse for finding happiness than attempting to look for it.

The act of searching fools you into believing it is out there. That it is something you *do not have*.

Just as struggling against your negative emotions feeds them, searching for happiness guarantees failure to find it.

Happiness can only arise by ceasing to battle reality. It grows when we acknowledge that things aren't perfect, but they are okay.

We must cultivate contentment where we are.

...

That said, if a movie is *clearly* terrible after thirty minutes, just walk out; you have better things to do.

No advice is *always* valid, even if it is mostly correct.

---

[85] The kilogrin, perhaps?

CHAPTER TWENTY-FOUR
Being Without Flaw

"It is clear that a thing is perfect so far as it exists" - Thomas Aquinas

A SHORT NOTE
To My Fellow Perfectionists

Is everything ideal?

A SHORT NOTE
To Everybody Else

Hello, non-perfectionists.

These few coming pages are mostly aimed at perfectionists, but I want to reassure you that it will become relevant to you shortly afterwards, so stick with it.

Yours imperfectly,

Neil

P.S. With hindsight, this note probably wasn't necessary. Presumably, you folks are forgiving of being left out for a portion of a chapter. That's the beauty of being a non-perfectionist, I guess.

P.P.S. In fact, I may have disappointed the perfectionists by sullying the pure beauty of <u>their</u> chapter with a note to filthy non-perfectionists. This chapter is no longer perfectly about them! Sorry, perfectionists. The next bit is for you, though.

A LONGER NOTE
To My Fellow Perfectionists

Hello again, perfectionists.

I felt that my earlier note to you lacked a certain something. While it was perfect for brevity, it lacked length.

And depth.

And purpose.

In fact, the more I look at it, the more easily I can see the countless aspects in which it was inadequate. Each time I look, it develops a new flaw.

And yet - at first - it seemed to *perfectly* encapsulate everything which ought to be said to my perfectionist friends.

We perfectionists cannot greet each other with a mere "How are you?" or "Is everything alright?"

Asking whether everything is ideal seemed like the... perfect... way to greet you all. But apparently not.

Perhaps it needed some more detail: "What areas are perfect, or otherwise?"

Or maybe it needed a specific query about how you are feeling. Does your body feel flawless at the moment? I hope there are no aches, pains, funny feelings, twinges or confusions.

I find it hard to focus whenever something like that comes along. I mean, it's probably not going to be fatal, whatever it is, but I suppose it might be. And, even if not, it's always distracting when your body doesn't feel like it's *supposed* to.

It's even worse when you forget what you're supposed to feel like in the first place. Am I normally this tired? This dizzy? Is it normal to feel imperfect? And therefore is it perfect to feel imperfect?

I'm sure I used to have more energy. Though I'm not sure when. It can't have been in the summer - any summer - because that's hay fever season.

Probably not in the cold season either, so it must have been in either spring or autumn. It doesn't seem likely that it was at a time when I was working, because then I'm normally tired and looking forward to a holiday.

But it probably wasn't when I was on holiday either. Holidays are tiring too. All that travel, and adventure, and fun.

So maybe my most recent day of feeling energetic and flawless was a day off. Except it can't have been a day when I did too much and tired myself out.

So it must not have been a memorable day, which is probably why I can't remember when it happened.

Now that I think about it, it seems like a waste not to have done something on the rare day when I felt perfect. I should have done more with it! It can't be a perfect day if I wasted it!

But then, I'm glad I didn't overdo it either. That wouldn't be ideal.

Anyway, I'm sure a day will come again when I feel absolutely physically perfect, and then I'll be *so* productive.

Although, should I aim to be productive on a day when I'm feeling so good? Perhaps I should rest. I have to be kind to myself. But I have to make the most of my life too!

I refuse to waste time, so I must work. But I must look after myself, so I must rest.

Speaking of productivity, I planned to achieve so much today. But I got distracted after breakfast, and now it's nearly lunchtime. I can feel that the *whole day* is wasted already.

Might be better just to leave it until tomorrow. I must do it all *properly.* If I were to squeeze a little bit of work into the remaining eight hours of the day I doubt it would be my best work. And work must *always* be my best work. Each time, it must be the best I've ever done.

Tomorrow it is, then.

I expect tomorrow will be a good day to make some life decisions too. I've been wondering: what should I be doing with my time?

Everything seems like a waste of time. A life of leisure is evidently wasted. But a life spent only working may bring deathbed regrets too. So I should prioritise leisure. But not at the cost of work. Or family. Or a social life.

I need new experiences too, but if I don't stick to what I'm doing I'll never do it perfectly.

It hurts to think about. When I'm doing one of these I'm neglecting all the others, so how can I do any of them perfectly? Worse - how can I do them *all* perfectly?!

Maybe I could convince everybody I know to work with me on a private island. Then I can have everything at once, perfectly. I'm sure *then* I wouldn't be so anxious about what I'm doing.

Unless I have a headache, of course.

Or if it's raining.

That would be terrible.

PERFECTIONISM ITSELF
No Subtitle Required

I'll keep this short.

Perfectionism is an enemy of contentment.

By 'perfectionism' I don't mean being uptight, obsessive or stressy (although it can certainly bring those traits out in us).

I mean taking a binary viewpoint: *this is either perfect, or a failure.*

Perfectionism wants us to believe that it only helps us to improve everything. What could be more enticing than that?

Perfectionism ignores the good times, the happy memories, the growth earned through struggle, in favour of a permanently-moving and impossible target. It has a harsh standard, and anything that doesn't meet this standard is failure.

A straight-*A* student feels an icy chill on receiving a *B+*. Ninety-nine people liked the presentation we made, but one person made a disparaging comment, so we fixate on that and fail to enjoy our success. A promising new partner turns out not to match the dream of them we invented, and a seed is planted in our minds that may one day destroy the relationship.

Perfectionism invents impossible standards and demands that all of reality matches up to them. And I mean *impossible*. It is impossible for anything to be perfect in every respect. Being perfect in one way is being imperfect on another scale.

And perfectionism will always choose a scale by which we fall short. No matter the situation, we can construct a way to look at it in which it is not quite perfect.

A perfect evening in is a terrible evening out. And a perfect dog is an awful cat.

Perhaps we wrote the perfect email. It was business-like, simple and accurate. We press send... Wait, should it have been funnier? More personable? Longer? Less committal?

There is no such thing as 'objective best'. One person's "best" is another person's "I don't care in the slightest." Whatever we do, and however we do it, it is always possible for a perfectionist to pick different criteria by which to criticise it.

And a perfectionist mindset will always find the least charitable way to look at anything.[86]

In any comparison between reality and imagination, the imaginary world is always able to win. We can always imagine a better world. Reality is never sufficient for a perfectionist.

Recently, I was swimming in a beautiful outdoor pool in Australia. The weather was gorgeous, and the pool was delightful. As I swam I felt happy.

But I couldn't help comparing this experience with my local swimming pool back home, and feeling sad that I was returning home soon.

Naturally I didn't judge the pool in Australia on its negatives; for example, at my local indoor pool I'm unlikely to get sunburn or to have to worry about possible skin cancer.

If we require perfection, we only look at the areas in which we are lacking.

Imperfect Examples in Brief

Uncertainty

I often attempt to impose certainty onto situations where there *has* to be uncertainty. This isn't confined to major life choices: I can agonise for hours about which restaurant to eat in.

My Inner Perfectionist can't tolerate the risk of failing to make the best possible decision.

Performance

Sometimes, perfectionism is about approval. If I make a mistake, other people might think less of me. Despite the fact I know rationally that my friends and family won't abandon me if I perform less than perfectly, some part of my brain is hard-wired to go into panic mode when I imagine publicly making a miscook.

MISTAKE, I meant mistake.

Please don't hate me.

---

[86] You might even say they're the best at this. But not perfect.

Health

If I'm not in a perfect state of health, I must be unhealthy. Since as a perfectionist I only have two states ('perfect' and 'everything else'), I exist basically in the same state as if I were dying.

Action

If I were only able to work in ideal circumstances I would be extremely unproductive. A healthy attitude recognises that there are times we must put up with less-than-ideal circumstances, and just get on with it.

Maybe I imagine I can only ask someone on a date once I've been to the gym and lost a few pounds. But I can't go to the gym until I've found the perfect gym. And I can't do that until I move house... and that means finding the perfect house... but I can't do that until...

There's always an excuse not to act to a perfectionist mind. Perfectionism can actually make you do less.

A Quick Alternative to Perfectionism

Perfectionists falsely believe that we need this mindset to function. But it's possible to live without perfectionism and still be the best we can be.

The solution is to subtly shift our focus from imagination to reality, which has the handy advantage of being, you know, real.

Recalibrating perfectionist thinking is necessary to make the next moment as good as it can be. But no better.

Inner critic: I thought you said "I'll keep this short"? This felt longer than I expected.

I tried. Nobody's perfect.

CHAPTER TWENTY-FIVE
Where NOT to Find Happiness: Part Three

"Happiness is like a butterfly, which when pursued seems always just beyond your grasp, but if you sit down quietly may alight upon you"
Anonymous, pre 1850

"What's so good about a butterfly landing on you?"
A cynic

A Short Recap To Hammer A Point Home

Perfectionism is a useful example of a custard trap that doesn't apply to everybody.

We've seen several times that we can't neatly divide the world into 'good' or 'bad'. Whether something is healthy always depends on us. The number of potential custard traps is infinite, so it's impossible to write about each of them.

Chapters I'm not going to write include *'Valuing What We Do Rather Than Who We Are', 'Status Games', 'Living Through Others Instead Of Ourselves', 'Addictions', 'A Healthy Approach to Anger', 'Requiring Control Over Everything'* and so on...

Each of these could be a whole chapter. Or probably a whole book. Perfectionism is the trap I chose to highlight, but it could have been anything.

Why highlight a trap that doesn't apply to everybody?

Because to live happily and securely we must learn for ourselves how to spot our personal custard traps. Escaping is almost always about changing our habits, particularly habits of thought.

This is tough enough, but most of the difficulty is in spotting the trap in the first place. And since I can't tell you what might be a trap, you have to recognise the shape of a custard trap when one shows up.

Let's look once more at the characteristics common to these traps.

Characteristics of General Custard Traps

Exhausting

Many traps begin as positive, useful modes of operation. But when we live on them constantly we become jaded and exhausted. Our energy is wasted on remaining afloat, instead of analysing the modes that tire us in the first place.

For example, constant perfectionism leads to constant criticism of anything and everything. It tires us out through eternal dissatisfaction.

Difficult to spot from within

It always seems that we have the correct approach to the world. For example, I don't realise I can take off my perfectionist spectacles because I am unaware I'm even wearing them.

This is the main feature that keeps us on the traps, and is why I have repeatedly stressed the importance of self-knowledge, self-examination and finding new ways to look at situations, however idiotic they may seem, or however sensible our current lens appears. Striving for new thinking makes us question the way we view the world, and opens us up to alternatives.

Maybe I don't have to be so hard on myself - is everybody as hard on themselves as I am?

Maybe I don't have to do everything perfectly - you mean everybody doesn't beat themselves up for imperfections?

Maybe I don't have to control everything - you mean everybody doesn't secretly want to control everything all the time?

And so on...

What are the questions you could ask yourself to find new ways of thinking?

Distracts from alternatives

The trap itself distracts us from the possibility of escape. We're too occupied by surviving the trap.

For example, perfectionist thinking undermines my happiness and makes me anxious. The fact that I'm anxious distracts me. I focus on that, rather than on the cause of anxiety, and so I don't notice that my thinking is the root of the problem. I definitely don't notice that I can change it. The trap protects itself from examination.

Conversely, once we've escaped some traps we have more energy to recognise and escape some more.

Self-justifying

There's usually some well-rehearsed line of defence in our minds when we initially challenge the trap.

These defences are basic, but are usually enough to dissuade us from attempting to change. Often we'll parrot a positive element of the trap, as if that validates remaining there:

"I have to remain perfectionist or I'll never get anything done, I don't know how everybody else lives so sloppily. Perfectionism just encourages me to do everything to a higher standard."

We overcome these weak defences by asking if we can have the proposed advantages without the negatives.

For example, "can we still do good work without viewing everything as either perfect or a failure?" Of course we can.

We have to look deep enough to bypass these shallow defences.

The response exacerbates the problem

In the truly fiendish custard traps, the way we respond to the trap strengthens the power of the trap. It's a vicious cycle.[87]

"I am anxious because I fear anxiety."

These self-feeding traps may not have started this way; perhaps our initial anxiety was of something else entirely, but over time it morphed into fearing anxiety itself. Now the custard trap gets deepened whenever we're anxious. To escape, we must find and break the link between our response and the trap.

What To Do About It

Once more, with feeling: Continual self-examination, including seeking fresh perspectives, will help you to spot the traps.

After a while, you will recognise the 'flavour' of your traps. Maybe a nagging realisation of wrongness in the back of your mind, or an anxious flutter in the chest. Paying attention to these feelings will help you spot the traps faster and faster.

Answer for yourself: is this, whatever it is, a trap for you, in this particular context? If so, how can you change your thinking, or look

---

[87] Or possibly a vicious circle. Either way, we can be certain that something is vicious, and it might be circular in shape. Sounds scary.

at it differently? Your aim is to keep the good parts, without the exhausting parts.

Try to apply this new thinking to your life, as an experiment.

If it helps, excellent. If not, find another way to frame your thinking.

None of these harmful habits are fundamental. With careful effort, we can replace them and live happier lives as a result.

What Now?

Now that we can recognise and escape our personal custard traps, we can turn our attention further outward still, towards the grand questions of life, death and meaning, without getting caught in petty traps of our own making.

The grandest traps of the universe itself are so much more interesting to escape from...

SPIRITUAL INSTRUCTION
The Boy & the Teacher

A boy approached his spiritual teacher.

"Master, why is it that all things must come to an end?"

The teacher, in his wise wisdom, wisely paused before he spake.[88]

"Because it is the nature of all things to end. Moreover, it is only *because* all things end that we appreciate what we have now."

The boy paused, uncertainly.

"So, it's good that things end, then?"

The teacher nodded sagely.

"Indeed it is."

The boy smiled widely.

He opened his hands, to reveal he was holding a pile of ashes, saying "Good, because while I was studying that ancient book you gave me, my candle fell and burned it to nothing."

The teacher smiled, pleased that the boy had understood today's lesson.

"You are forgiven. Thank you for teaching me the value of my book this morning. Through such loss, may I achieve detachment."

The boy returned the smile to his teacher.

Emboldened, he spoke once more unto his master.

"Also, I borrowed your new car and smashed it to pieces. I'm not sure who I hit with it, but I think it might have been your mother."

The police were called immediately, and the boy served a long sentence for theft, criminal damage and accidental manslaughter.

Even the wisest teachers have their limits.

---

[88] The teacher did like spaking.

CHAPTER TWENTY-SIX
Dying of Laughter

"The cost of a thing is the amount of life which is required to be exchanged for it."
Henry David Thoreau

I was once hospitalised by a fish.

I was very young at the time, so I can't recall all of the details, but I remember toddling around in a kitchen, some sort of incident, and suddenly a hot fish fell and burned my back.

I was taken to hospital, hopefully to be recorded somewhere in Official Statistics as the only person to be injured by a fish that year.[89]

At the age of (around?) three, I was already unable to get into a difficult situation without it somehow being funny. It seems to be one of the Laws of the Universe that bad things happen to everyone, but whenever they happen to me I can't even tell people about it without them having to hide their laughter, instead of feeling appropriately sympathetic.

I can't decide how to feel about this. But it does mean I have plenty of practice at taking dark aspects of life and finding humour in them, so let's attempt the Final Boss of dark aspects of life: Death.

Discussing such dark, difficult matters inevitably leads to stock phrases. Any second now, I'm going to talk about overcoming inner demons, facing the darkness inside or gazing into the abyss.

It seems universal to tell stories about young heroes facing major existential threats,[90] and discovering an inner strength they had

---

[89] Although, admittedly, only very mildly.
[90] Making them "Jung" heroes, right?!

always secretly possessed. This universality suggests it's important to face deep existential questions. So let's talk about them.

Inner critic: That's... not very logical. All cultures recognise the importance of building private places to poo, but that doesn't mean you need to do it right now.

Oh! That reminds me of an *excellent* story of something that happened to me in Peru...

Inner critic: Oh god. Forget it!! Talk about the death thing, already. Here, I'll do a title for you:

Death, and Stuff. Now!

We have already discussed how repressed angst due to existential concerns can undermine our contentment.

Un-repressing[91] this angst and facing the underlying concerns is a tough sell. We have an understandable aversion to death.

We slide past talking about it, usually opting to either deflect the topic with a joke, or to parrot a relevant phrase and move on. Attempts to have deep conversations about death are sensibly avoided by all concerned.

Unfortunately, death is inevitably a concern to all of us. And not only later, when it eventually comes, but now. Just as isolation can affect us in surprising ways, our instinctive terror of death can surface in apparently unrelated terror.

Arguably, you could make a case that my over-fixation on a sports team failing to win a trophy could be rooted in repressed death anxiety; perhaps I have projected my subconscious desire for immortality onto my favourite team, and their constant abject failure to win reminds me of the inevitable failure of my own hopes to live forever. And so I am sadder when they lose than the loss warrants.

Inner critic: Hold on, hold on... Are you seriously claiming that sports fans sad after a defeat are secretly mourning their own demise? Just as I was starting to warm to you, you come up with more of your nonsense.

Don't be silly. I don't mean that every negative emotion is automatically an expression of death anxiety! Just that if this idea

---

[91] Yes it's a real word, or real enough.

of death anxiety surfacing in unrelated ways is true, then it could be.

Perhaps if I have adequately addressed the issue, I will have a more proportionate amount of disappointment in my favourite sports team's uselessness.[92]

Death Musing

Rather than using my patented method of rigorously constructing an argument on a given topic, we're just going to meander around the topic of death for a while.

Inner critic: Pfffffft. Hahaha.

Thinking about death has the potential to be painful and unpleasant. There is a reason we instinctively develop defence mechanisms against thinking about it: it is *scary.*

In the modern world we see more fictional fatalities and less actual death than any human society in history. Yet, while most of us would barely blink at a movie scene where the hero takes out tens of nameless minions, we recoil strongly from thoughts of death closer to home.

This is partly due to movies being fictional, of course, but I suspect part of it is an instinctive flinch away from thinking about death at all.

Our experiences of death are generally impersonal and highly sanitised. Even the language we use is euphemistic: we prefer the hero to "take out" rather than "kill" minions.

Talking about death is an awkward taboo even with close friends. Most of us brush against it so rarely that we are uncertain how to act when it does - inevitably - show up in our lives.

While I'm not advocating for constant celebrations of death, we ought to occasionally puncture this bubble to drain some of the attached emotion in a healthy manner.

Our instinctive repression tries to convince us to maintain this bubble. This automatic repression makes me suspicious. If we can't face reality as it is - the good and the bad - then we are not free to

---

[92] At the time of writing, they're terrible. I'm writing a chapter about the actual death of humans, and the bit that is making me saddest is thinking about how bad they are. They're THAT bad.

live our lives. We are controlled by a childish fear. Maybe we can come up with a more adult response.

Inner critic: This seems unlikely in your case. But go on...

Is the repression of death truly universal? I mean, right at the beginning of the book I mentioned that I have occasional suicidal thoughts. Doesn't the existence of suicide imply some sort of un-repression of death?

I suspect that whatever underlies these thoughts differs greatly from person to person, so I can only speak for myself. And due to my fortune that these painful feelings rarely last longer than a day when they show up, my experience is limited.

Still, a perspective I've found helpful is to turn my view inside-out, by recognising that (for me) suicidal thoughts arise out of desire for life.

That may sound stupid. But the desire to escape my life - or to escape *myself,* as it sometimes feels - arises only *because* I care.

Caring about anything always opens us up to possible pain, and if we care about something as massive as our lives, the pain can become great enough to make death appear preferable to continuing to suffer. For me, remembering that this pain arose from valuing life can be helpful to manage the feelings.

While this is a genuinely useful perspective shift for me, I'm aware that to others it may sound trite or useless. I'm sharing it in case it can be useful to anybody else. But if it doesn't seem relevant or helpful, then please ignore it.

Deflating the Bubble

Returning to the topic of death more generally, it's interesting that so many fictional heroes are fearless in the face of death. At the risk of just making up theories,[93] maybe we want to be like them: able to look death in the eye and grin.

Or, at least, not run away screaming, defecating and crying, like at the end of a first date.[94]

---

[93] To pre-empt the inevitable interruption from my inner critic: you're right, nothing has stopped me so far.

[94] I have been informed that first dates are not supposed to end this way. I'll believe it when I see it.

Even if we've never encountered bereavement personally, we have all developed unconscious coping mechanisms towards death. Given that we likely never chose these reactions, it seems reasonable that revisiting our attitude towards death as adults may help us to develop a healthier, stronger perspective.

I don't think it matters what perspective you choose towards death; our goal, for now, is only to spend some time out of our death-repression bubble and come out on the other side intact.

It seems to me that there are two equally valid basic approaches, assuming you agree that hiding our heads in the sand isn't the most adult and healthy decision we could make.

1) Team 'Death is Sort of Good'

To this school of thought our mortality helps us to lead happier and more fulfilled lives.

Fans of this perspective would say things like "without death, life would lack meaning."

I can empathise with this. It is plausible that since death is an inevitable part of the natural cycle, without it we would never change. And science fiction has explored the idea that if we all lived forever we'd get bored.

Maybe another reason to be on 'Team Death is Sort of Good' is that a brush with death can inspire us to make radical life changes afterwards.

Lastly, Team Death probably have the coolest outfits.

2) Team 'Screw Death'

This team would claim we shouldn't go as far as actually painting the grim reaper and his enterprises as a *good* thing.

In this approach, death isn't something to be meekly accepted; it's an infuriating and purposeless tragedy. A sad fact of the universe we live in, but nothing more.

Sure, with this perspective we're forced to accept that death *exists* - it's pointless to resist reality - but to this team it is always bad. No good comes of it that we couldn't have gotten anyway. To this school of thought "being bored as an immortal" merely displays a lack of imagination.

They would argue that we don't have to thrust ourselves into potentially fatal situations to make radical life changes; only to make an effort to grasp our mortality.

And..?

It doesn't matter which of these perspectives appeals to you, or if you don't much like either. I'm not trying to convert you to a side. It doesn't matter if we see death as good, bad, helpful or unhelpful; it just *is*. In order to accept that bare fact, we must occasionally confront it.

Both of these approaches - as well as multiple religions and societies across human history - underline the importance of accepting the fact of death.

I once visited the intensely provocative Capuchin Bone Crypt in the church of Santa Maria della Concezione, in Rome. This place sounds macabre: a crypt filled and decorated with the bones of ancient monks. Amongst the bones is a plaque, which reads

"What you are now, we once were; what we are now, you shall be"

Terrifying, right? A literal warning from beyond the grave.

Yet visiting this space doesn't feel like experiencing a real life ghost story. And I don't believe the monks intended the plaque as a threat.

The crypt is oddly beautiful, and exploring it is a peaceful experience; I recommend visiting, if you ever get the chance. There is an unconventional freedom that comes from looking our fears in the eye.[95]

Something about the calm acceptance of the monks reaching across the centuries is comforting. The acknowledgement that they have gone before us into death is irrationally reassuring.

Another ancient practice for confronting mortality is the Buddhist tradition of 'charnel ground' meditations. Delightfully, they would visit open graveyards and meditate among the decaying bodies. I suppose the idea is that if you can achieve inner peace in a graveyard then you can do it anywhere, like the meditation equivalent of training for a marathon while wearing lead boots.

---

[95] Or in the socket.

These traditions have in common the idea that acceptance of death - in fact, a conscious meditation on the idea of death - is healing.

ASIDE: Hold on, what about the afterlife?

It's easy for a discussion of death to get morphed into a discussion of the afterlife. In fact, I bet that the most common response to talking about death is to invisibly slide the discussion onto the afterlife instead. We distract ourselves by debating, or imagining, what happens after we die, while failing to notice that this is actually a separate topic.

The fact of our death is irrelevant to the question of what comes after. Whether we personally believe in an afterlife or not, it is an unarguable fact that we will face death in this life. And if we never truly consider that fact on its own, we are ignoring reality.

I'm not offering opinions on whether the afterlife is real. We can all believe what we like. I'm saying that it's a separate question to the one we are exploring.

What happens after death is undeniably important, and we should decide for ourselves what we believe. But it's not the same as developing an adult approach to the unavoidable reality of death. Believing they are inextricably linked and must be discussed together is an instinctive distraction we use against confronting our fear.

If you find yourself being wholly distracted by life after death you might want to explore questions like "is my belief (or disbelief) in the afterlife a healthy, strong coping mechanism for me? Or am I avoiding the fact of death by focusing instead on the afterlife?"

I know it can be hard to honestly answer that question, but if we are to spend time out of our death-repression bubble we must not be swayed by other topics, even related ones like the afterlife.

Actually Approaching Death

So what do we do now?

It's tempting to slip into binary thinking, as if our only option apart from repression is to join some sort of death cult where we wear skulls and black robes and dance like zombies under a new moon (actually, this sounds quite fun, as death cults go).

But there's good news: merely having this conversation[96] at all is helpful. The hidden terror of death is fed by our inability to talk about it, and it's this bubble of avoidance I'm attempting to pop, a little.

The main idea, beyond just talking and thinking about it, is to stretch our acceptance muscles. Death is the ultimate inevitability, and there is nothing to gain from denying its reality.

NOT AN EXERCISE: Laughing in the Face of Death

I have absorbed from somewhere the twin ideas that laughter is healing, and that there is something noble about laughing in the face of death.

So, as an experiment, and in the spirit of science, just now I genuinely attempted to laugh out loud at death for two minutes. Here's what happened:

I pictured the inevitability of death, reminded myself of the end of all things and of my life in particular, and then flipped the mental switch from 'terrifying' to 'hilarious' and began laughing aloud.

At first the laughter was a little forced, but after a few laughs I became genuinely amused by the fact I was even trying this. Everything became more and more hilarious until I reached a peak and started to wonder how much time had passed. My mind drifted mid-laugh to consider that two minutes is much longer than you think it is before you start.

Still, I pressed beyond this obstacle and made a stronger effort to visualise death on both personal and universal scales, and to find the fact that we cannot escape it hysterically funny. For a moment, I wavered back to the standard negative emotions associated with death, then suddenly it became funny again that life is guaranteed to end and I hit another wave of genuine laughter.

This carried me right through to a mini-wave of embarrassment, and then I found *that* funny and laughed until the timer went off.

---

[96] I'm aware that this book is a very one-sided conversation between you and me. But if you feel resentful that I'm not listening to you as much as you'd like, I equally feel as if I'm doing all of the work. There are two sides to every story.

What did I learn? Well, I think it might have helped. Maybe. A bit.

It was a novel way to spend two minutes, anyway. And there's some original research for you.

We can reuse the strategy we developed earlier of associating positive concepts with our most formidable fears. Just as existential isolation can be fuel for loving one another, a shared fear of death can bring a similar sense of connection. The moments when we feel least afraid of anything are those when we feel most connected to others.

Seeking out these moments of connection and tapping into love for our fellow humans is the truest solution to death anxiety. But only if we're giving and receiving affection in the knowledge and acceptance of death, and not as a means of hiding from it.

EXERCISE: Loving in the Face of Death

It would be convenient to rewire our brains to have a more peaceful association with death. Actually, it'd be convenient if we could physically rewire our brains *at all.* We could do so much! But, since medical technology has selfishly failed to make this a simple procedure, we are required to put some work in.

So, to manually come to peace with death, we need to spend a little time meditating on the idea of death, while mentally drawing on times of love and connection.

What does that mean, practically?

1) Visualise death without judgement. Don't flinch away from the idea.

2) Remind yourself that you can label it as good ("a fitting end to a well-lived life"), bad ("a terrible enraging travesty of injustice"), but that you can accept it either way.

3) Observe your emotions - whether fear, anger, or whatever - and watch them come and go.

4) Once you've watched some emotions ebb and flow, try to hold onto the idea of death with one part of your brain, and to reach for memories of love, connection and happiness with another part.

Inner critic: Are you sure that's even possible?

Probably. I mean, I can simultaneously think about a hippo while remembering a time I felt angry, so it seems reasonable that we can do the same thing with "death" and "love" instead of "hippo" and "anger", right?

Inner critic: Why did you do that? Aren't you just going to feel angry whenever you see hippos now?

I'm not sure. It felt like a good idea at the time.

Inner critic: You're weird.

What next?

I realise it's quite laughable to attempt such a large topic as death in a single chapter.

Inner critic: If only it had been actually laughable at any point...

I don't expect to have come close to solving death anxiety, but I hope I've successfully suggested that it may be an area worth personally exploring, as well as hinting at some ways to begin.

More than any other part of this book I think that this chapter may warrant some follow-up. If this has stirred some interest in you, I would like to recommend the book *Staring at the Sun* by existential psychotherapist Irvin Yalom. It's excellent and approachable, and explores these ideas far beyond the meandering opening up of the topic presented here.

Let's move to the comparatively easier topic of figuring out what to do with our lives, and what the Meaning of it all even is, anyway.

"Death must be so beautiful. To lie in the soft brown earth, with the grasses waving above one's head, and listen to silence. To have no yesterday, and no tomorrow. To forget time, to forgive life, to be at peace."
Oscar Wilde

TEMPORARILY
A Breakthrough

"When we are tired, we are attacked by ideas we conquered long ago."
Unknown provenance, often attributed to Nietzsche

He got it. Finally. He *really* got it.

The ego is the creator of all problems. Now he'd *finally* realised this *obvious truth*, he had shed his ego without a second thought.

He would never again experience difficulty.

He smiled beatifically as he walked through the city.

He went to sleep that night, enlightened.

But he pissed the bed in his sleep.

CHAPTER TWENTY-SEVEN
Valuing Time

"Time is gonna take so much away, but there's a way that time can offer you a trade:
You gotta do something that you can get nicer at,
You gotta do something that you can get wiser at,
You better do something that you can get better at
'Cause that's the only thing that time will leave you with.

It might be cabaret, it could be poetry,
It might be trying to make a new happy family,
It could be violin repair or chemistry,
But if it's something that takes lots of time, that's good,
'Cause time is gonna take so much away,
But there's a way that time can offer you a trade.

You have no choice, you have to pay time's price,
But you can use the price to buy you something nice.
Something you can only buy with lots of time,
So when you're old you blow some whippersnapper's mind.

One good idea could cost you thousands of your days,
But it's just time that you'd be spending anyway.
You have no choice, you have to pay time's price,
But you can use the price to buy you something nice"

- selected excerpts from 'Time Trades' by Jeffrey Lewis

As I have already confessed, haircuts are always a source of some trauma to me. I seemingly missed instructions everyone else received on how to know what you want, and how to ask for it.

I appreciate that this doesn't make me sound like a well-adjusted adult. But I've come to terms with it, and have settled on an inoffensive way to lose some hair that doesn't lead to mockery in the barber shop, or on the streets afterwards, so I suppose I'm at peace with it now.

During one particular haircut, I happened to glance up at the mirror shortly after my fringe had been cut. I had avoided the barbers for months, so this was my first glance at my forehead in a long time.

To my mild shock, there was something that looked a bit like... wrinkles... across my forehead.

I don't put much stock in my appearance. And I didn't think I was upset at the thought of growing old. But this moment, at the ripe old age of thirty-one, hit me surprisingly hard, like a retired boxer leaping at me in a public bathroom.[97]

Perhaps it was the fact that my life was in a state of flux at the time, but I had a sudden vision of myself ageing, becoming infirm, and dying.

Inner critic: Nicely emotionally balanced, as usual, Neil. Not written a chapter on 'how to have a functioning sense of perspective' yet?

By the end of the haircut, I had recovered my grip on reality. Sure, this was a minuscule reminder that I am slowly ageing. Exactly like every other person in the world. It'd be more weird if I *wasn't*.

I grinned, as I walked home, at how silly I'd been. It wasn't that bad, really. In fact, it was quite amusing.

Later that day I was having a cup of tea with my mother, and thought I'd amuse her with the story.

"You'll never guess, mum, but I had a funny moment before when the barber cut my fringe back. I looked up at the mirror, and..."

"Oh, have you finally noticed that you're receding?"

My mum calmly unleashed a conversational torpedo right into my newfound psychological weak spot. My jaw fell open.

"Re... receding...?!"

I dashed to a mirror to check. Was I receding? I couldn't tell. Time for another temporary panic!

This could be a reminder not to worry about the inevitable (particularly when it doesn't matter; we are no less valuable or lovable with wrinkles, bald patches, or any other signs of age) but, for me, this story is about time.

Time is a persistent fear of mine. A recurring thread picked at by the anxious voices in my head is the idea that I'm running out of

---

[97] Don't ask.

time, that I've achieved nothing, that I've wasted time, that I'm wasting time now.

Small scale time-wasting generates intense guilt and anxiety. And the larger question of how to spend my life has always been painful. I made life choices, but I have never been sure why I did so.

I believe I mentioned that I spent some years as a travelling Catholic evangelist. It was a strange but interesting period, and one I look back on with much affection.

During this time I attended an event in an Eastern Europe monastery. On arrival, I was warned that there was a strict curfew, and that monks would patrol the corridors at night to ensure we were all quietly in bed.

So it was quite a surprise when an eminent elder conference attendee took me aside to whisper conspiratorially:

"The Lithuanians have brought beer. Come to Room 317 after the bell rings. Don't be seen!"

My misspent youth playing videogames prepared me well for sneaking through the monastery that evening; keeping to shadows, following the path of the shuffling monks searching for misbehaviour, knowing exactly where to drag the bodies to hide them if one should accidentally spot me.[98]

I arrived at Room 317, having evaded the mild disapproval of any monks, and knocked on the door.

It was like any other party from my youth. Hordes perched on beds in a tiny dorm room, handing around beers from a smuggled crate.

Except the people doing the smuggling were a group of nuns from Eastern Europe, everyone here was way older than me and therefore should presumably have known better,[99] and - crucially - at most parties I had previously attended we didn't have to silence ourselves every time we thought we heard a monk wandering around outside.

I chatted to a nun and drank my illicit beer, and wondered exactly how I got here, and what it said about what I was doing with my life.

---

[98] This last bit may actually be from a videogame, not from reality, now I come to think about it.

[99] Of course, we never know better, and it wouldn't be much fun if we did.

My purpose has always been somewhat confused. In early 2014, I semi-accidentally enrolled on a master's programme at an Australian university, after an email conversation got a little out of hand. Many years before this, I chose my first degree after opening a university prospectus at random to the physics page, and thinking it seemed interesting. Before *that*, I went to South America for a year because the top internet search result for "what should I do next year" suggested to do so.

It appears that my life story is a series of random blunders from one experience to the next. Physics, Catholicism, programming, driving across Australia, stand-up comedy, accidentally starting another degree...

It won't surprise you that I've frequently criticised myself for this. I couldn't see a consistent thread tying my life together, and I interpreted that as a harsh indictment of myself and my lack of direction.

Inner critic: As if there's any other way to view it..!

Well...

Inner critic: No, don't worry, I know the drill by now.

There is an alternative viewpoint, and it would be more loving of me as an inner critic to occasionally choose that viewpoint.

Oh, wow. You've really been listening!

Inner critic: You're still an idiot, though.

Oh...

Inner critic, muttering: Love you, really...

What? Did you say something?

Inner critic: No. Go away! Don't you have some half-formed opinions to foist onto people, or whatever it is you're doing?

I suppose. Sorry about that, everyone.

As I was saying, I couldn't explain why my life choices were like this. Until I realised that there *is* a thread that ties it all together: I value having as wide a variety of experiences as possible.

I didn't understand how important that value was. In fact, I had missed the crucial importance of 'values' altogether.

Now that we're confidently escaping custard traps and striding towards solid ground, we are in a position to evaluate the direction to head in, which is determined by our values.

Wait, What Are Values?

Values are deeper than goals. A goal is a concrete *thing* you can measure: a mountain you've climbed, a family you've started, a song that you've written. Each of these goals arises out of a value (or multiple values), such as valuing physical challenges, or loving relationships, or creative expression.

Dr Russ Harris[100] offers the best visualisation of values I have heard: values are a *direction*, while goals are places we visit along the way.

These directions could be anything. Maybe family, solitude, or self-respect. Perhaps they are leisure, musical expression, technology, local community or world peace. Anything that gets you excited, passionate and joyful is a good place to start looking.

Knowing our values is like owning a personalised compass that aids our decision-making. When we have a choice to make, we can compare the direction each option takes us in against the direction suggested by our values: "Does this job offer take me in the directions I value, or not?"

Even smaller decisions are made easier with our value compass: "I have chosen to respect my value of health more, so I will turn down this distressingly delicious piece of cake and exercise for a minute instead."

This is still a tough choice, but made easier by reminding ourselves of our chosen values. Our values are the best decision criteria for accepting or rejecting opportunities that come our way, however large or small.

It's up to you to decide what's important to you. This is crucial; for a fully contented life, *your* values are the ones that you need. Not society's, not your partner's, not anybody else's!

It's tempting to abdicate responsibility and look to external influences to tell us what we ought to value, what we ought to find important and what we ought to want. But living with inauthentic values isn't living our own life.

Now we've spent so much time learning to love ourselves, we can live what is truly important to us.

---

[100] Yes, the one who helped us with defusion and acceptance earlier, well remembered.

Of course, should we want to, we're able to re-evaluate our values with people who are important to us. Maybe you value sharing in the values of others and helping them achieve their goals. That's fine; as long as you've *chosen* to value that, and not simply absorbed it from dominant personalities around you.

My Cat's Values

In school, we had an endless series of lessons on values. Each lesson we would write lists titled 'My Values', 'My Parents' Values', 'My Brother's Values', 'Some Guy Down the Road's Values'... it went on seemingly forever.

At the time, this felt futile, but now I realise how valuable it could have been if I'd had the capability to know at the age of fourteen what my values were. (Again, this isn't a general insult to teenagers, just an admission that everything I personally thought I knew at that age was pretty much wrong.)[101]

Had I correctly identified my values back then, I could have spared myself years of angst due to self-criticism over my life choices. I took a long time to realise I was actually responding to an important value.

It would have been much easier to make all forms of decisions if I had a known set of values to judge the options by.

EXERCISE: A Quick Values Review

Everybody seems to agree you must operate out of your values to live a fulfilled, authentic life, but I found it frustrating how nobody seemed to clearly explain how to discover what they are. Most advice seems to assume I just *know* what is important to me, but it didn't seem that easy in practice:

I want to start a family. But also build a career.

I want to get fit. But I want to eat what I want and be lazy.

I want to travel. But I want to put down roots.

How am I meant to pin down my values out of this contradictory mess of wants?

---

[101] This is the best lesson I would teach myself now if I went back in time, though I doubt I'd listen. I barely listen to myself now, after all.

If you aren't sure what your values are, then make it a project to discover them. The payoff is worth it; they will inform everything you choose to do - or to stop doing! - afterwards.

Admittedly, fully discovering our values is a complex and time-consuming process. I can't walk you through every step in this chapter, but I hope to encourage you to start.

On a piece of paper, write whatever comes to mind in response to the question: "If I could choose any values, which ones would I like to have?"[102]

For some unfathomable reason, we find it easier to answer this variant than the question "What are my values?" despite the fact that it's basically the same damn question phrased very slightly differently.

Actually, it makes sense that it would be easier. "What values would I choose?" is aspirational. It allows us to imagine a perfected version of ourselves. Someone who is already living exactly according to their values. And the person we would *like* to be is always easy to imagine. If nothing else, their non-existence taunts us whenever we make a mistake.

Meanwhile, the seemingly simpler question "what are my values?" confronts us with our deficiencies. It's a scary blank canvas, which offers a chance to be wrong, and so we naturally shy away from answering it. So, stick to "what values would I choose if I could have any?" and write down whatever pops into your head.

There are no rights or wrongs. Just splurge a stream-of-consciousness and trust that whatever you write will have importance for you. Don't attempt to be comprehensive. Definitely do not attempt to think! If you find yourself pausing to think, then resume writing without further debate, as far as is possible.

Once you're done, re-read what you have written. Do any themes reoccur? How could you summarise the top few values that appear?

Take even frivolous themes seriously, as they could be clues. If you found yourself unexpectedly writing about valuing colours and shapes and beauty, perhaps aesthetic concerns are important to you. Maybe you value your environment, or creating art, or... what? What is it?

---

[102] This question is adapted from 'The Happiness Trap' by Russ Harris.

Perhaps you wrote about something serious, such as wishing to value family more highly: this is an evident pointer to an underlying value.

Think of this review as beginning a conversation. It may crystallise facts you always knew but didn't *know*... like, for me, my 'revelation' that I value variety of experience so highly. With hindsight, it's obvious that this value has informed all of my life choices.

It may, excitingly, reveal a hidden passion your subconscious has been nagging you about. Who knew you valued hat manufacture so highly?! Time to turn that into a goal.

Keep exploring to identify the direction of your values as precisely as possible. That inner compass will be extremely helpful.

The Sexiness of Concrete Actionable Goals

I'm serious. Concrete actionable goals are exciting.

Self-knowledge, self-growth and all the rest of it mean nothing without translating to actual action and change. The effort must lead to tangible improvements in our lives.

Two types of action are of particular interest to us:

1) Ongoing Antidotes to Trouble

This first type of goal is about consolidating our escape from custard traps. We want to generate automatic, habitual corrections to any negative traps we tend to fall into.

Perhaps there is a particular trigger that sets us to thinking negatively, setting off a spiral of anxiety. We want a concrete goal that follows the formula: "every time I encounter that trigger I will do *xyz*", where *xyz* represents the antidote we have prepared in advance. These automated anti-custard habits will maintain our contentment.

We want to simply use the knowledge we have gained so far. If we know a particular thought upsets us, one goal could be "when I think *this*, I will defuse from it using my favourite defusion technique."

Or, we may generate these antidotes out of our values. For example, we may value gratitude, but be very easily influenced by consumer culture, and constantly feel lacking due to susceptibility to advertising. A useful actionable goal might be "spend a moment feeling grateful whenever I see an advertisement for something I want."

In this way, we turn advertisements - which usually drag us onto the custard - into triggers for inner peace. We have successfully used our value of gratitude to turn custard into solid ground.

2) Positive Expressions of Our Values

It's not enough to only avoid the custard; we want to build something incredible on solid ground. Looked at another way, what places do we want to visit as we travel in the direction of our values?

It may be helpful to group our values into broader regions: social, career, family, ambitions, creativity, and so on. Then we reflect on how successfully we're travelling towards our values in each group.

For example, maybe we're doing very well in valuing our personal health through exercise and rest, but in the social sphere we realise that we are not investing in our friendships as much as we'd wish.

Friendship is a value, so let's choose a goal for it: maybe we want to make more local friends, or perhaps we want to invest more time in the friendships we have already.

This process may sound almost insultingly obvious, but, in fact, so many factors affect our time, attention and emotions that we often stumble blindly around in the vague direction of our wants.

Consciously taking time to assess our current circumstances against our values is a much better way to create goals that build the life we want.

EXERCISE: Two Mildly Sexy Goals Lists

Let's write two lists, one of each type of the goals above.

The first list will define antidotes to turn our custard traps into automated positives.

Think about what situations or topics make you anxious, or otherwise drag you onto the custard. Can you identify specific triggers?

Once you have some triggers (the list doesn't have to be exhaustive or perfect - you can refine them later) it's time to create antidotes. What thought or action would dissolve the negativity, or even have the exact opposite effect? Think of gratefully reminding yourself of everything you have whenever you see an advertisement, or repeating an affirmation of your self-compassion whenever you compare yourself to another.

How can you remind yourself to apply the antidote every time the trigger occurs?

List all of these in three columns: TRIGGER, ANTIDOTE and REMINDER.

Since triggers are occasionally invisible to us (such as negative thoughts we aren't paying attention to at the time), the reminder is what you notice *first*. It's the thing that you experience.

For example, a reminder might be "spiralling anxiety" and the trigger might be "thoughts that I'm going to die." If you suddenly feel anxious, and realise that these particular unpleasant thoughts have surfaced again, then it's time to apply your antidote. Perhaps it's "compassionately remind myself I've been through this before." Use whatever works best for you. You can always update this list with better antidotes as you find them.

Once you have the list, each week, pick *one* trigger (so it's not too overwhelming), and try to consciously apply your antidote whenever it occurs. And, naturally, don't feel guilty or beat yourself up for forgetting. Just imagine how peaceful it would feel to have positive feelings after all of these triggers and keep at it.

Secondly, on another sheet of paper, let's choose some goals of the second type.

This list is a snapshot of small goals at a moment in time, and it will change frequently.

To create it, consider your values, and identify *no more than two* which you are not travelling towards as fully as you could.

From these couple of values, come up with *no more than two* small, positive, achievable and measurable goals that you can do in a short period of time - say, one week.

For example, you may value physical health but not be living that value as much as you'd like. So you might decide to go for a walk three times this week. As long as it's realistic, helpful and takes you in the valued direction, anything is fine.

At the same time next week, assess how well you did. If you achieved them, fantastic! Come up with a couple more.

If not, no problem. Be forgiving, try again, and come up with *even smaller, more achievable* goals. Continue this process of a weekly small goals list, and before long you'll be living a life full of your values.

Inner critic: You make this sound simple. It's not this easy.

No, it isn't. Resistance is always a factor. But without pushing ourselves to take concrete steps forward we will not achieve change. And without change we'll remain stuck. Adding small weekly expressions of our values is a solid foundation for happiness.

See if you can replace this list week-in, week-out with a new list of actions for the week. The first list won't change much, but it may evolve as you find more effective antidotes or new triggers... or remove a trigger.

Imagine how much you could achieve if you continually make concrete progress towards your values, while converting your most common traps into strengths.

Keep both lists somewhere visible and compassionately encourage yourself to continue working on both.

Goals Mean Failure (and that's okay)

Many years ago I took up swimming with the goal of getting fit. I hated it. I pushed myself to complete length after length, counting each one and desperately wishing it was over as soon as it began. I resented every single stroke, spending the entire time wishing I was anywhere else.

However, I felt great afterwards... but not because of the endorphins rushing through my body, as promised by exercise enthusiasts everywhere. It was simply because I had stopped bloody swimming.

Years later, I took up swimming again but with the mindset of simply enjoying myself, seeing how far I could go only as a by-product. There was no desire to avoid failure, or to achieve success. I was amazed to find that I enjoyed it.

We require goals to achieve anything at all. Even "be content" requires a concrete action of some kind, like "take a few seconds to be grateful."

But goals also open us up to the possibility of failure, which can be frightening. In order to avoid the paralysis of goallessnessless[103] we need a positive attitude towards failure.

As a barely-recovering perfectionist you can imagine that comfort with failure doesn't come easily to me.

Luckily, failure is just a label that we ascribe to a certain outcome. There's no "failure particle" that exists in the universe and attaches itself to us when we mess up.

If we put the worst results of the worst project we've ever worked on under the world's most accurate microscope we couldn't find a single mote of failure in there.

Failure exists *only* in our minds. (And in the minds of others, but that's even less important.)

This is a tough concept to swallow for anybody who is success or perfection-oriented so I'm going to say it again.

Failure does not *exist*, anywhere. It is not a real, tangible thing. It is just a label.

Not only is it only a label, it's a completely arbitrary label. If I write a song and decide it must have ten thousand downloads to be a success, is it a failure if only nine thousand ever hear it? What about five thousand? Or fifty?!

At what *numeric point* do I flip from success to failure? Is 9,999 still a failure, because it's less than the amount I decided in advance?

If you think so, imagine a parallel universe where everything was the exact same. The same number of people download and like my song. It has the same measurable level of success... except beforehand I only wanted ten people to download it.

If, in both universes, my song had five thousand downloads, in one it's a wild success, and in the other it's a huge failure.

Does that not sound bizarre? That every event occurs identically except for a single thought I had beforehand - an imagined number of people in my mind - and yet that thought is exclusively

---

[103] Sorry... I enjoyed typing that word and got carried away.

responsible for the labelling of 'success' or 'failure' and all the emotions those labels imply?

Failure is only a thought. We are not required to believe it, and certainly not to berate ourselves for it.

This is why we must detach ourselves from the outcome of our goals. If we're detached we won't be sucker-punched by failure, but pick ourselves up and carry on. In fact, we won't even need to pick ourselves up, because we won't be disappointed. Letting go of the end result frees us from fear of failure.

It's okay to risk failure; in fact, nothing worthwhile can be achieved without vulnerable exposure to the possibility of failure.

Unfortunately, this is fuel for resistance. When we're feeling anxious, the last thing we want is more vulnerability. We want to minimise risk, maintain control, stay safe.

But we are already familiar with the paradoxes at the heart of our emotions. Openness to vulnerability makes us less fearful, and therefore more likely to attain our goals. Attaining our goals then makes us more content, and thus less vulnerable to emotional struggles.

Openness to failure makes us less likely to fail, and openness to vulnerability makes us less emotionally vulnerable.

Can You Summarise All Of This, Please?

Why, yes I can, and thank you for asking.

- Time is valuable. Spending it is inevitable, so we should aim to get something back from the way we spend it.
- Our values act as an internal compass, pointing in the directions we should spend time travelling in.
- Goals are concrete, actionable expressions of our values.
- Having goals opens us up to failure, so sometimes we hide from even having goals.
- This is unavoidable: without willingness to be vulnerable we cannot achieve anything.
- We must be open to the possibility of failure.
- Luckily, failure is only an arbitrary label.
- Hooray!

RESIGNATION

THE FRANKLY UNBELIEVABLE
ADVENTURES OF McBIGGS
Hero-At-Last

McBiggs blasted yet another Thing into goop and glanced at his Super Serious Laser.

3% left.

He hoped it would be enough. There was one final corridor between him and the armoury. Cautiously, he pressed his fingers to the sensors and hid as the door slid open.

He peeked, heroically, through the gap. *Nothing.* Or No Thing.

He smiled grimly, and stepped into the final corridor.

Slither.

That noise came from behind. But his goal lay ahead, and he was *so* close. Forget that accursed Thing. He couldn't spare the time, or the shots. He needed the armoury. *Now.*

He dropped his shoulder and sprinted. Just a few more steps...

He squeezed the door control, diving through the blessedly opening portal as soon as the gap was large enough.

Slither. Slither. Slither.

No.

No.

No.

Not this. Not after everything.

The armoury was crawling with Things.

For some reason, there were at least as many in here as he'd fought in the whole rest of the ship to get here.

They seemed not to have seen him, yet, distracted as they were by something strapped to the far wall. But it wouldn't be long before one of them looked up. He had maybe a few seconds to think.

The door clunked shut behind him.

He couldn't go that way, anyway. That Thing that had been chasing him would be blocking the corridor by now.

He hardly had any shots left. Certainly nowhere near enough to secure the armoury. Never mind making it to the bridge to figure out just what the *hell* had happened today.

A slithering noise alerted him that the Things had noticed his presence. They began to ooze towards him. McBiggs wondered, briefly, about using his final couple of shots. But what was the point? It was over.

His heart dropped to his stomach, and something released inside his mind.

For the second time in a day... in fact, for the second time *ever*... McBiggs gave up.

A lightness came over him.

He flung his Super Serious Laser to the floor and spread his hands wide, grinning at the approaching, slithering, monstrous Things.

"Alright, Things. Come and get me..."

PART FIVE
FINALITY

*"An end is that which is naturally after something itself...
and with nothing else after it"*
Aristotle

NEVER GIVES UP

WALKING ON CUSTARD
Gotta Keep Going

Left. Slap. Right. Slap.

Left. Slap. Right. Slap.

Her foot hit the surface. It hardened, slightly, as it had a thousand (ten thousand? a million?) times before. She drew a shallow breath. The surface beneath her softened, and she lurched involuntarily. Again.

Quickly, she brought down her other foot.

Custard spattered in all directions as it hardened once more. She had long since failed to notice the unpleasant dampness of her shoes, the sickly sweet smell, or the occasional taste of the infernal stuff as it hit her in the face.

Nothing mattered except staying afloat.

Slap. Slap. Slap.

It was automatic now. It was impossible *not* to keep going.

Her legs ached. She wondered what it'd be like to sleep, to rest. She vaguely thought it must be nice, though privately she no longer believed it had ever been possible.

Slap. Slap. Sploosh.

Her heart faltered. She'd been too slow. Choking with familiar terror, her foot plunged beneath the surface and she stumbled forward, tottering into the liquid with her knees, and then the rest of her body. What was this, the hundredth time she'd fallen like this? The thousandth?

If she'd ever kept count of her falls, she'd forgotten about it.

Wearily, she rolled herself back onto her feet.

Gotta keep going.

Left. Slap. Right. Slap.

Left. Slap. Right. Slap.

CHAPTER TWENTY-EIGHT
The Meaning of Everything

"But I do know that about ten times as many people find their lives dull, and unnecessarily dull, as ever admit it; and I do believe that if we busted out and admitted it sometimes, instead of being nice and patient and loyal for sixty years, and then nice and patient and dead for the rest of eternity, why, maybe, possibly, we might make life more fun." - Sinclair Lewis

Life is an endless parade of mystery. In the 1960s, there was an outbreak of hysterical laughter in Tanganyika, Africa which spread from person to person with no apparent cause. The unstoppable laughter reportedly lasted for years before winding down, leaving a trail of chaos and disruption wherever it went.

I've never experienced anything so widespread, but I seem to attract occasional mysterious happenings. One such incident occurred in Germany at a ludicrously large convention for a million Catholic youth, back in the time when I attended such events. After a day of exploring, some of my group were heading back to the town we were staying in.

Unfortunately, at the train station we encountered a crowd filling the entire concourse. The transport system was completely overwhelmed. Asking around, we learned that some people had been waiting for hours without any sign of movement. We were a long way from seeing a platform, let alone a train. There was no hope for getting home any time soon.

I'd mentally relinquished the rest of the day to tedious stressful waiting, when a priest from my group confidently ran off, shouting "FOLLOW THOSE NUNS!" and waving frantically at us.[104]

He had spotted a group of nuns wandering down an empty passageway. I was sceptical that following random religious ladies down what appeared to be a service corridor would be helpful. But,

---

[104] This sort of thing used to occur remarkably frequently in my world.

in response to my quizzical look, the priest merely nodded confidently, enigmatically saying "Nuns always know..."

I found this odd too, but in the absence of any better ideas we followed them down the corridor, past some doors, around some twisty-turny corners, before emerging onto a platform with a sleek, clean, and *gloriously empty* train before us. A sign indicated that this train was going express to our destination.

We took our seats - seats! - on the carriage, and I accosted the priest. "How on *earth* did you know?!"

His reply, infuriatingly, was that nuns had an eerie intuitive sense of how to handle these situations. My inner sceptic wanted to doubt this ("How would anybody have special knowledge of handling packed train stations in foreign countries, and *why nuns in particular?*") but - irritatingly - he had been proven absolutely correct in this instance.

So I let it go.

Inner critic: So, what's the moral of this story? If you want to dishonourably jump a queue and get onto a train - when it almost certainly wasn't your turn - then following a group of nuns is the best way to do it?! That doesn't sound like a lesson applicable to, well, anything.

No!

Obviously not.

In that moment, it was a relief to temporarily lay aside doubts and plans and to follow the nuns to where I wanted to go.

If only life were always so simple; that someone, or something, could show us the way, guiding us around obstacles and helping us to our destinations. But life *isn't* that simple.[105]

The greatest navigation system I could imagine would be to know the Meaning of Life. This sense of deep purpose would percolate into our values, and we'd have natural guidance for everything from life decisions through to daily choices.

There'd be greater benefits too. Without meaning, we lack foundation, and too easily slip into depression and anxiety. Wondering "what's the point of everything" can be a slippery slope into yet another existential crisis.

---

[105] Except, apparently, in highly specialised, weird and unlikely moments such as this one.

So, to both assist in avoiding the pain of meaninglessness, and to inform our choices, we come to discuss the Meaning of Life itself.

I admit, it is a little selfish of me to have kept this secret until now. You've read however-many-pages of varying levels of nonsense, only to learn at this advanced stage that I've been keeping the Meaning of Life from you all this time.

Inner critic: That is just typical of the kind of selfish... wait, we know the meaning of life?!

Ha. Have you been ignoring all my clumsy foreshadowing until now?

The Meaning of Meaning

We won't be delving into the philosophical deep-end.[106]

I'm more concerned with finding a practical, hopefully-helpful approach to the question of meaning than with breaking insightful new ground. Luckily, we can get a reasonable amount done in the intellectual shallows.

Meaning is a nebulous concept, so let's begin pinning it down with an obvious premise:

Some things are meaningful. Other things are not meaningful.

Okay, that didn't help much. Let's move up a gear:

Meaning exists in neither subject, nor object, so we must reject our intuitive, yet false, dualistic approach.

Curses, that didn't help either. It's simply a fancy way of pointing out that meaning doesn't physically exist, so it must be a construct of our minds. Again, it's true, but not very useful.

The trouble is that meaning is a highly overloaded word, by which I mean it has far too many, er, meanings.

We use the same word for 'what a word signifies' (the meaning of a word) as we do for 'universal sense of purpose' (the meaning of life), and this can create confusion. Our minds aren't always able to maintain strong boundaries between different interpretations of the same word.

Even if we simply restrict ourselves to talking about the 'life's purpose' kind of meaning, we readily conflate two distinct levels, which I am going to call *personal* and *universal.*

---

[106] For the extremely practical reason that I am incapable of doing so, as a mere dabbler in philosophy.

Splitting out these levels helps to answer some big questions.

Two Levels of Meaning

The first level of meaning - *personal* meaning - is simple.

Some things are meaningful and others aren't, in our personal experience. Perhaps I'm suddenly struck by a beautiful view and I feel deeply connected to nature, and this event takes on some personal significance.

Experiences don't have to be shared to be meaningful. A thousand others may pass that same view on that same day without feeling anything special. But this doesn't remove the meaning for me.

So personal meaning is entirely subjective; our mind creates it. We can see this from the fact that anything can be imbued with meaning. A picture of a banana might be meaningful to one person, but that doesn't mean that pictures of bananas are meaningful in general. Anything can have personal meaning.

We tend to think things that have larger effects are necessarily more meaningful, but personal meaning doesn't require important or lasting consequences. There's no shame in finding significance in a fleeting moment, even if it seems small or unimportant.

Despite the seeming arbitrariness of it, personal meaning is of huge importance. It provides our motivation. Our values (as discussed earlier) aren't universally shared - some of us work to help the disadvantaged, some for streamlining a business, others for saving the rainforest, and others for serving great coffee.

But for each of us, our motivation is fuelled by the personal meaning we extract from these values. These moments of personal meaning are crucial for our motivation. If we think what we're doing doesn't matter, we take little joy from it.

The arbitrariness of personal meaning becomes a real benefit here, as things don't have to be 'important' in any eyes but our own.

If we get great personal meaning from our life's work of growing massive onions, then it doesn't matter that nobody else shares it. The meaning is personal to us, but it is worth no less for that.

So far, so simple. But on the deeper level of "meaning", which I am calling *universal meaning*, things get a little more complicated.

Perhaps Excalibob had a deep personal experience after communing with nature,[107] or when he helped a sick dog down at the Local Home for Sick Dogs, but what's the meaning of that? Why does his meaningful experience matter at all? Come to that, why does anything matter at all?

Questions like "why does anything matter at all?" are a consideration of *universal* meaning. They lead to further questions like "is there a God?" and "what's the point of humanity?"

And to massive, massive arguments.

Just looking in the vague direction of these questions for mere milliseconds is enough to get sucked into heated debates about "the point" of everything.

There are - shall we say - mildly differing opinions about our overall purpose, and how we ought to be achieving it. If the internet has taught us anything, it's that *any* discussion eventually derails into a violent screaming match on life's big questions. Entire websites devoted to nothing but happy kittens have gone up in physical flames after one user innocently asks "so, who here is religious?"

So far in this book, I have repeatedly used a trick when confronted with such debate fuel: sidestepping the question, by acknowledging its importance, while simultaneously saying that it doesn't matter. (See, for example, the earlier mention of the afterlife.)

Depending on your view, this sidestepping technique is either a heroic avoidance of pointless arguments, or a cowardly refusal to take sides and start shouting.

Now, we can use this distinction between universal and personal meaning to ~~justify my cowardice~~ dissolve the arguments; these big questions are *universally* important, but they needn't *personally* matter.

We must keep these levels separate. Left unchecked, universal meaning can bleed into and override our sense of personal meaning. The resulting feeling of 'nothing I do matters' is toxic to our happiness, and can kill our ability to care about anything.

---

[107] Not a euphemism.

You might think I'm saying that only people who think there's no purpose to existence could fall into this sort of existential crisis. But, actually, pretty much *any* universal meaning you can think of could be used to override our personal meaning:

There is no god; we all die in the end, nothing matters.

There is a god, but if he knows everything, then my future is already determined; what's the point in anything; all my choices are meaningless, nothing matters.

Physics dictates that every choice I make is simply electrical currents moving along established pathways in my brain; all life is pointless.

And so on. Note that I'm not claiming any of these things are true or false. I only want to show that a wide range of beliefs can trigger a crisis of meaning. I expect most beliefs could be twisted into such a crisis.

The solution to this problem isn't "change your universal belief," it's "stop letting universal beliefs override your personal meaning."

Keep the levels separate.

The fact that any universal belief can cause a crisis of personal meaning also means that no universal belief *necessitates* such a crisis.

We can believe we live in a universe with or without free will, or that there is or isn't a god, or whatever we like. And whatever we choose, we can still experience personal meaning and the happiness that comes with it.

None of these views can stop us from being happy, if we don't let them. We aren't required to choose any particular answer to existential questions to retain personal meaning and maintain our motivation.

Of course, it's EASIER to be happy if your system of universal belief is "the universe loves me and wants to surround me with cupcakes, rainbows and cuddles."

But not all of us are lucky enough to actually believe anything so positive. Life supplies us with too much challenging evidence otherwise. Even if our own lives are pretty good, accidentally reading a newspaper or watching the news provides a constant reminder that the universe isn't always a nice place to everybody.

If you have managed to maintain an optimistic sense of universal meaning despite all this, then that's excellent. I am a little jealous of your positive outlook. For everybody else, we must remember this: *No matter what we believe about the universe and life in general, we can enjoy moments of personal meaning.*

It's so easy to forget to keep these two levels separate, and to go from "I'm not sure whether there's any purpose to life" to "Nothing I do matters, there is no joy anywhere."

These do not follow from one another! Existential despair doesn't have to suck all the happiness from our daily existence.

Undoing An Existential Mix-up

Luckily, if we do mix our levels and trigger unpleasant existential misery, there is a way to escape.

Losing belief in life's ultimate meaning isn't logically compatible with losing motivation, energy and hope. If we *truly* believe there's no universal meaning, then it doesn't have to affect our emotional state at all.

In a world without meaning, the fact that "life is meaningless" is itself meaningless! We may as well continue finding personal significance in whatever we like.

It may be arbitrary, but if everything is arbitrary, then happiness is just as arbitrary as being miserable. So we may as well choose happiness.

To put it another way: "What's the point of anything? Everything sucks" is a judgement which requires us to care.

You can't say "everything sucks" without caring about the state of 'everything'. The state of everything has meaning to you. If you truly didn't care, you wouldn't even have that opinion.

The fact that we care, and hurt, when we believe life is meaningless shows that it is not meaningless to US.

But Seriously, What's It All About?

Decoupling personal meaning from universal meaning frees us to maintain our contentment without depending on our particular beliefs about the universe.

Since some of us tend to get lost in big questions and accidentally think ourselves into an unhappy hole, it's useful to have a practical escape from such a hole.

Unfortunately, it's considered mildly tricky to solve the question once and for all by, say, proving the existence of God.[108]

But what if we *really* want an answer to the universal purpose of everything? Can we find one?

Let's look at what we know about the universe. No matter what happens, eventually the Sun will expand and swallow the Earth.

I was going to make a joke about how this would make for a terrible motivational poster, but as I just said: it doesn't have to affect our personal motivation!

Inner critic: Wow. You avoided instantly contradicting yourself, for once. This is a proud moment for me.

Sometime later, the Sun will itself die. Eventually all stars will die. Maybe the Universe will contract in on itself and the cycle will begin again, but it appears more likely that entropy will win in the end and the universe will smooth out to a sort of tedious paste. If all this is true... how can *anything* be meaningful?

Instinctively, we feel we need something objective to show us what matters. It feels as if there has to be something out there, outside the universe, which imbues all of this with meaningfulness.

We would like God, or aliens, or a mystical guru to show up with all the answers. A group of Cosmic Nuns for us to follow through the Great Train Station of Existence.

It is so tempting to desire such an objective answer. But imagine if that actually happened. Being told what is meaningful would be no help at all. If the Meaning of Life was discovered, objectively, certainly, written on some giant stone monolith atop some mountain - or wired into all of our brains - then we'd have no choice except to get on with whatever we're told.

---

[108] I have discovered a truly remarkable proof which this footnote is too small to contain; with apologies to Fermat.

"And lo, apparently The Meaning of Life is having a tidy desk and being kind to named sea creatures."

And so we all develop an organised in/out desk system and kiss Keith the Seahorse every day. Being handed the meaning of life on a plate would be dull. Having universal purpose decreed on our behalf would sap all meaning from our choices.

Instead, it's the *absence* of outside-mandated universal meaning which allows us to cultivate personal meaning.

In a world without obvious universal meaning, where all choices look the same, the time we spend on any one choice makes it unique to us. We cultivate love and meaning by choosing to care; *not the other way around.*

We create a positive feedback loop when we choose to care. When we act, something magical happens: we begin to care about whatever we are doing.

We don't sit in an empty room, waiting until we spontaneously care about something, and then go do it. It's the other way around. We start doing things, and then we care about them. The more we do, the more we care.

If we choose not to act, then we shrink away and care less.

The entire universe eventually ending in heat death doesn't prevent us from acting now. We can still do whatever aligns with our values, and thus nourish our care for whatever that is. We can still love the people around us. Personal meaning gets us out of bed in the morning, not universal.

It is a common truism that we ought to 'find and live our purpose.' Sometimes the pressure to do this can be counter-productive, as it seems to put an obligation on us to be useful, to fix the world, to do something. It can be a stick to beat ourselves with. *"I don't know my purpose, or if I do, it isn't very impressive. I'm useless."*

But we are not required to be useful. We don't have to be anything. Reality is much more freeing than this.

If we have a grand sense of life's purpose that flows naturally out of our beliefs regarding universal meaning, then that's great. This can be a real source of inspiration and personal meaning.

However, it is also a paradoxically fragile place to stand. If our perspective changes, we can fall into a dark place of apparent emptiness. This is less a custard trap, and more a trapdoor that can be pulled from underneath us at any time.

On the other hand, letting go of the answers to big questions, and choosing to cultivate personal meaning no matter what, is always a solid place to stand.

From there we can ask the big questions - Is God real? What is the destiny of humanity? Does any of this really matter at all? - from a secure location.

We don't have to fear accidentally undermining the ground we stand on. We can be playful about it, grasping lightly at different answers.

Through the magic of acting towards our values, whatever we are doing becomes imbued with meaning. Significance and joy flow into our lives, and we experience that delicious sense of connection with the universe.

Inner cynic: Sigh. We've lost him again. He's experiencing delicious senses of connection with the universe, apparently.

When we act, we naturally cultivate meaning, purpose and love. And we always have the chance to act.

AT LAST..
The Meaning of Life

Here we are nearing the end.

I've been promising the Meaning of Life all the way.

And I realised, too late, that this meant I'd have to figure out the actual Meaning of Life.

And so I did. Sort of.

It turns out that it's all deeply personal, and that we must choose the answer for ourselves.

So my answer is only for me, Neil Hughes. It seems you're going to have to figure things out and cultivate meaning for yourself.

How embarrassing. I'm sorry.

But, actually, I'm *glad* it turned out this way. I'd *hate* to tell you what ought to be important to you. Choosing it for yourself is what makes it meaningful. You owe it to yourself to choose great things. Even if your inner critic isn't so sure.

By now, I definitely don't need to tell you that I don't have all the answers. But even if *nobody* has all the answers, everything is still okay.

Flinching from the big questions of life makes them seem scarier than they are. Looking directly at them, and saying "I don't have an answer yet, but I can be happy anyway", is as good as an answer, for now.

I hope I've shown you how to escape some traps you might hit along the way. We've explored a variety of them, from over-identifying with our thoughts, to having to be perfect, to worrying about death, and even despairing that life lacks all meaning.

What helped me escape from each trap is wondering: *how can I look at this differently?* Each time, it turned out that I could find strengths and ideas buried in the trap itself. I could leave the exhaustion of the trap behind, and move towards more solid ground.

As much as my inner critic wants me to conclusively solve all the problems of the universe forever, I think even he agrees that this will have to do for now.

Inner critic: I guess...

Shall we hug, inner critic? It would make a good ending.

Inner critic: No. Really. Let's not. Leave me alone!

This is progress, I guess.

Maybe a hug would have made for a nice emotional climax if this were a story, but this is real life. Mostly.

Everything isn't sorted. But I'm not as anxious as I once was. And I don't fear the return of anxiety; if it shows up again, I have the tools to get through it.

This is solid ground, more or less. I hope to see you there too.

In the beginning, I said that nobody can undertake the journey off the custard for you. That this is something we all have to do for ourselves.

It turns out that the same is true of nurturing the meaning in our lives.

We all have to do it alone.

But at least that means we're all doing it together.

WALKING OFF CUSTARD
A Guide for Peaceful Humans

Left. Slap.

Right. Slap.

She took another step. Forward.

Slap.

And another. Forward.

Slap.

One more.

Crunch.

Crunch!? Automatically, her other foot followed.

Crunch.

She paused. And looked down.

The ground beneath her was hard. And *green*. It didn't give way underneath her. *Solid ground.*

A hand touched her shoulder. She looked up into a smile.

A welcoming face. "You made it!"

Her aching leg muscles twitched, confused by the sudden absence of activity. Dimly, through the haze of exhaustion, she began to realise the implications.

I can stop...

People milled around her, grinning and hugging and cheering and congratulating her. There'd be time to meet them later.

Right now, she allowed herself to dip and touch the grass, before rolling onto her back to watch the sky for a moment.

It was time for a rest.

WHATEVER HAPPENED TO McBIGGS?
Hero-At-Rest

*"It is only by being in trouble that people can understand how
far from easy it is to be the master of one's feelings and thoughts."*
Chekhov

Somewhere in space, McBiggs and a Thing were looking at each other. They had been like this for some time.

McBiggs smiled.

So did the Thing.

At least, McBiggs thought it was a smile. He still wasn't sure.

But he was happy.

Faraway, across the vastness of space, a kindly old shopkeeper smiled to herself as she put away her telescope.

That little boy had turned out alright, after all.

AND FINALLY
A Note to the Reader

Hello.[109]

It feels a little silly addressing you after talking to you this whole time. Nonetheless, I want to say, sincerely and gratefully, thank you so much for taking the time to read this book.

I hope you enjoyed it.

More than that, I hope it's been useful to you. As I've stumbled my way through the writing process, my motivation has been fuelled by imagining that somebody, somewhere may someday feel better as a result of reading it.

If you have any stories or thoughts to share, then I'd love to hear from you. Email me on: *neil@walkingoncustard.com*

And, of course, if you did enjoy this book, then please share it, review it, and tell your friends. And tell me too! As I write this note, I have no idea how - or if - I'm going to convince anybody to read these ramblings, so I'd be very grateful for any encouragement you can provide.

Lastly, my inner critic wants me to pass on that he is, frankly, shocked that you read this far. And a little bit disappointed by your lack of taste in books. But he says hello too.

Thank you all for reading, and much love,
Neil

www.walkingoncustard.com/mailing
neil@walkingoncustard.com

---

[109] Are you supposed to start notes to the reader by saying... oh, forget it.

FURTHER READING
For Anyone Interested

Most of the 'research' for this book was conducted before I ever dreamed I might write a book at all. As far as I knew, I was looking for help with my own struggles anywhere it could be found. It was only much later that I wondered about sharing my story.

I read a tonne[110] of books, blogs, websites, forums, pamphlets and long-forgotten comments scrawled on strange and not-so-strange parts of the internet. I first heard the idea of feelings being rooted in thoughts some years ago from a website that no longer exists (or at least, that I can no longer find: it was just a bunch of text, pre-Web 2.0).

I listened to experts and random strangers alike, and absorbed and rejected common wisdom, depending only on whether or not it helped. I even enjoyed reading about a dimensional shift that the Earth is apparently due to undergo soon, which is something nice we all have to look forward to.[111]

As a result, this book is a melange of ideas that helped me personally during the years I spent working through my own anxiety.

I'd like to mention some sources - mainly books - which were the most helpful at the time, and which likely provided the seeds for many of the ideas in this book.

I mentioned two books several times in the text: *Get Out of Your Mind and Into Your Life* by Steven Hayes, and *The Happiness Trap* by Russ Harris.

Both authors kindly gave me permission to adapt some of their ideas for inclusion in this book. In particular, Russ Harris allowed me to borrow his image of The Struggle Switch, and Steven Hayes

---

[110] Not a literal tonne, especially as most were e-books which would have weighed very little. It's not important at all that you know this.

[111] Citation needed.

allowed me to adapt his mindfulness exercise for remaining in the present moment. As well as these, I learned about the concept of *defusion* from both these books. I recommend them as excellent resources for mind management, and for living a full life rooted in our personal values.

If you found my attempts to introduce the topics of isolation and death interesting, then I'm sure you'd appreciate the books of Irvin Yalom. I read these some years ago, in particular *Love's Executioner, Staring at the Sun* and his textbook *Existential Psychotherapy.*[112] They are wonderful, warm and insightful reads. Start with *Love's Executioner.*

I mentioned perfectionism as a quick example of a custard trap, and would like to recommend *Present Perfect: A Mindfulness Approach to Letting Go of Perfectionism and the Need for Control* by Pavel Somov, which explores the topic in considerable depth. Naturally, he does it much greater justice than I was able to in just a few pages.

I found *The Mindful Path Through Worry And Rumination* by Sameet M. Kumar comforting at a difficult time. I recall particularly appreciating how compassionately it is written and the practical introductions to meditation.

I have read a large part (but far from all) of the online writings of Eliezer Yudkowsky, in particular his *Sequences,* which were originally published on *Overcoming Bias.* Clearly, I never absorbed his ability for intellectual rigour (!) but I'm working on it.

And I'd like to mention a few further books that I found helpful and inspiring at the time of reading, including *Daring Greatly* by Brene Brown, *The Road Less Travelled* by M. Scott Peck and *The Power of Now* by Eckhart Tolle.

Lastly, the 'Spiritual Instruction' story I wrote was loosely a parody of an ancient story from the *101 Zen Stories* compilation. Of course, I can't recommend the original author, but apparently these stories go back at least as far as the 13th century Japanese master Muju, who I expect was a very cool guy. Must be nice to have a story you wrote down be referenced 700 years later.

Inner critic: Don't get any ideas...

---

[112] Yes, I read textbooks for fun. I'm cool.

SCIENCE & RANDOM BITS

I didn't want to spend this book throwing study after study at you, but I would like to point to a few sources for interesting claims I referred to in passing.

On happiness actually increasing with income, contrary to common wisdom (albeit at a logarithmic rate):

As mentioned in the text of the chapter, this inconvenient study is:

'Subjective Wellbeing and Income: Is There Any Evidence of Satiation?' by Stevenson & Wolfers, University of Michigan (2013)

On many people preferring to electric shock themselves than remain in solitude for a few minutes:

Full disclosure: I only read the abstract of this one, which mentions the interesting result I quoted.

'Just think: the challenges of the disengaged mind', Timothy Wilson et al, Virginia University (2014)

On 'Que Sera Sera' being a proverb of English roots:

Linguistics is awesome, and this paper on the origins of 'Que Sera Sera' was a really interesting (if unnecessary) distraction while I was supposed to be writing:

'"Que sera sera": The English Roots of a Pseudo-Spanish Proverb' Proverbium, 30, by Lee Hartman (Southern Illinois University) (2013)

On an epidemic of laughing occurring in Tanganyika:

Full disclosure again... I only verified that a paper was published under this title, which was enough for my purposes of pointing out the existence of weird events:

'An Epidemic of Laughing in the Bukoba District of Tanganyika', Central African Medical Journal, By A. M. Rankin (Maskerere University College) and P.J. Philip (1963)

On various musings about ancient Greek and Latin:

At the time of writing, I wasn't sure where I'd heard of this etymological relation between *caritas* and *agape*. Luckily, I remembered before going to print, and oddly enough, it came from a half-remembered letter written by Pope Benedict XVI which I had read about ten years earlier: *Deus Caritas Est.* For some reason, the relation between those words stuck in my head ever since, even if nothing else did.

Inner critic: Hold on... THAT was your research? A bunch of books, a few papers, and a letter you only partly remember?
AND you admit to reading only portions of two of those papers... while a third is totally irrelevant?!

Basically, yes! If you'd been paying more attention, you'd have noticed I'm not really writing an academic work here. I just wanted this section to honour the people whose work helped me through difficulty, and/or inspired me to write something of my own.

Speaking of people...

QUOTES & EPIGRAPHS

I quoted a few living artists over the course of the book: Jeffrey Lewis, Luke Smith (of Luke Smith & The Feelings), Thom Tuck and Rónán Johnston (and Emmaus), who all kindly gave permission to use their words.

They are fantastic musicians and comedians who are all making the world a better place. I recommend that you check them and their work out.

Any other quotes are from public domain works, or apocryphal popular sayings, or things I obviously made up.

A FINAL, FINAL THANKS

To anybody mentioned, and, for completion, to anybody *not* mentioned too. Because why not.

Congratulations for anybody who's still reading, for somehow making it to the end of this informative, but dull, section.

I hope you have a lovely rest-of-your-day.

Neil Hughes finds it difficult to describe himself, especially in the third person. He has spent time as a computer programmer, a student of physics, a semi-professional evangelist and even occasionally as a stand-up comedian. He now writes part-time, programs part-time and tries not to worry too much about it all. After many years living all over the place, he has returned to the north-west of England where he hopes to do various things that help people to be happy. He wishes there was a way to say this without sounding so painfully cheesy.